I0214417

Partnership in Ministry

Partnership in Ministry

A Study of Networking and Collaboration in Paul's Ministry and Their Implications

Paul H. Byun

PICKWICK *Publications* • Eugene, Oregon

PARTNERSHIP IN MINISTRY
A Study of Networking and Collaboration in Paul's Ministry and Their Implications

Copyright © 2023 Paul H. Byun. All rights reserved. Except for brief quotations in critical publications or reviews, no part of this book may be reproduced in any manner without prior written permission from the publisher. Write: Permissions, Wipf and Stock Publishers, 199 W. 8th Ave., Suite 3, Eugene, OR 97401.

Pickwick Publications
An Imprint of Wipf and Stock Publishers
199 W. 8th Ave., Suite 3
Eugene, OR 97401

www.wipfandstock.com

Paperback isbn: 978-1-5326-0985-5
Hardcover isbn: 978-1-5326-0987-9
Ebook isbn: 978-1-5326-0986-2

Cataloging-in-Publication data:

Names: Byun, Paul H., author.

Title: Partnership in ministry : a study of networking and collaboration in Paul's ministry and their implications / Paul H. Byun

Description: Eugene, OR: Pickwick Publications, 2023. | Includes bibliographical references.

Identifiers: ISBN: 978-1-5326-0985-5 (paperback) | ISBN: 978-1-5326-0987-9 (hardcover) | ISBN: 978-1-5326-0986-2 (ebook)

Subjects: LCSH: Bible. NT—Criticism, interpretation, etc. | Bible.—Epistles of Paul—Criticism, interpretation, etc.

Classification: BS2506.3 B95 2023 (print). | BS2506.3 (epub).

05/15/23

Scripture taken from the New American Standard Bible®, Copyright © 1960, 1962, 1963, 1968, 1971, 1972, 1973, 1975, 1977 by The Lockman Foundation. Used by permission. https://www.lockman.org.

Scripture quotations from The Authorized (King James) Version. Rights in the Authorized Version in the United Kingdom are vested in the Crown. Reproduced by permission of the Crown's patentee, Cambridge University Press.

Scripture taken from the New King James Version®. Copyright © 1982 by Thomas Nelson. Used by permission. All rights reserved.

Scripture quotations marked (NIV) are taken from the Holy Bible, New International Version®, NIV. Copyright © 1973, 1978, 1984, 2011 by Biblica, Inc.™ Used by permission of Zondervan. All rights reserved. worldwide.www.zondervan.com.

Scripture quoted by permission. Quotations designated (NET) are from the NET Bible® copyright ©1996, 2019 by Biblical Studies Press, L.L.C. http://netbible.com. All rights reserved.

Contents

Preface

THIS BOOK CAME OUT of my PhD dissertation at Southwestern Baptist Theological Seminary. The contents of the dissertation reappear here in a slightly changed format and style. One day, in the beginning of my PhD study, I was in Dr. Son's office talking about Paul's missionary works. A short conversation led me to realize that New Testament scholars tend to view Paul's ministry in light of a conflict with his opponents, still acknowledging the partnership character of Paul's ministry. I also realized that there has been no book-length of research into the subject, i.e., Paul's ministry in the context of partnership and relationship. That was when and why the present study started.

In this book, I seek to demonstrate Paul's partnership ministry according to three ministry areas—Paul's coworkers, financial assistance, and communicative activities—each against its social and religious backgrounds. After introducing the methodology and significance of the present study (chapter 1), chapter 2 determines Paul's partnership ministry by examining the mission of Paul's coworkers, locally and trans-locally. Chapter 3 looks into the networking and collaboration of Pauline churches through financial assistances that took place either to support Paul's missions or to help other believers in need. The next chapter (chapter 4) investigates Paul's communicative activities—i.e., letter-writing, visitations, and conferences—which reflect the vitality of networking, coordination, and cooperation among the churches. The final chapter (chapter 5) concludes that Paul's churches, owing to the partnership ministry of

Paul, maintained local and trans-local relationships and collaborations, availing themselves of the social conventions of the first-century world. This conclusion will challenge Pauline scholarship to view Paul's ministry not from his opponents but from his friends, and to consider New Testament church relationships not in the frame of conflict but of partnership.

I need to express my gratitude to those who helped me finish this study project. I am grateful to Dr. Mark Taylor, who was my professor in ThM and PhD seminars on 1 Corinthians, which evoked my interest in Paul's ministry. He also reviewed and guided my dissertation with accuracy and mercy. I have to mention Dr. S. Aaron Son, who has been my academic advisor and thesis supervisor from the beginning. I thank for his conscientious comments on my work. Further, he always encouraged and supported me that I could persist. Completion of this project is deeply indebted to him. I'd like to give special thanks to Wipf and Stock Publishers for publishing my dissertation. Finally, I owe my greatest gratitude to my wife, Sarah. When I worked hard and even lazed around, she has been always on my side and did not spare anything for the progress of my study. I can never thank her enough. "Partnership in Ministry" could come out with such faithful and sacrificial supporters. Of course, I know who has been behind all this. Thanks be to God!

Abbreviations

1–2 Clem.	*1–2 Clement*
Ant.	*Jewish Antiquities* (Josephus)
AJECS	Ancient Judaism and Early Christianity Series
AB	Anchor Bible
ABD	*Anchor Bible Dictionary*. Edited by David Noel Freedman. 6 vols. New York: Doubleday, 1992
ANTC	Abingdon New Testament Commentaries
AYB	Anchor Yale Bible
BAR	*Biblical Archaeology Review*
BDAG	*Greek-English Lexicon of the New Testament and Other Early Christian Literature*. Walter Bauer. Revised and edited by Frederick W. Danker. 3rd ed. Chicago: University of Chicago Press, 2000
BECNT	Baker Exegetical Commentary on the New Testament
BHH	*Baptist History and Heritage*
BRev	*Bible Review*
BSac	*Bibliotheca Sacra*
CBET	Contributions to Biblical Exegesis and Theology

CBR	*Currents in Biblical Research*
CIG	*Corpus Inscriptionum Graecarum*
CIJ	*Corpus Inscriptionum Judaicarum*
CJ	*Concordia Journal*
CJZ	*Corpus jüdischer Zeugnisse aus der Cyrenaika*
ConBNT	Coniectanea Biblica: New Testament Series
CRINT	Compendia Rerum Iudaicarum ad Novum Testamentum
CTJ	*Calvin Theological Journal*
CTQ	*Concordia Theological Quarterly*
Dial.	*Dialogue with Trypho* (Justin Martyr)
DPL	*Dictionary of Paul and His Letters*. Edited by Gerald F. Hawthorne, Ralph P. Martin, and Daniel G. Reid. Downers Grove, IL: InterVarsity, 1993
EDNT	*Exegetical Dictionary of the New Testament*. Edited by Horst Balz and Gerhard Schneider. 3 vols. Grand Rapids: Eerdmans, 1990–1993
Embassy	*On the Embassy to Gaius* (Philo)
EvQ	*Evangelical Quarterly*
ExpTim	*Expository Times*
Flac.	*Pro Flacco* (Cicero)
Flaccus	*Against Flaccus* (Philo)
GNT	Good News Translation
HCSB	Holman Christian Standard Bible
Hist. eccl.	*Ecclesiastical History* (Eusebius)
HNTC	Harper's New Testament Commentaries
HTR	*Harvard Theological Review*
ICC	International Critical Commentary
IG	*Inscriptiones Graecae*
JBL	*Journal of Biblical Literature*
JECS	*Journal of Early Christian Studies*

JETS	*Journal of the Evangelical Theological Society*
JGRCJ	*Journal of Greco-Roman Christianity and Judaism*
JNES	*Journal of Near Eastern Studies*
JSNT	*Journal for the Study of the New Testament*
JSNTSup	Journal for the Study of the New Testament Supplement Series
JTS	*Journal of Theological Studies*
J.W.	*Jewish War* (Josephus)
KJV	King James Version
L&N	*Greek-English Lexicon of the New Testament: Based on Semantic Domains*. 2 vols. 2nd ed. New York: United Bible Societies, 1989
LCL	Loeb Classical Library
Let. Aris.	*Letter of Aristeas*
LNTS	Library of New Testament Studies
LTQ	*Lexington Theological Quarterly*
NAC	New American Commentary
NASB	New American Standard Bible
Nat.	*Natural History* (Pliny the Elder)
NCBC	New Century Bible Commentary
NET	New English Translation
NICNT	New International Commentary on the New Testament
NIDB	*New Interpreter's Dictionary of the Bible*. Edited by Katharine Doob Sakenfeld. 5 vols. Nashville: Abingdon, *2006–2009*
NIGTC	New International Greek Testament Commentary
NIV	New International Version
NJB	New Jerusalem Bible
NKJV	New King James Version
NovT	*Novum Testamentum*
NovTSup	Supplements to Novum Testamentum

NRSV	New Revised Standard Version
NTS	*New Testament Studies*
PNTC	Pillar New Testament Commentary
REB	Revised English Bible
ResQ	*Restoration Quarterly*
RSV	Revised Standard Version
SCJ	*Stone-Campbell Journal*
SEG	*Supplementum Epigraphicum Graecum*
SJT	*Scottish Journal of Theology*
SNTSMS	Society for New Testament Studies Monograph Series
Spec. Laws	*On the Special Laws* (Philo)
SWJT	*Southwestern Journal of Theology*
TDNT	*Theological Dictionary of the New Testament*. Edited by Gerhard Kittel and Gerhard Friedrich. Translated by Geoffrey W. Bromiley. 10 vols. Grand Rapids: Eerdmans, 1964–1976
ThTo	*Theology Today*
TNTC	Tyndale New Testament Commentary
TynBul	*Tyndale Bulletin*
WBC	Word Biblical Commentary
WMANT	Wissenschaftliche Monographien zum Alten und Neuen Testament
WTJ	*Westminster Theological Journal*
WUNT	Wissenschaftliche Untersuchungen zum Neuen Testament
WW	*Word and World*
ZECNT	Zondervan Exegetical Commentary on the New Testament
ZNW	*Zeitschrift für die neutestamentliche Wissenschaft und die Kunde der* älteren *Kirche*

1

Introduction

Issues and Thesis of the Study

WHAT TYPE OF RELATIONSHIP did New Testament churches have with one another?[1] Was it, as Baur and his followers have claimed, a relationship of conflict and competition?[2] Or was it a loose aggregation of individual churches scattered over the Greco-Roman world?[3] Or can it be rather described as a cohesive partnership for the common cause of the gospel of Christ? Given the diversity and fluidity of early Christianity, it would be hard to give an immediate answer to these questions. With a number of sporadic accounts referring directly to church-to-church actions in the New Testament, it seems difficult to delineate the relationship of New

1. In the present study, "New Testament churches" denotes all the churches or Christian communities mentioned in the New Testament, explicitly or implicitly. The time span is from the beginning of the church up to the end of the first century when the New Testament books were completed. Sometimes "early churches" or "the earliest churches" is used in place of "New Testament churches."

2. F. C. Baur, the founder of what has been known as the Tübingen School, asserted that the early church was divided into two opposing parties, Petrine/Judean Christianity vs. Pauline/gentile Christianity. Baur's theory will be discussed below in the section of "Scholarly Context of the Study."

3. For example, Ascough argues that "Paul never assumes that his own communities were in contact with one another" (*Paul's Macedonian Associations*, 106).

Testament churches with certainty.[4] In fact, New Testament scholars have not yet reached a consensus on this subject.

On the other hand, although holding different views on the church relationship, most scholars recognize a certain level of partnership in Paul's missions. A careful reader of the New Testament can find a large number of references and clues that imply the act of communication and cooperation among Paul, his coworkers, Pauline churches, and non-Pauline churches.[5] Even a cursory reading of Acts and Paul's letters will reveal that Paul carried out his ministry along with his coworkers and in partnership with local churches.

Most of the tangible and firsthand sources for New Testament church activities are found in the record of Paul's ministry. Furthermore, as Meeks observes, a "coherent and identifiable segment of early Christianity" can be found most appropriately in the "missionary activity of Paul of Tarsus and a broad circle of co-workers and the congregations they established."[6] In this sense, studying Paul's missionary works is almost like studying New Testament church activities. The present study is founded on the premise that close attention to Paul's partnership ministry offers a richer understanding of New Testament church relationships. Paul's partnership ministry will furnish a window through which one can see how the New Testament churches were related with one another.

There arise some questions about the ministry of Paul. In what concrete ways was the partnership ministry practiced? How extensive was it and how did it link the New Testament churches together? This volume explores the various activities of Paul, his coworkers, and local churches to determine the scope and methods of Paul's partnership ministry. Besides, one may question how the socio-religious system of

4. Simply put, there are only a few New Testament passages that refer to church-to-church actions per se, such as "Church A cooperated (or fought) with Church B" or "they had much (or little) communication with each other." A typical example of church-to-church interaction would be the financial assistance of the Antioch church for the church at Jerusalem (Acts 11:27–30; 12:25).

5. Although there may be a subtle difference in nuance between "Paul's" and "Pauline," the present study will use these two expressions interchangeably. Regarding the definition of "Paul's/Pauline churches," see the section "Qualifications of the Study" below.

6. Meeks, *First Urban Christians*, 7–8. He explains the validity of choosing "Pauline Christianity" for the study of "First Urban Christians": (1) Paul's mission is "intrinsically fascinating"; (2) it is "the best-documented" with at least seven undisputed letters of Paul, which are "the earliest of all extant Christian writings"; and (3) Pauline Christianity is "entirely urban," befitting the theme of his discussions.

the Greco-Roman world influenced the partnership ministry regarding community, communication, and cooperation. These questions will guide the present discussion.

Overall, the present study seeks to underscore the act of networking and collaboration among the New Testament churches. When done properly, it will demonstrate that Paul's churches, occasioned and mediated by the partnership ministry of Paul, were engaged in networking and collaboration far more closely than has generally been assumed, not only among themselves but also with non-Pauline churches.

Method and Approach of the Study

Partnership in Paul's ministry is prominent particularly in three areas: (1) Paul's coworkers; (2) financial assistance for and through Paul's ministry; and (3) communicative activities such as letter-writing, visitations, and conferences. The present study takes up these three areas—three mediums of networking and collaboration—for the analysis of Paul's partnership ministry and church relations. First, Paul's coworkers functioned as the links for the networking of Paul's ministry. The partnership ministry can be traced by observing the activities of those coworkers. Second, financial support for Paul's missions indicates that the gospel ministry was not of an individual or of one group, but of several Christian communities in "partnership for the gospel."[7] Almsgiving was an important project in Paul's ministry. It implicated "economic mutualism," the practice of financial partnership among early churches.[8] Third, the spirit of partnership is evident from the great number of biblical references to letters, visitations, and meetings in the New Testament. By investigating these communicative activities, one will be able to find the intensity of partnership in the ministry of Paul and local churches. In sum, the research into these three subjects—Paul's coworkers, financial assistance,

7. After exploring a number of Pauline passages of financial support for missions, Dickson concludes that the passages reveal "the apostle's conception of congregational involvement in the advancement of the gospel, or 'partnership for the gospel'" (*Mission-Commitment*, 212).

8. Meggitt, *Paul, Poverty and Survival*, 157–63. By "economic mutualism," Meggitt means "the implicit or explicit belief that *individual and collective well-being is attainable above all by mutual interdependence*" (italics in original). He points out that the early church mutualism—economic partnership—is found not only in Paul's "collection" project across trans-local regions, but also in the practice of financial assistance within individual communities.

and communicative activities—will provide the source material which is useful in drawing a clearer picture of Paul's partnership ministry and of the early church relationships.

In addition, the present study is conducted with another categorization in view. Whenever possible and advisable, the discussion proceeds according to the scope of ministry. First, locally, house churches in an area maintained their local network and collaboration through, for example, community meals, joint worship services, and charity.[9] Second, trans-locally, Christian communities in different regions communicated and cooperated together for various purposes.[10] Third, these trans-local relations occurred not only within Paul's churches but also between Pauline and non-Pauline churches.[11] Thus, the three areas of partnership ministry will be treated, as far as possible, in the order of the scope of ministry. This approximate classification will be helpful to grasp the breadth of Paul's partnership and overall church relationships.

The ministry of Paul and local churches can be identified and discerned from actual events and incidents as documented in the New Testament. Accordingly, the primary method of this study is to examine relevant texts in the New Testament, particularly in Acts and Paul's letters. The first step is to search for the biblical data which refer or allude to Paul's coworkers, travels, relationships, financial aids, letters, meetings, and so forth. Then, the biblical data will be categorized according to the three areas of ministry—coworkers, financial assistance, and communicative activities—and also, whenever possible, according to the three scopes of ministry—local, trans-local, and beyond Pauline missions. Lastly, the assorted data will be probed to determine how Paul carried out his missions in partnership with others, and how the partnership ministry brought about networking and collaboration among the New Testament churches, locally and trans-locally.

9. It is commonly believed that there were multiple house churches in each major city that Paul evangelized. For example, Paul's letters show the presence of several house assemblies in the cities of Philippi (Phil 1:1), Corinth (1 Cor 14:23), Rome (Rom 16), and so on.

10. For example, the Antioch church sent a relief fund to the Jerusalem church (Acts 11:29–30). Apollos, recommended and encouraged by the Ephesian church, went to Corinth and proved himself to be "a great help" to the Corinthian church (Acts 18:27–28).

11. For example, the "collection" was contributed by Paul's churches to support the church at Jerusalem (Acts 20:4, 17–24; 1 Cor 16:1–4, 17; 2 Cor 8–9; Rom 15: 25–27, 31).

Another concern of the present study is to determine how the existing social and religious conventions were germane and contributive to the partnership ministry of Paul and the local churches. Therefore, it surveys the first-century environment in which Paul and the New Testament churches carried out their ministries. There has been much study on the possibility of parallels between Paul's churches and Greco-Roman socio-religious entities.[12] Particularly, informed by the recent scholarship that has emphasized the Jewish background of early Christianity, the present study seeks to understand Paul's partnership ministry in light of the practice of Jewish communities in the Diaspora.[13]

The three areas of Paul's partnership ministry—Paul's coworkers, financial assistance, communicative activities—constitute the three major chapters of this volume. After this introductory chapter, chapter 2 investigates the first area of partnership ministry, missionary activities of Paul's coworkers. They are examined according to their main ministry fields: (1) those who worked primarily in a local setting (e.g., Philemon, Nympha, Euodia); (2) those who were engaged in trans-local activities (e.g., Timothy, Titus, Epaphroditus); (3) those whose work extended beyond Paul's churches (e.g., Barnabas, Silas, Aquila).[14] This classification

12. Ascough, in *What Are They Saying*, suggests four equivalent social models—voluntary associations, synagogues, philosophical schools, and mystery cults, devoting a chapter to each model. Also, see Meeks, *First Urban Christians*, 75–84; Adams, "First-Century Models," 60–78; and Harland, *Associations, Synagogues, and Congregations*.

13. Concerning the Jewish background of the earliest church, Meeks notes that "Because Christianity was an offshoot of Judaism, the urban Christian groups obviously had the diaspora synagogue as the nearest and most natural model" (*First Urban Christians*, 80–81). Also, Lüdemann affirms that the early churches were "grounded in the whole fabric of Judaism" (*Primitive Christianity*, 146). For more thorough treatment, see Barclay, *Pauline Churches and Diaspora Jews*; and Nanos and Zetterholm, *Paul within Judaism*.

14. This categorization is based solely upon biblical references. A definite demarcation is unlikely because of limited information. In some cases, therefore, the distinction of "local coworkers" and "trans-local coworkers" is not so clear. For example, Paul commends Phoebe, "a servant of the church in Cenchrea," to the believers in Rome (Rom 16:1). Most scholars agree that she was the letter carrier (messenger) to Rome (Rom 16:1–2). Thus, she ministered both locally and trans-locally. Likewise, Onesiphorus, a house church leader/patron at Ephesus, traveled to Rome and "often refreshed" Paul in chains (2 Tim 1:16–18; 4:19). Even though the individuals have visited Rome and might have done some work there, they are still categorized, in this book, as the "local coworkers" since their ministries seem to have centered on their local churches. See Appendix 1 and 2, which list Paul's coworkers based on their primary field of ministry.

is chosen not because it best represents the spectrum of Paul's coworkers but because it fits into the aforementioned methodology—the advancement of thesis according to the three scopes of ministry. The first section discusses Paul's coworkers in the local ministry. Except for the occasional role as church messengers sent to Paul or to other communities, they normally served as the hosts/hostesses of local house churches. The second section deals with another group of coworkers who are categorized as "trans-local" since their activities spanned the wide area of the Mediterranean basin. Paul's travel companions belonged to this group along with the envoys sent by Paul to the churches or by the churches to Paul.[15] The last section also discusses trans-local coworkers, but especially those whose missionary activities transcended the boundary of Paul's ministry. They had ministry relationships not only with Paul but also with other apostles and other Christian communities.

Chapter 3 examines the sharing of financial resources among Pauline as well as non-Pauline churches. First, it briefly reviews the socio-economic condition of the Mediterranean world, such as famine, poverty, and the financial status of the population, particularly, the Christians in urban areas. It also reviews the economic support system of Greco-Roman voluntary associations and Jewish communities in the Diaspora. The second section deals with various biblical texts pertaining to the practice of financial assistance among local believers. It reflects the relationship of house churches within a city area. In the third section, the financial collaboration of churches is investigated with regard to their support for Paul's missions. It seeks to find how the Christian communities financially assisted Paul's ministry, thereby joining together in Paul's missionary efforts. The last section discusses the contributions to the poor in Jerusalem made first by the Antioch church and then by Paul's churches. Scholars have debated what Paul's motive for the "collection" was and how it turned out as a result. While most studies have taken "basically theological" approaches, the present study focuses on its

15. A clear-cut division of the roles is elusive because of their similarities and overlaps on some occasions. For example, it is most probable that the travel companions of Paul on the way to Jerusalem were also envoys/representatives of the local churches who had been enlisted for the sake of Paul's collection project (Acts 20:4). Whereas Epaphroditus was an envoy sent from Philippi to Rome to help Paul (Phil 2:25; 4:18), Erastus served as an envoy from Corinth *and* as Paul's travel companion as well (Acts 19:22; 2 Tim 4:20). See Appendix 2 "Paul's Trans-Local Coworkers."

historical aspects and implications for the interdependent relationship of New Testament churches.[16]

Chapter 4 investigates written and verbal communications, such as letter-writing, sending and receiving envoys, visitations, and church conferences, which occurred in connection with Paul's ministry. The first section, for contextual understanding, discusses the social mobility of the first-century world—travels, writing of letters, interrelationship of voluntary associations, and most importantly, social networks of the Diaspora Jews. The second section presents Paul's letters in terms of their communal characteristics. It shows how Paul's letters were conducive to inter-church awareness as one body of Christ, locally and trans-locally. In the third section, Paul's visits to local churches and Jerusalem are probed. The study will ascertain the connectedness of local churches and the solid relationship between Paul and the Jerusalem apostles. The last section treats three conferences—the Jerusalem conference (Gal 2:1–10), the Antioch incident (Gal 2:11–14), and the Jerusalem Council (Acts 15)—and affirms the principle of cooperation operative between Jewish and gentile Christians.

Chapter 5 summarizes and evaluates what is found from the present research. Once Paul's partnership ministry has been explained in the context of inter-church actions, this study will be able to make an informed judgment on the relationship of New Testament churches. Its implications are discussed for further studies: (1) many interpersonal or inter-group accounts in Acts and Paul's letters can be interpreted in light of a cooperative church relationship; (2) early Christianity is to be construed with the paradigm of unity rather than with the Bauerian concept of opposition; (3) the twenty-first century churches can find some models of communication and collaboration in the practice of New Testament churches.

Scholarly Context of the Study

There have been scholarly discussions related to the present study of New Testament church relationships. Baur's hypothesis—antithetical dynamics between Paul and Peter/James—has been the major factor that has

16. Horrell, "Paul's Collection," 76. He argues that scholars have proposed mostly theological reasons for the collection project. Three major ones are: (1) an eschatological interpretation rooted in a particular view of salvation-history; (2) the concept of the unity of the Church as the body of Christ; and (3) an act of charity, which is of itself fundamentally theological ("materialist theology").

influenced the modern scholarship of early Christianity. His analysis has an important bearing on the relational structure of New Testament churches. More recently, some scholars have shown interests in the social aspect of early Christianity. Their works often deal with the dynamics of interpersonal and inter-community relationships existent among New Testament churches and church leaders. A brief survey of these scholarly discussions will be helpful to see the point of the present study in its broader context.

F. C. Baur and Early Church Relationships

The topic of partnership in Paul's ministry ultimately subsumes the ministry relationship between Paul and the Jerusalem apostles. This issue has been controversial since the middle of the nineteenth century when Baur advocated a dialectic theory of early Christianity. According to Baur, the earliest Christians were the law-observant Jews who followed Jesus as their Messiah. Paul, however, led a group of law-free Christians and separated from traditional Judaism. Thus, a serious tension built up between Paul and the Jerusalem apostles, and it continued down to the second century until the two parties were reconciled into the "old Catholicism." Baur applied Hegel's dialectic philosophy to the analysis of the development of early Christianity—the synthesis of two opposing theses, Palestinian/Jewish/Petrine Christianity and Hellenistic/gentile/Pauline Christianity.

Baur's proposal has been criticized by many scholars for being too selective in the use of evidence and too simple in its historical reconstruction to represent the actual scene of first-century churches.[17] An early critique came from his own student, Albrecht Ritschl. Arguing that "unification even for external reasons always comes about only where the same inner reason is at work," Ritschl affirmed a fundamental partnership between Paul and the Jerusalem apostles based upon "the identical content of the gospel of all apostles."[18] A century later, against the Baue-

17. For example, Hengel's study has weakened the foundation of Baur's model, Judaism vs. Hellenism. Surveying a wide range of Greek classics and Second Temple Jewish literature, Hengel concludes that "from about the middle of the third century BC. all Judaism must really be designated 'Hellenistic Judaism' in the strict sense" (*Judaism and Hellenism*, 104). Hence, the concept of the traditional model—distinction and dialectics—has become questionable.

18. Kümmel, *New Testament*, 163.

rian trend in academia, Johannes Munck emphasized that "Paul is not an opponent of Jerusalem, and the earliest disciples there are not opponents of Paul."[19] The "Judaizers" were, according to him, but a minority group of the Jerusalem community with little connection with Peter or James. Like Ritschl, Munck maintained that Paul differed from the Jerusalem apostles in strategy, not in principle. They were on the same front fighting against the Judaizers.

Even in the midst of criticism, Baur's paradigm of two opposing parties has persisted into the present-day New Testament scholarship. Gerd Lüdemann, for example, examines all the cases of "anti-Paulinism" in Paul's letters and extra-biblical literatures and concludes that "both the liberal and conservative wings of Jerusalem Jewish Christianity had shared an anti-Pauline attitude" in opposition to Paul's apostleship and his law-free mission.[20] The Jerusalem church, according to him, became increasingly antagonistic to Paul and ultimately rejected the collection fund from gentile churches.[21] Michael Goulder is a recent advocate of Baur's argument. He considers the conflict between Paul and the Corinthian church to be indistinguishable in nature from the conflict in Galatians. Opponents in both churches were linked with the Jewish mission led by Peter, competing for converts. In some distinction from Baur's philosophical approach, relying on the exegesis of Pauline texts, Goulder redraws Baur's demarcation line between the two "competing missions."[22]

Even though not many students of early Christianity endorse Baur's hypothesis, his analysis of the Antioch incident (Gal 2:11–14) continues to influence much of the present-day New Testament scholarship. For example, James D. G. Dunn examines the major verbs in Galatians 2, which indicate Paul's relationship to the Jerusalem apostles, and concludes that after the Antioch incident Paul who had been on a friendly footing with

19. Munck, *Paul and the Salvation*, 284.

20. Lüdemann, *Opposition to Paul*, 115. The opponents in Galatians 2 (Acts 15) are differentiated from those in Corinth who had a more liberal theology; however, both of them are viewed alike as anti-Pauline Jewish Christians under the sway of the Jerusalem apostles.

21. Lüdemann, *Opposition to Paul*, 59–62.

22. By "two competing missions" Goulder means the conflicting relationship between the mission of Paul and that of the counter-missionaries sent by the "pillars" in Jerusalem. His view of the ministry relationship of New Testament churches is readily noticeable from the titles of his major books, *St. Paul versus St. Peter: A Tale of Two Missions* and *Paul and the Competing Mission in Corinth*.

Peter and James shifted to a stance of independence and separation.[23] Nicholas Taylor, while denouncing Baur's treatment of early church history, acknowledges the fatality of the Antioch dispute: "Paul's break with the Antiochene church therefore required a complete reorientation."[24]

A more amicable relationship between Paul and the Jerusalem church has been put forward by other scholars. F. F. Bruce regards Peter as a bridge-builder, who catalyzed the partnership between the Jewish Christians led by James and the Hellenistic Christians led by Paul.[25] Richard Bauckham finds in Acts and Galatians no indication of conflict and division in the mainline movement of early Christianity. Paul, Peter, and James all agreed on the doctrine of salvation as well as on the ethical and liturgical significance of Jewish traditions.[26]

From this brief account of Baur's thesis and varying repercussions thereof, arise several points of note for the present study. First, Baur's theory, particularly his reconstruction of the Antioch incident, still provides a frame of reference to Paul's relationship with the Jerusalem church. Second, therefore, most scholars consider the Antioch incident to have been so critical as to have resulted in a permanent split between the ministry of Paul and that of Peter and James. Third, it is noticeable that almost all the arguments have been dependent on the exegesis of Gal 2:11–14 and Acts 15. The discussion has focused on a few questions as to who were the "certain men from James" (Gal 2:12)[27] and why Peter withdrew from the table fellowship with the gentile Christians. Fourth, Baur's hypothesis has been evaluated by many scholars with a bent for ideological and theological import rather than with meticulous socio-historical facts.[28] Fifth, the paucity of textual sources and their seemingly contradictory nature have brought about many different interpretations and different

23. Dunn, "Relationship between Paul and Jerusalem," 461–78.

24. Taylor, *Paul, Antioch and Jerusalem*, 24.

25. Bruce, *Peter, Stephen, James, and John*, 39–48. See also Hengel, *Acts and the History*, 92–98. He argues that Peter took a mediating position in the matter of Jewish vs. gentile conflict. Peter, according to Hengel, had a "lax" stance over the Torah and "never shared the strict standpoint of the Judaists" (97).

26. Bauckham, "James, Peter, and the Gentiles," 91–142.

27. Biblical texts in this book are mostly from my own translation or NASB unless otherwise noted.

28. The theological and philosophical tendency of the debate is self-evident with the Hegelian construct of the agenda. In this connection, Johnson points out that "More important, the Tübingen school paid attention only to ideas. It paid little attention to persons, and even less to places and social institutions" ("Koinonia," 306).

reconstructions of the situation at Antioch. With Baur's analysis still influential, the question of early church relationships remains a matter of scholarly debate.

Social Dynamics in Paul's Ministry

In keeping with the sociological approach to New Testament studies, some scholars have paid particular attention to the dynamics of social relations operative in the community of Paul's ministry.[29] One of the pioneering studies was done by John H. Schütz in his *Paul and the Anatomy of Apostolic Authority*. Its main thesis is that "for Paul, the authority of the apostle is an interpretation of power—the power of the gospel."[30] Building upon Weber and other sociologists, Schütz lays out the interrelationship of power, authority, legitimacy, leadership, and change. Although the context of his analysis is relevant to the social relations in Paul's world, the major portion of his study is confined to a theological and hermeneutical treatment of the subject. Schütz's work is focused "on Paul's assertions of authority, rather than on the communities and relationships within which that authority is exercised."[31]

In the third chapter of *Paul and the Dynamics of Power*, Ehrensperger discusses "The Exercise of Power–Networking in the Early Christian Movement." Exploring Paul's relationships with his coworkers, churches, and the apostles at Jerusalem, the author portrays Paul as an apostle "who is part of a network of people, closely related and in contact with others, interacting and communicating within this network."[32] She analyzes the literary style of Paul's letters—co-senders, greetings, and sibling

29. The use of sociological analysis as an interpretive tool for NT texts has its root already in the latter part of the nineteenth century. Early scholars include, for example, sociologist Max Weber, historian Ernst Troeltsch, and New Testament scholar Adolf Deissmann. In the 1970s, however, emerged systematic applications of the social science to the study of New Testament world and exegesis. The sociological approach has become one of the most important methodologies in biblical studies for the past half-century. For its leading scholars and works, see the next section, "Need and Significance of the Study."

30. Schütz, *Anatomy of Apostolic Authority*, ix. He discusses three significant terms—"the gospel," "the kerygma," and "the apostle"—in relation to Paul's self-understanding of apostleship. Basically, Paul understood apostolicity in terms of preaching the gospel.

31. Taylor, Review of *Anatomy of Apostolic Authority*, by Schütz, 85.

32. Ehrensperger, *Paul and the Dynamics*, 36.

terminology—and then concludes that although there was an asymmetrical power balance between Paul and his communities, it was not a relationship of "power over" but rather based on mutual trust.[33] Regarding Paul's relationship with Jerusalem, Ehrensperger emphasizes that Paul sought "interdependence *for* mutual recognition within the apostolic group," but not "independence *from* or superiority *over* other apostles."[34] It is notable that Ehrensperger underscores a relational and collaborative aspect of Paul's ministry. However, the basic setting of her study still concerns the use of power and authority, a hierarchical relationship.

More comprehensive and significant to our discussion is the work of Bengt Holmberg, *Paul and Power*. This book does not concern the theology of the church or of its ministry; it is mainly "a historical study of the structure of authority in the Primitive Church as reflected in the Pauline epistles."[35] It consists of two parts, "Distribution of Power in the Primitive Church" and "Structure of Authority in the Primitive Church." Holmberg presents, in the first part, an exegetical and historical study of early church relationships, and in the second, an analysis of the collected data in light of Weber's concept of "charismatic" authority.[36] The socio-historical study of the first half, which is more relevant to the present study, discusses the dynamics of interpersonal and intergroup relations in three areas: (1) between Paul and the Jerusalem Church; (2) within the region of Pauline churches (trans-local); and (3) within the local Pauline churches.[37]

While considering Paul's ministry as independent of the Jerusalem church, Holmberg claims that Paul has acknowledged the authority of the apostles at Jerusalem and continued to turn to them for their approval. Paul's visitations to Jerusalem and conferences with the leaders

33. Ehrensperger, *Paul and the Dynamics*, 61–62.

34. Ehrensperger, *Paul and the Dynamics*, 43.

35. Holmberg, *Paul and Power*, 3. By "authority," Holmberg means "social relations of asymmetric power distribution considered legitimate by the participating actors," and by "structure," "a totality or system of interdependent qualities or phenomena."

36. Holmberg, *Paul and Power*, 137. "Charismatic" authority is an authority based on "devotion to the exceptional sanctity, heroism, or exemplary character of an individual person, and of normative patterns or order revealed or ordained by him."

37. This categorization corresponds, in reverse order, to the present study methodology, which seeks to lay out its discussion along the similar line of ministry scopes. However, Holmberg's discussion of the local level, "The distribution of power within the local Pauline churches" (chapter 3), is not about the inter-church relationship of a local Christian community. Rather, it deals with the origin and function of "charismatic" and "institutional" offices in the early church.

there, according to Holmberg, indicate the asymmetrical balance of power between the Jerusalem church on the one hand, and Paul, Pauline churches, and the Antioch church on the other. Whereas Jerusalem regarded the "collection" as a "duty" of the gentile churches to acknowledge the former's spiritual supremacy, Paul and the gentile churches might have given it "a more theological interpretation," recognizing "Jerusalem's actual importance in God's election-and salvation-history."[38] According to Holmberg, the Jerusalem church was in the position of power and authority due to its apparent closeness to the ultimate source of the authority, Jesus Christ.

Holmberg analyzes the interrelationship of Paul's churches by evaluating his coworkers and the local churches. Coworkers are divided into two groups based on the nature of their relationship with Paul.[39] The local churches are examined also in their relations to Paul. Holmberg approaches the study by investigating the apostle's self-understanding and the power he exercised in relation to his churches. Meanwhile, the study of the relationship within a local community is not about how the local house churches interrelated with one another. Instead, Holmberg makes a "brief analysis of the intra-church differentiation of functions (or "ministries") in Pauline churches."[40]

The dominant theme of Holmberg's study is expressed in the book title *Paul and Power*. It is about Paul's power and influence exerted through his personal presence, representatives, letters, and financial assistance. Holmberg's analysis of ecclesial relationships centers on how the relational concept of power and authority has been built up and distributed among the churches and the leaders. It is his intention to approach the historical data in the book of Acts and Paul's letters with an eye for "explicit and implicit relations of superiority and subordination."[41] That

38. Holmberg, *Paul and Power*, 41.

39. Holmberg, *Paul and Power*, 61–62. One group includes those who are "entirely at his [Paul's] disposal" and personally close to the apostle—i.e., Erastus, Tychicus, Mark, Epaphras, Timothy, and Titus. The other group comprises Barnabas, Silvanus, and Apollos, whose missionary activities were "not at his [Paul's] disposal."

40. Holmberg, *Paul and Power*, 96. He lists and explains the commonly accepted church positions/functions of the early church—apostles, prophets, teachers, leaders/administrators, and other functions referred to in 1 Cor 12–14.

41. Holmberg, *Paul and Power*, 8–11. Before setting out to investigate NT texts of ecclesial relationships, Holmberg discusses the concept of "power." "Power" is, according to his definition, "an actor's ability to induce or influence another actor to carry out his directives or any other norms he supports," and this power is indicated foremost by

is, Holmberg's study starts from the presupposition of an asymmetric relationship of power.

Due to the nature of underlying perspectives, the studies of social dynamics have certain limitations in representing Paul's ministry partnership, which was the manifestation of friendship and teamwork rather than the structure of power and authority. It is not that Holmberg has little regard for the intimate and corporate nature of church relationships. He makes clear that "it is necessary to keep in mind the fact that the relationship was deeply personal,"[42] and that "many different authority relations are not mere isolated occurrences of authority but are interrelated parts of an organic whole."[43] Nevertheless, since Holmberg's outlook is aligned to the Weberian theory of power, his analysis is bound to reflect a hierarchy of relationship, thereby obscuring the significance of correlation and collaboration among the parties involved in the community of faith. Baur looked at the early church through the framework of dialectics, and Holmberg, through the sociology of power and authority. With the Bauerian and Weberian perspectives still prominent in the analysis of early church relations, there arises a need for a new approach to the study, which is not based on philosophical method or political structure, but primarily on historical realities substantiated by copious and concrete evidence, e.g., letters, envoys, inter-group relations, assistance, visitations, meetings, and other relational activities.

Need and Significance of the Study

Over the past century, numerous works have been produced for the historical reconstruction of early Christianity. The majority of them concerned the process of early church formation and institutionalization. More recently, the sociological approach to New Testament studies has flourished, resulting in many works on the social background of early church development.[44] Particularly, a number of socio-historical studies

"phenomena belonging to relations of explicit superiority and subordination."

42. Holmberg, *Paul and Power*, 61.

43. Holmberg, *Paul and Power*, 196.

44. Among those socio-cultural studies, the following books are significant and relevant to the present study: Judge, *Social Pattern of Early Christian Groups*; Holmberg, *Paul and Power*; Theissen, *Social Setting of Pauline Christianity*; Meeks, *First Urban Christians*; Malherbe, *Social Aspects of Early Christianity*; Stark, *Rise of Christianity*; Ehrensperger, *Paul and the Dynamics*; Porter and Land, *Paul and His Social Relations*.

successfully delineated the life of early Christian communities such as those in Corinth, Rome, and Ephesus.[45] By focusing on the individual communities, however, these studies have done little to illuminate how the Christian communities related together and formed a ministry of partnership locally and trans-locally. Considering the enormous studies on the development of early churches, surprisingly little effort has been made to ascertain the relational aspect of New Testament churches. In fact, no scholarly book has been published on the subject of inter-church networking and collaboration.[46]

As mentioned in the beginning, partnership in Paul's ministry is well recognized among New Testament scholars. Given its wide recognition, however, there has been not much scholarly work on the subject. Furthermore, since the concept of Paul's partnership ministry tends to focus narrowly on the teamwork of Paul and his associates, its study has not dealt with the whole purview of partnership ministry, and even less with its implications for early church relationships. Monographs or articles have been published, yet only on one aspect of partnership ministry, e.g., on letter-writing, on Paul's coworkers, or on the "collection." These particularistic studies are intended to pursue the task of their own agenda, not the ministry of partnership as a whole. A comprehensive study on various aspects of partnership ministry is needed to grasp the whole picture of Paul's ministry and church relationships.

In addition, the present work is significant since it may effectively challenge Baur's thesis, which carries a renewed weight in recent scholarship.[47] Were the first-century churches divided into two camps that

45. Studies on these Christian communities include, for example, Murphy-O'Connor, *St. Paul's Corinth*; Hemer, *Letters to the Seven Churches*; Lampe, *From Paul to Valentinus*; and Trebilco, *Early Christians in Ephesus*.

46. To the knowledge of this writer, there is no book-length publication available, which is devoted entirely to the relationship or collaboration of the first-century churches. An unpublished PhD dissertation bears a title that relates to the issue of church relationships: Lawrence Malcom Stewart III, "Communication Networks and Social Cohesion in the Early Church." Its main discussion, however, is not about biblical accounts of inter-church relationships or collaborations that actually happened in the early church. It is rather a social analysis of "social cohesiveness" that rests on the network of house churches and its master builders, "psychagogues" (Christian teachers). The dissertation devotes much space to the discussion of second-century church affairs. Nevertheless, it contains some useful material for this study: "Paul's Relations with His Converts" (61–65); "Levels of Relationships" (65–82); and "Continuing Contact with Converts" (83–90).

47. Tyson, "Legacy of Baur," 125–44. In recent works of New Testament scholars, such as John Knox, Gerd Lüdemann, Michael Goulder, C. K. Barrett, and Jacob Jervell,

competed with each other? Was the Antioch incident, as many scholars accept, the epitome of such confrontation? The survey of scholarly context in the previous section raised some concerns about the way these questions have been treated in the past. Many arguments and debates have rather centered on a few biblical passages. The assessment has been influenced by theological presuppositions. The result is varied suppositions and continuing debates.

The relationship between Paul and the Jerusalem apostles, which necessarily involves the relationship between Pauline and non-Pauline churches, should be understood in the context beyond a few incidents of limited information. It needs to be examined with a more extensive database, i.e., all biblical accounts of contacts and interactions between Paul and other apostles/coworkers, and between various Christian communities. Out of this integrated study of relational activities, an image of first-century church relationships will surface. Interpersonal and inter-church relations are first a matter of historical affairs and events. That means that Baur's relational paradigm can best be supported or refuted by the whole case of the partnership activities and events that took place among the first-century churches including Pauline and non-Pauline communities.

One of the most notable developments in twentieth-century Christendom was the ecumenical movement, with an increasing concern for the unity of the church. For the cause of both theological and missiological progress, the partakers advocated inter-church conversation and cooperation. Also, numerous and divergent studies have been made to promote the local, trans-local, and universal unity of the church. Many of the studies leaned to the theological and hermeneutical analyses of the ecumenical ideal, giving little attention to the practical side of the ideal. In this connection, Kloha makes a crucial observation: "Perhaps the most overlooked aspect of the life of the NT church is the fostering and maintaining of relationships among geographically distant congregations. . . . A second significant aspect of the life of the NT church was the relationship among local 'house-churches' in a given city."[48] The present study seeks to shed light on the overlooked aspect of church life by investigating the networking and collaboration of the New Testament churches. This study may then point to a direction for the ecumenical movement based on biblical models and instructions.

Tyson observes "something of a revival of interest and appreciation [about Baur's theory]" (131).

48. Kloha, "Trans-Congregational Church," 185.

Sources of the Study

Numerous accounts in the New Testament, explicit and implicit, constitute evidentiary materials for the reconstruction of early church activities.[49] Hence, the primary source for research is Paul's letters, which convey many occasions of interactions among Paul, coworkers, other apostles, and the local churches. In the course of discussion, all canonical books ascribed to Paul will be taken as his own writings.[50] Whatever the case of authorship may be, it will make little difference to the conclusion of this study, since the issue at stake is the theme of relationship and collaboration reflected either in the writings of Paul or of his disciples.

Along with Paul's letters, the information in the book of Acts will be utilized. Critical New Testament scholarship has questioned the book's historical reliability because of its alleged differences from Paul's letters in several historical contents. Many scholars, therefore, have inquired into Paul's letters for historical data, while discrediting the book of Acts as secondary or even useless.[51] More recently, however, a number of studies have demonstrated that the differences might be only superficial or much less significant than previously thought.[52] Based on this understanding, this book appropriates all the accounts of the book of Acts for the historical reconstruction of Paul's partnership ministry and early church relationships.

49. Most biblical texts relevant to the present study are listed in the appendixes: Appendix 1 "Paul's Coworkers in the Local Ministry"; Appendix 2 "Paul's Coworkers in the Trans-Local Ministry"; Appendix 3 "Biblical Accounts in Relation to Financial Assistance"; and Appendix 4 "Paul's Letters: Senders, Receivers, and Persons in Greeting."

50. Many NT scholars consider six of the thirteen canonically Pauline books as pseudonymous, i.e., Ephesians, Colossians, 2 Thessalonians, and the Pastoral letters (1 & 2 Timothy and Titus). However, given the lack of substantial and decisive evidence that would disprove Pauline authorship, the present study develops its thesis on the assumption that Paul, along with his coworkers, wrote all the thirteen letters.

51. Already in the middle of nineteenth century, F. C. Baur questioned the historicity of the book of Acts. Distrusting its historical accounts, he rejected all attempts to reconcile the Paul of the letters with the Paul of Acts. About a century later, in *Chapters in a Life of Paul*, John Knox also claimed that the study of Paul, particularly Pauline chronology, should not depend uncritically on the book of Acts for historical information.

52. For this viewpoint, see Thompson, "Paul in the Book of Acts," 425–36. He lists several major differences, which the contemporary scholarship claims to find in the book of Acts and Pauline letters, and then gives his own arguments against each of them. For a helpful survey of recent scholarship on Acts, see Walton, "Acts: Many Questions, Many Answers," 229–50 (particularly, 240–44).

Besides biblical texts, several sources provide useful information. First, Jewish literature includes many historical accounts concerning the first-century Jewish communities in the Diaspora. It will be worthwhile to survey this literature since the Jewish communities had a significant bearing on the first-century churches. Second, recent years have seen a number of books published on synagogues and voluntary associations.[53] In these books, numerous archaeological, epigraphic, and numismatic materials are collected and organized for ready use in exploring ancient social institutions. The present study turns to these source books to survey the socio-cultural backgrounds of what and how Paul's churches practiced in partnership with other churches. Third, the contemporary social custom is normally what originated and developed from the preceding generations. This means that the early second-century Christian literature provides useful sources for the study of first-century church activities. The most important of them are the writings of the Apostolic Fathers, which were temporally adjacent to the later writings of the New Testament.[54] These post-apostolic sources will be noted whenever necessary to corroborate the biblical testimony of early church networking and collaboration.

Qualifications of the Study

One might ask how legitimate the phrase "Paul's/Pauline churches/communities" is. Some scholars are wary of this designation on the grounds of its semantic quality that may isolate a particular group ("Pauline") from the overall Christian movement.[55] Some others do not favor the

53. Notable among them are, in the order of publication, Meyer, *Ancient Mysteries*; Williams, *Jews among the Greeks and Romans*; Runesson, Binder, and Olsson, *Ancient Synagogue*; Kloppenborg and Ascough, *Greco-Roman Associations*; and Ascough et al., *Associations in the Greco-Roman World*.

54. "Apostolic Fathers" refers to a collection of post-apostolic writings immediately subsequent to the writings of the NT, possibly with some overlap. 1 Clement was written circa 95 AD about the time when the book of Revelation and the epistles of John were completed. These writings were "revered and, in some cases, rivaled the very writings that now make up the canon of the NT." Evans, *Ancient Texts*, 269.

55. See Horrell, "Pauline Churches," 185–203. Sketching Paul's early letters (1 Thessalonians, Galatians, 1 and 2 Corinthians, etc.) in terms of the concept of "Pauline," Horrell convincingly points out a potential pitfall in that nomenclature. The crux of the matter is that "the 'networks' . . . were not, it seems, separate and isolated networks of Pauline workers, Petrine adherents, and so on, but instead—notwithstanding certain 'team-like' allegiances—facilitated contacts within and across the early Christian movement" (195).

term because it obscures the individuality and diversity of various Christian communities in one quick "Pauline" brush.[56] Nonetheless, it would be quite valid to use the description "Pauline" or "Paul's" given the unique position and significance of his ministry in the development of early Christianity. The majority of scholars customarily mention "Pauline churches" to denote simply the Christian communities founded and nurtured primarily by Paul and/or his coworkers, with no theological strings attached. The present study also adopts this general concept of Pauline and non-Pauline distinction.

To this simple category belong the churches at Galatia, Corinth, Thessalonica, Philippi, Ephesus, and Colossae. Of course, the Christian communities at Rome and Antioch were no less significant in Paul's missions. Paul wrote his longest letter to the Roman Christians, and many of his coworkers served the house churches in that city. The Antioch church commissioned Paul to undertake missionary journeys. Nonetheless, the churches at Rome and Antioch were not founded or educated primarily by Paul. In this sense, these two important churches will be regarded as distinct from those called "Paul's/Pauline churches." Since the two churches are not Pauline but closely related to Paul, they functioned as an important bridge connecting Pauline and non-Pauline missions.

The word ἐκκλησία, which occurs twenty-three times in the book of Acts and sixty-two times in Paul's letters, is used primarily to denote "a local assembly or gathering of Christians in a particular place: it is thus not a metaphor, but a term descriptive of an identifiable object."[57] Likewise, the present study uses the word to mean "house church" when the assembly takes place at home, and "church" when the assembly implies the whole group of Christians in a city. Sometimes fluid expressions are used to avoid monotony: "house assembly" or "house gathering" in place

56. See Barclay, "Thessalonica and Corinth," 183–96. In a comparative study of the churches at Corinth and Thessalonica in light of their respective social settings, Barclay argues that the Corinthian church ought not to be assumed as a typical example of Pauline churches. All of the so-called "Pauline" communities had different origins, circumstances, and issues of their own. Discussing the divergent development of the two Pauline churches, he concludes that it is misleading to "generalize about 'Pauline Christians'" (196).

57. O'Brien, "Church," 124. Besides the community of Jesus' followers, however, Luke in the book of Acts employs the same word to denote the Israelites wandering in the wilderness (7:38), a meeting of a synagogue (13:43), a simple gathering of people (19:32), and a civic assembly of gentiles (19:34). Luke does not take ἐκκλησία as an official term exclusively reserved for the Christian church.

of "house church"; "Christian community" or "faith community" corresponding to "church"; and "early churches" or "the earliest churches" instead of "New Testament churches."

Pauline chronology is significant for reconstructing the history of early Christianity. Paul's partnership ministry was carried out through the activities of sending and receiving letters, missionaries, and financial gifts, all of which are grounded in Pauline chronology. For the chronological layout, this study accepts and utilizes the historical veracity of the book of Acts and Paul's letters alike. Although a definite chronology is unfeasible, arguments in this study comply with these assessments: (1) the Jerusalem visit of Gal 2:1–10 is identified with the famine visit of Acts 11:30; (2) the Antioch incident and the writing of Galatians occurred after the so-called first missionary journey but shortly before the Jerusalem Council (Acts 15); and (3) Galatians was written to the churches in southern Asia Minor (South Galatian hypothesis). In addition, the present study posits that Paul wrote the "Prison Letters" (Ephesians, Philippians, Colossians, and Philemon) during his imprisonment in Rome.

2

Collaboration through Paul's Coworkers

THERE ARE VERY FEW scholarly works of book-length written on Paul's coworkers.[1] Yet, one can find a good number of articles and essays on this subject.[2] In his influential article, Ellis profiles Paul as "a missionary with a large number of associates" and "scarcely ever found without companions."[3] That is, Paul's ministry was carried on with and through many coworkers. Since most of the coworkers were associated with certain Christian communities, the ministry of Paul's coworkers provides plausible information about the local churches and their mutual relationships. Therefore, the present chapter examines Paul's coworkers as to how their activities are indicative of or contributive to early church relationships in both local and trans-local dimensions.

1. Three book-length works are available: Ollrog, *Paulus und seine Mitarbeiter*; a slender volume by Bruce, *Pauline Circle*; and a PhD dissertation by Maness, "Pauline Congregations." More recently, a series of short works on individual coworkers have been published under the series title, "Paul's Social Network: Brothers and Sisters in Faith" by Liturgical Press.

2. Noteworthy of them are Ellis, "Paul and His Co-workers," 437–52; Holmberg, *Paul and Power*, 58–69; and Ehrensperger, *Paul and the Dynamics*, 35–62. Some missiological works on Paul provide useful information concerning Paul's mission strategy and his coworkers, e.g., Gehring, *House Church and Mission*, 119–55, and Schnabel, *Early Christian Mission*, 1425–45.

3. Ellis, "Paul and His Co-workers," 439.

This chapter consists of four sections. The introductory section discusses Paul's coworkers in terms of their functions, categorization, and relationship with their local churches. It includes the discussion of the Greco-Roman household structure and the house churches in Paul's missions.[4] The second section seeks to determine, as much as possible, church relationships within an area (i.e., among the house churches) by investigating the local ministry of Paul's coworkers. The third section discusses trans-local church relationships indebted to the trans-local coworkers whose mission field encompassed multiple Christian communities. The fourth section also discusses trans-local church relationships, but the ones beyond the boundary of Paul's missions. It examines those coworkers who were relatively independent of Paul or in companionship not only with Paul but also with other apostles and non-Pauline churches.

Paul's Coworkers

For the development of discussion, this section first lays out the definition and functions of Paul's coworkers by surveying various Greek terms for "coworker" used in the book of Acts and Paul's letters. Then Paul's coworkers are categorized roughly into three groups according to their primary field of ministry. Also, a study is done to understand the place of Paul's coworkers within the life and ministry of the local churches. Lastly, a subsection is given to introduce the concept of household and house churches in the setting of the first-century Greco-Roman world.

Functions of Paul's Coworkers

Depending on how one defines "Paul's coworkers," their total number varies.[5] In the present study, the term "Paul's coworkers" is used to refer

4. In this chapter, the term "house church" may be used interchangeably with "house group" or "house fellowship" or "house assembly" according to its context. The "local churches" may imply the local "house churches." Sometimes, "the churches" mean "the house churches." Generally speaking, the "church" in this study denotes the original meaning of ἐκκλησία ("assembly" or "gathering") in relation to Christ-believers.

5. According to Ellis, the total number of Paul's coworkers may become "ninety-five (Redlich) or eighty-one (Pölzl) depending on how broadly one defines the term," while he himself gives a chart of thirty-six coworkers, eliminating "the names mentioned only in Acts and those with unspecified and general relationships to Paul"

to those who are described in the New Testament, explicitly or implicitly, as Paul's colleagues, assistants, or friends who are involved in the apostle's missionary works, such as, traveling, preaching, teaching, communicating written and/or verbal messages, and any other mission-related activities. By this general definition, approximately seventy-five persons can be included in the list of Paul's coworkers.[6]

Ellis identifies thirty-six coworkers of Paul under nine different designations.[7] The four most frequent and significant of the designations are συνεργός ("coworker"), ἀδελφός ("brother"), διάκονος ("minister"), and ἀπόστολος ("apostle"). Συνεργός/συνεργοί is used when "Paul refers to those who helped him in spreading the gospel as *his fellow-workers*."[8] They may refer to the colleagues who are "equal to one another" as are Paul and Apollos in 1 Cor 3:8–9.[9] Ollrog's view of coworkers is noteworthy. He claims that συνεργοί are those who minister as God's representatives on the same "work" of missionary preaching. The term συνεργός is not to be defined by the team concept of "togetherness" at work, but by the common "work" itself. So it relates firstly not to the form of cooperation, but to the common content, that is, the gospel of Christ.[10] According to Ollrog, συνεργός stands for more than a companionship; it represents the commonality of the gospel ministry commissioned by God.

Another significant term for Paul's coworker is ἀδελφός/ἀδελφή, which generally denotes a fictive kinship of brothers and sisters in Christ. Paying particular attention to the word, Ellis suggests that "'the brothers' in the Pauline letters often refers to colleagues in the Christian mission" rather than all believers.[11] Similarly, Aasgaard argues that although the sibling metaphor does not represent special tasks or offices, there is "a tendency towards using the metaphor in such a restricted sense: Paul

("Coworkers, Paul and His," 183–84). Besides, Peerbolte enumerates fifty-seven coworkers appearing in Paul's letters (*Paul the Missionary*, 228–30).

6. About seventy-five names of Paul's coworkers are listed in Appendix 1 "Paul's Coworkers in the Local Ministry" and Appendix 2 "Paul's Coworkers in the Trans-Local Ministry."

7. Ellis, "Paul and His Co-workers," 438. The nine designations for Paul's coworkers are ἀδελφός ("brother"), ἀπόστολος ("apostle"), διάκονος ("minister"), σύνδουλος ("fellow slave"), κοινωνός ("partner"), ὁ κοπιῶν ("toiler"), συνστρατιώτης ("fellow soldier"), συναιχμάλωτος ("fellow prisoner"), and συνεργός ("coworker").

8. BDAG, s.v. "συνεργός."

9. Ellis, "Paul and His Co-workers," 440.

10. Ollrog, *Paulus und seine Mitarbeiter*, 67.

11. Ellis, "Paul and His Co-workers," 448.

employs it to assign to them a particular status and authority."[12] As Paul sometimes uses the term "son" to designate his close associate/convert (1 Cor 4:17; 1 Tim 1:2, 18; 2 Tim 1:2; Titus 1:4; Phlm 10), the sibling language ἀδελφός/ἀδελφή may indicate, on certain occasions, the coworker who is in close relationship with Paul in ministry.[13]

In Paul's letters, διάκονος occurs often in conjunction with συνεργός (1 Cor 3:5, 9; 2 Cor 6:1, 4; cf. 1 Cor 16:15–16), suggesting that the term διάκονος may signify not simply a church worker or servant but a person holding a specific position and role in connection with Paul's missions. Commenting on this term, Schnabel emphasizes that "Missionary work is always 'service'" focused primarily on "the preaching and teaching ministry."[14] Διάκονοι are found not only among itinerant workers but also among the workers in local congregations, such as Phoebe (Rom 16:1) and the "deacons" in the church at Philippi (Phil 1:1).[15]

Ἀπόστολοι as Paul's coworkers include Apollos, Barnabas, and Silas in the sense that they were, according to Ellis, the "apostles of Christ" who have "seen Jesus our Lord" (1 Cor 9:1; cf. 15:5–8) and have been commissioned by the Lord.[16] In addition to this special class of coworkers, the book of Acts and Paul's letters refer to other ἀπόστολοι, "apostles of the churches" who were commissioned by local churches and sent out to assist Paul's ministry. Greeting the Roman Christians, Paul salutes

12. Aasgaard, *Beloved Brothers and Sisters*, 297. Concerning the particular use of ἀδελφός, Aasgaard observes two patterns of construction: (1) "brother"/"sister" combined with the personal pronoun "my"/"our" as for Phoebe (Rom 16:1), Titus (2 Cor 2:13), Epaphroditus (Phil 2:25), and Timothy (1 Thess 3:2); and (2) "brother"/ "sister" with the definite article (ὁ, ἡ) only, e.g., Quartus (Rom 16:23), Sosthenes (1 Cor 1:1), Apollos (1Cor 16:12), Timothy (2 Cor 1:1; Phlm 1), and Apphia (Phlm 2).

13. However, more scholars take the term simply as an affectionate way of addressing fellow Christians. For example, Banks says that the designation is "Paul's favorite way of referring to the members of the communities to whom he is writing" (*Paul's Idea of Community*, 50–51). Similarly, Horrell argues that "he refers to individual believers, specific or nonspecific, as ἀδελφός or ἀδελφή," and the term represents "a basic identity-designation of those who are members of the Christian communities" ("From ἀδελφοί to ἀοἶκος θεοῦ," 299–300).

14. Schnabel, *Early Christian Mission*, 1437. Similarly, Ellis contends that "the *diakonoi* appear to be a special class of co-workers, those who are active in preaching and teaching" ("Paul and His Co-workers," 442).

15. Ellis, "Paul and His Co-workers," 442–43.

16. Ellis, "Coworkers, Paul and His," 185. From the context, it is likely that Paul regards Apollos as one of "us apostles" (1 Cor 4:9). Barnabas and Paul are described as being on a par with "the other apostles and the brothers of the Lord and Cephas" (1 Cor 9:5–6). Paul and Silas are mentioned as "apostles of Christ" (1 Thess 2:6).

Andronicus and Junia as "outstanding among the apostles" (Rom 16:7).[17] Epaphroditus is called "your apostle (ἀπόστολος)," namely, the one sent by the Philippian church to Paul (Phil 2:25).

In relation to both Paul and the local churches, therefore, the function of Paul's coworkers can be outlined: (1) local church leaders who continued the gospel missions Paul had initiated in the community (e.g., Stephanas, Epaphras, and Philemon); (2) travel colleagues who accompanied Paul's missionary campaigns (e.g., Barnabas, Silas, Timothy, Tychicus) and his personal envoys to the local churches (e.g., Timothy and Titus); (3) missionary assistants to Paul sent out from the local churches (e.g., Epaphroditus and Epaphras); (4) messengers of the local churches sent to Paul (e.g., Stephanas); and (5) coworkers who were involved in the composition of Paul's letters.[18]

Categorization of Paul's Coworkers

Paul's coworkers show a wide range of differences in intimacy, dependency, and duration in their relationship with Paul. Scholars have employed various criteria for grouping Paul's coworkers. Ollrog assorts them into three groups according to the significance and nature of their ministry: (1) "inner circle" who were engaged in Paul's ministry quite intimately and for a considerable length of time (Barnabas, Silas, and Timothy); (2) "independent coworkers" who also ministered outside Paul's missionary sphere (Apollos, Priscilla and Aquila, Titus); and (3) "community envoys," the largest group who worked in their local communities and

17. Most scholars are certain that the phrase means "prominent among the apostles" rather than "outstanding in the eyes of the apostles." The couple probably belonged to the group called "all the apostles" in 1 Cor 15:7. Dunn, *Romans 9–16*, 894–95. Also, see Cranfield, *Epistle to the Romans*, 789.

18. The involvement takes three forms—co-senders, secretaries, and couriers. First, eight of the thirteen letters refer to co-senders (1 and 2 Corinthians, Galatians, Philippians, Colossians, 1 and 2 Thessalonians, and Philemon). These co-senders may have played some roles in the composition of the letters. Second, like his contemporaries, Paul often employed a secretary in writing letters (e.g., Tertius, Rom 16:22). The precise role of the secretary might have varied from letter to letter, from a simple dictation to some participation in the composition. Third, Paul usually sent letters through his coworkers, who would not only deliver Paul's letters but also represent Paul as his envoys (e.g., Tychicus, Epaphroditus, and Onesimus). Look up more discussions in chapter 4, section "Collaboration through Letters" and Appendix 4 "Paul's Letters: Senders, Receivers, and Persons in Greeting."

sometimes worked with Paul by the commission of the local churches (Epaphras, Epaphroditus, etc.).[19]

Ellis identifies twelve major coworkers who were associated with Paul until his death and makes distinctions among them: association from the Antiochian period (Mark and Titus); from the second missionary journey (Timothy, Prisca, Aquila, Aristarchus, and probably Luke and Erastus); from the time of Roman imprisonment or possibly from the earlier Ephesian ministry (Demas, Epaphras, Tychicus, and Trophimus). Five of these—Erastus, Mark, Timothy, Titus, and Tychicus—were in "an explicit subordination to Paul, serving him or being subject to his instructions."[20] Barnabas, Silas, and Apollos, meanwhile, are taken as a distinctive group of coworkers who also worked independently of Paul.

In the present study, as mentioned in the preceding chapter, Paul's coworkers are categorized according to their ministry scope: (1) local ministry (e.g., Philemon, Nympha, Euodia); (2) trans-local ministry (e.g., Timothy, Titus, Epaphroditus); and (3) ministry beyond Pauline churches (e.g., Barnabas, Silas, and Aquila). First, the evidence of inter-church relationship gleaned from the "local" coworkers mostly represents the relationship of house churches in the local area. Second, the ministry of "trans-local" coworkers crosses over distant localities and involves multiple Christian communities. Their activities show the network and collaboration of Paul's churches scattered around the Mediterranean basin. Third, the ministry of the independent coworkers, who also ministered beyond the scope of Pauline missions, intimates the contact and cooperation between Pauline and non-Pauline missions.

Paul's Coworkers and the Local Churches

Most missionary events and incidents recorded in the New Testament took place in and around Paul's life and work. In other words, nearly all the sources for the knowledge of the early church missions come from Paul's letters and the book of Acts, which were written from the perspective of Paul and his travel companion, Luke. Accordingly, it is not surprising that one can find in the New Testament only a few accounts which straightly describe local church activities or inter-church actions per se. It is only through Paul's missionary works and pastoral activities

19. Ollrog, *Paulus und seine Mitarbeiter*, 93–96.

20. Ellis, "Paul and His Co-workers," 437–39.

that one manages to figure out how the local churches acted themselves and interacted with other local churches.

It should be noted that once a house church was established in a local area through Paul's missionary works, its worship and ministry continued under the leadership of those now called "Paul's coworkers."[21] Probably, Paul himself may have served as one of the church leaders in the cities where he stayed for an extended time.[22] Paul and his coworkers did not band themselves into a separate group of missionaries. Together with the local believers, they belonged to the same circle of worship and prayer. Their evangelistic and missionary outreach was that of the local churches, too. The financial project of Paul and his coworkers was also the ministry of the local churches. In short, it is most probable that the ministry of Paul and his coworkers was inseparable from the ministry of the local churches as long as they stayed in the local area.

Ollrog's study cast light on the intertwined nature of Paul's coworkers and the local churches. During his missionary campaigns, Paul's work in a city normally resulted in a house fellowship in the community.[23] Paul then sought to utilize the house assembly as a base camp for spreading the gospel further to its neighborhood and surrounding areas. It was, according to Ollrog, usually at this stage that a number of coworkers were enlisted to extend the gospel ministry.[24] That is, the status and ministry of coworkers were grounded in their local churches, respectively. After a certain period of assisting Paul's missions, they eventually returned to their home churches. Since they represented their local churches, their ministry is to be construed as that of the local churches. So, Paul's "coworker mission" (*Mitarbeitermission)* was nothing but the "community mission" (*Gemeindemission*). By means of these coworkers, Paul bound

21. As will be noted in the following subsection, the house assemblies were mostly led by the household patrons/patronesses, who came to be known as "Paul's coworkers." White rightly observes that "Paul's expressions of local leadership are often found in the context of house church patronage [as in 1 Cor 16:16] . . . Given this use of authority language, in the absence of direct references to 'office,' the house church patrons must be looked upon as local church leaders" ("Social Authority," 218).

22. Paul was one of the church leaders ("prophets and teachers") at Antioch (Acts 13:1). Likewise, he must have led the local church ministries while at Corinth and Ephesus.

23. For example, Paul's missionary works produced a Christian fellowship in Lydia's household at Philippi (Acts 17:15, 40), in Stephanas's at Corinth (1 Cor 1:16; 16:15–18), and in Philemon's at Colossae (Phil 1:2).

24. Ollrog, *Paulus und seine Mitarbeiter*, 111–18.

his mission with the communities, and the communities associated with the mission of Paul. This collaborative system between Paul, coworkers, and the local churches was a "primary sense of coworker mission," which constituted the basic framework of Pauline ministry.[25]

Utilizing Ollrog's argument of *Mitarbeitermission* based on *Gemeindemission*, Maness develops his thesis that the concept and praxis of Paul's coworkers are to be understood in light of "three determinants"—Paul, congregation, and coworkers themselves.[26] While Ollrog's study focused on a portion of the coworkers who were more community-based, Maness puts all the coworkers on his evaluation scale and explains the relational dynamics between Paul, his coworkers, and the local churches. He draws a rather simple conclusion: (1) the ministry of Paul's coworkers is influenced by three factors—local churches, Paul, and coworkers; (2) there is no one single factor that overwhelms the others; and (3) different coworkers show different orders of the factors in the degree of influence.[27] Although Maness' study differs from Ollrog's in focus, scope, and result, it brings to light the significance of ministry relationships among Paul, his coworkers, and, particularly, the local churches. Like Ollrog, Maness affirms the important place of local churches in the ministry of Paul and his coworkers.

This ministerial integration and collaboration are adequately attested in the book of Acts and Paul's letters: (1) Paul's missionary journeys were initiated and commissioned by the Antioch church (Acts 13:1–3; 15:40); (2) Paul, during the so-called second missionary journey, functioned as a courier of the Jerusalem church, delivering the decision of the Jerusalem Council to gentile Christian communities (Acts 16:4); (3) many of Paul's coworkers were emissaries from certain local churches; (4) many of Paul's coworkers were the leaders of their local churches; (5) Paul and his coworkers on their journeys often stayed at the residence of local churches (1 Cor 16:6); (6) most greetings in Paul's letters reveal that he and his companions were with local believers; and (7) local churches sent Paul money and personnel, joining in the "collection" for Jerusalem (Acts 20:4). The ministry of Paul and his coworkers—pastoral, evangelistic, and missionary—was done in the midst of and in connection with the local churches.

25. Ollrog, *Paulus und seine Mitarbeiter*, 125.

26. Maness, "Pauline Congregations," 2.

27. Maness, "Pauline Congregations," 3.

The Greco-Roman Household and Paul's House Churches

It is a scholarly consensus that the basic unit of the Greco-Roman society was the household (οἶκος).[28] From individual families to the whole Empire, the entire society was based on the structure of the first-century household. The ancient household was large, usually including not only the immediate family members and relatives but also slaves, former slaves (freedmen/freedwomen), servants, hired laborers, tenants, and sometimes friends and business associates.[29] This broad and open constitution of the Greco-Roman household entailed a certain social context in which "to be part of a household was thus to be part of a larger network of relations."[30]

A household was under its patronal householder who possessed the authority over the household members and, at the same time, took responsibility for their protection and support.[31] Although the majority of patrons were men, "there is sufficient evidence to indicate that wealthy women, too, gave public benefactions and received similar kinds of honors as a result."[32]As the household was the basic unit of Greco-Roman society, the patron-client relationship was "the backbone of the social system, operating at all official and unofficial levels."[33] The household structure and its patronal system were interwoven with each other, comprising the socio-economic matrix that sustained the cohesion and control of the Roman Empire.

28. See, for example, Klauck, *Hausgemeinde und Hauskirche*, 15–20; Elliott, *Home for the Homeless*, 170–81; and Osiek and Balch, *Families*, 48–54.

29. Meeks, *First Urban Christians*, 75–76.

30. Meeks, *First Urban Christians*, 30. Meek discusses two kinds of relations, (1) vertical relationships of protection and subordination between *paterfamilias* and slave or between patron and client, and (2) connections on more or less equal terms between a household and others, that is, "links of kinship and of friendship, which also often entailed obligations and expectations."

31. Thus, the patronal system was based on "a long-standing personal relationship in which mutual fidelity is assured for the benefit of both parties." Osiek and Balch, *Families*, 50.

32. Osiek and Balch, *Families*, 50. For instance, in the New Testament, several women appear to have had a patronal position: Lydia and possibly Euodia and Syntyche at Philippi (Acts 16:15, 40; Phil 4:2–3); Phoebe at Corinth/Cenchrea (Rom 16:2); and Nympha at Laodicea (Col 4:15).

33. Osiek and Balch, *Families*, 216. In addition, the patronage system was "the principal way of obtaining and using status and power" in politics, economics, education, and personal relations.

The household structure was crucial, particularly, to social entities such as voluntary associations, philosophical schools, and Jewish synagogues. As Craffert notes, "they were located for the most part in private homes, linked to household conventions, and dominated by patron-client relationships and the system of honour and shame."[34] Various religious groups utilized the house setting for worship and community activities, as "the Jewish communities often assembled in house-synagogues."[35]

Since early Christians "lived and operated within the bounds of society at large," it was not peculiar for the Pauline communities, like other social and cultic groups, to utilize existing households as the bases of their religious activities.[36] In the same vein, Craffert affirms that "all the evidence suggests that the household structure provided the basic social setting both for the expansion and for the assembly of the Pauline communities in the cities of the Greco-Roman Empire."[37] Furthermore, the household was not just a natural choice for a worship place; it enhanced Christian gatherings and missional outreach to the community. Blue, thus, argues that "the early believers met in houses *not by default alone* but deliberately because the house setting provided the facilities which were of paramount importance for the gathering."[38]

The adaptation of the household setting by the earliest churches is well attested in the New Testament. It is certain from Luke's accounts that the first Christians of Jerusalem met at homes owned by fellow Christians (Acts 1:13–14; 2:46; 5:42; 8:8; 12:12). The significance of the household is apprehensible in the frequent references to a person's conversion "together with the whole household" (Acts 11:14; 16:15, 31–34; 18:8).

34. Craffert, "Pauline Household Communities," 315.

35. Blue, "Influence of Jewish Worship," 473.

36. White, *Social Origins*, 140.

37. Craffert, "Pauline Household Communities," 325. See also Meeks, *First Urban Christians*, 75–77; Banks, *Paul's Idea of Community*, 37–41; White, *Social Origins*, 103–10; Gehring, *House Church and Mission*, 179–90.

38. Blue, "Acts and the House Church," 121. According to Blue, Christian believers met in homes (or renovated homes) "until the early decades of the fourth century when Constantine began erecting the first Christian Basilicas" (120). For the reasons for meeting in houses in early Christianity, see Blue, "Influence of Jewish Worship," 474–75. He explains four factors that led early Christians to employ domestic facilities as their worship center: (1) houses were immediately available for use; (2) the house church setting was "relatively inconspicuous," avoiding unnecessary publicity and possible persecution; (3) early Christians adopted the custom of Jews who also met at home, "the house-synagogue"; and (4) most importantly, houses were expedient to prepare and provide for the Lord's Supper and fellowship meals.

More importantly, four passages in Paul's letters explicitly refer to house churches in connection with their hosts/hostesses, using the characteristic expression ἡ κατ' οἶκον + genitive personal pronoun + ἐκκλησία ("the church at one's house").[39]

The possessive case ("*one's* house") signifies the presence of a central figure in the assembly. Blue makes a perceptive observation that the book of Acts mentions Aquila and Priscilla, Jason of Thessalonica, Simon the Tanner, Lydia and the Philippian Jailor "not merely out of gratitude for offering Christian leaders a place to sleep, but probably because they opened their homes for meetings of their local Christian communities."[40] It is to be noted that many of Paul's coworkers played the role of house church patrons/patronesses in their local settings.[41] They were key ministry leaders of the local house churches.

Besides the household setting, biblical evidence strongly suggests the existence of multiple house churches within a city or a province.[42] Most scholars agree with Meeks that "the number of household assemblies in each city will have varied from place to place and from time to time, but we may assume that there were ordinarily several in each place."[43] White acknowledges "several such house church cells in any locality, particularly in larger cities like Corinth, Rome, or Ephesus."[44] Not only in the larger cities, but also in less strategic areas such as Laodicea and Crete, there seem to have been a cluster of house fellowships.[45] Throughout Paul's

39. The four passages are: "with the church at their [of Aquila and Priscilla] house" (1 Cor 16:19); "the church at their house" (Rom 16:5; cf. 16:14–15, 23); "the church at your house" (Phlm 2); and "the church at her house" (Col 4:15).

40. Blue, "Acts and the House Church," 119.

41. Important among them are Priscilla and Aquila who ministered in Corinth (Acts 18:1–3), Ephesus (Acts 18:18–19; 1 Cor 16:19), and Rome (Rom 16:3–4); Gaius (Rom 16:23) and possibly Chloe (1 Cor 1:11) and Stephanas (1 Cor 16:15) also in Corinth; Philemon in Colossae (Phlm 1:1–2); Phoebe in Cenchrea (Rom 16:2); Lydia in Philippi (Acts 16:15, 40); and Nympha in Laodicea (Col 4:15).

42. The evidence of multiple house churches is apparent from the biblical accounts of Acts 14:23; Rom 16:5; 1 Cor 16:19; 2 Cor 8:1, 19, 23; Gal 1:2; Col 4:15–16; Phlm 2.

43. Meeks, *First Urban Christians*, 76.

44. White, "Social Authority," 215. For example, "over the decade of Paul's activity at Corinth at least five different house churches are known," including Prisca and Aquila (Acts 18:3), Titius Justus (Acts 18:7), Stephanas (1 Cor 16:15), Gaius (Rom 16:23), and Phoebe of Cenchrea (Rom 16:2).

45. There were several house assemblies in the Lycus valley, which met at the house of Philemon (Phlm 1–2), Nympha, and "the brothers at Laodicea" (Col 4:15). Paul's instruction for Titus to appoint elders "in every city/town" (κατὰ πόλιν) suggests that

ministry, therefore, "alongside the local church as a whole, there existed house churches in which most of the activities and life of the church took place."[46] The presence of multiple house churches suggests, in all probability, the presence of certain communication and interaction between the house churches.[47] The following sections investigate several Pauline communities as to how the local believers, that is, house churches, were related to one another in the local community.

Paul's Coworkers in the Local Ministry

One of the strategic patterns for Paul's missions was to establish a house church or churches "in the major provincial centers" of the Roman Empire.[48] Visiting a major city, Paul won converts, began house gatherings, and "appointed co-workers, local converts who participated in the local mission and continued it after the Apostle moved on."[49] This section discusses Paul's coworkers whose major task was to minister to their local churches. When "church relationship" is mentioned in the context of a local community, it means the relationship of house churches in the local community. Accordingly, this section investigates the local ministry of

there were multiple house churches in the island of Crete (Titus 1:5). Luke's account, "Paul and Barnabas appointed elders for them in each church" (Acts 14:23), suggests that a number of house churches were planted in the region of Galatia.

46. Gehring, *House Church and Mission*, 157.

47. In the case of Roman Christianity, however, most scholars admit its divided nature, i.e., the lack of a centralized structure. Concerning the separateness of the church, Lampe argues that "There is nowhere any indication of a central location for the different groups scattered over the city. Each circle of Christians may have conducted worship services by itself in a house or apartment, so that it can be referred to as a house community" (*From Paul to Valentinus*, 359–60). Nevertheless, it should be noted that the lack of centralized organization does not necessarily mean a lack of communication and interaction between the house churches. Paul, in Rom 16, refers to multiple churches at one time, which is sensible only on the assumption that the churches had some kind of mutual awareness and relationship for the sharing of the letter. Lampe himself acknowledges that "Early Christians in Rome formed various house churches. . . . These house churches, scattered over the city, were only loosely connected. Some sent portions of their eucharist to other Christian groups in the city to express fellowship and unity with them. Written material was also shared among the Christian groups in Rome" ("Early Christians," 26).

48. Marshall, "Luke's Portrait," 103. Likewise, Gehring argues that Paul preached the gospel and established churches "in one city in each province, usually in the respective capital—Thessalonica, Corinth, Ephesus" (*House Church and Mission*, 179).

49. Ellis, "Paul and His Co-workers," 451.

Paul's coworkers in light of the house church relationship. Three major cities in Paul's missions are chosen for discussion—Philippi, Corinth, and Ephesus/Lycus Valley.[50]

Philippi

The information about Paul's coworkers in Philippi is found in Luke's account (Acts 16:11–40) and Paul's letter to the Philippians, particularly Phil 4:2–3. During the so-called second missionary journey, Paul and his coworkers arrived at Philippi, "a leading city of the district of Macedonia" (Acts 16:12). Lydia, a female merchant of purple cloth from the city of Thyatira, heard and believed the gospel message from Paul, and she and her whole household were baptized (Acts 16:14–15). Lydia was relatively wealthy businesswoman who could afford to take in Paul's missionary team and provide a domestic space for the "brothers" to assemble there (Acts 16:40). It is most likely that she was a patronal householder, and her household functioned as one of the active house churches in the city.[51]

In the letter to the Philippians, Paul specifically mentions four of his Philippian coworkers, Euodia, Syntyche, Clement, and Epaphroditus besides the unnamed recipient of the letter ("you, true yokefellow") and "the others, my fellow workers" (Phil 4:2–3). Both Euodia and Syntyche were individually addressed in the letter that would be read publicly in the church, which suggests that each woman was in the leading position of the Philippian church. Paul describes the two women as those who "have strived alongside me" (συνήθλησάν μοι) together with Clement and other coworkers (συνεργοί). The phrase "in the gospel" (ἐν τῷ εὐαγγελίῳ) carries a notion of "personal involvement in missionary proclamation."[52] Therefore, both Euodia and Syntyche, as Paul's coworkers (συνεργοί), must have continued the work of evangelism and church planting in and around

50. Paul's churches were located in three provinces—Macedonia, Acaia, and Asia. Three cities—Philippi, Corinth, and Ephesus/Lycus Valley—are selected out of the provinces, respectively. These three cities may best represent their localities, and biblical data is readily available for those churches.

51. Luke introduces another household of Christian converts. Paul and Silas were put into prison. Following the incident of earthquake, the city jailer and all his family were converted and baptized. Although speculative, it is possible that his household grew into another house church in Philippi (Acts 16:25–34). See Gehring, *House Church and Mission*, 132.

52. Dickson, *Mission-Commitment*, 141. Also, see Hawthorne, *Philippians*, 180.

Philippi. Paul's address to "overseers and deacons" (Phil 1:1) implies the plurality of house churches in the city. So it may well be that the two women ministered in the community as evangelists and house church leaders.

The Philippian believers had a cordial relationship with Paul and supported the apostle's ministry: they were in "participation (κοινωνία) in the gospel" by continuing the evangelistic work after Paul's departure (Phil 1:5); they financially supported Paul's missions in Thessalonica (Phil 4:16), in Corinth (2 Cor 11:9), and for the Jerusalem believers (2 Cor 8:1–5); and they sent out one of their valuable members, Epaphroditus, to assist Paul in Rome (Phil 2:25–30; 4:18). Although the Philippians devotedly collaborated with Paul, there was some disunity among themselves, particularly between Euodia and Syntyche, at the time when Paul was writing the letter.

The main thrust of Phil 1:27–30 is to "stand firm in one spirit, with one soul, striving together for the faith of the gospel" (v. 27). This theme of unity and collaboration, with the connecting particle οὖν (Phil 2:1), extends to a fuller discourse in chapter 2. Paul exhorts the Philippian believers to be in unity (2:1–4). In this context, Euodia and Syntyche are exhorted "to be of the same mind in the Lord" (Phil 4:2). Examining the literary characteristics of the letter, Dahl points out "a remarkable correspondence between the initial, general exhortations in Philippians 1:27—2:5 and the special appeal to Euodia and Syntyche in the context of 3:20—4:3."[53] That is, one of Paul's concerns underlying the letter is the discord among the believers. Paul appeals not only to the women involved but also to another leader, the "true comrade," to help the women (Phil 4:3).[54] What Paul seeks from the Philippian church is unity and collaboration between the church leaders. Given the prominence of the two women, we can reasonably assume that the disagreement was "a threat to the unity of the church as a whole."[55] As Dahl observes, the disunity between Euodia and Syntyche was not merely "a personal quarrel" but

53. Dahl, "Euodia and Syntyche," 9. He continues to claim that "even the general exhortations in Philippians have been formulated in a way that relates to the conflict between Euodia and Syntyche."

54. It is intriguing that Paul singles out one person as the letter recipient ("you, true comrade") in a letter addressed "to all the saints in Christ Jesus who are in Philippi, with the elders and deacons" (Phil 1:1). Attempts have been made to identify the "true comrade" with no conclusive answer. What is certain is that Paul urges one of his co-workers in Philippi to help Euodia and Syntyche to recover their mutual relationship.

55. O'Brien argues, "Otherwise, it is difficult to explain why their names were mentioned in a letter to be read publicly in church" (*Epistle to the Philippians*, 478).

"related to their work and trials for the sake of the gospel," reflecting "a conflict between two rivals."[56]

There is no way to ascertain from biblical or extra-biblical sources whether Euodia and Syntyche resolved their disagreement. It is to be noted that Paul does not make any "explicit reproaches or complaints" against the Philippian church, and there is no evidence for "opposing factions" within the community.[57] Luter argues that "the present-tense" disunity was not "chronic,"[58] and Martin reasons that "the disappearance of these two women from the scene suggests that Paul's plea was heeded."[59] Considering the cordial relationship between Paul and the Philippians, a positive outcome may be conjectured: Euodia and Syntyche, who had "strived together," might have heeded their fellow workers' encouragement as well as Paul's exhortation, and come to "the same mind in the Lord" (Phil 4:2–3). As is shown in the expression "your fellowship (κοινωνία) in the gospel from the first day till now" (Phil 1:5), the Philippian church had maintained a good partnership with Paul in the gospel ministry, and, as such, its house groups probably stayed, overall, in a positive relationship with one another for the cause of the gospel ministry.

Corinth

Paul's greeting to "the church of God, which is in Corinth, with all the saints in all Achaia" (2 Cor 1:1) suggests the presence of a large Christian community in the metropolitan area. In Corinth, according to Linton, existed as many as six house churches that met probably in the house of the leading Christians of the city—i.e., Aquila and Priscilla (Acts 18:2–3), Titius Justus (Acts 18:7), Crispus (Acts 18:8), Chloe (1 Cor 1:11), Stephanas (1 Cor 1:16; 16:15), and Gaius (Rom 16:23).[60] In the port city of Corinth, Cenchrea, Christians met in the house of Phoebe (Rom 16:1–2).

Given the context of multiple house churches in Corinth, Paul's word in 1 Cor 14:23 is noteworthy: "if, therefore, the whole church comes together in one place." Most scholars agree that Paul's description implies the existence of "other gatherings as subgroups" and "the whole church"

56. Dahl, "Euodia and Syntyche," 6–7.

57. Dahl, "Euodia and Syntyche," 10.

58. Luter, "Partnership in the Gospel," 419–20.

59. Martin, *Philippians*, 152.

60. Linton, "House Church Meetings," 233.

means "the assembling of the several house fellowships" that makes up the church at Corinth.[61] Murphy-O'Connor explains the distinction of these two types of gathering: "the formulae 'the whole church' and 'the church in the home of X' (Rom 16:5; 1 Cor 16:19; Col 4:15; Phlm 2) should not be equated, but contrasted."[62] Blue's suggestion is more specific: in writing the present clause (1 Cor 14:23), Paul "envisions the entire Christian community (i.e., all the smaller house churches) assembling in Gaius' house."[63] It can be said that in Corinth "church gatherings consisted of more regular small house groups interspersed with less frequent (weekly, monthly?) gatherings of 'the whole church.'"[64]

Though some scholars belittle internal factions in the Corinthian church,[65] the majority view is that there existed a discord between the groups in the congregation. Carson portrays the Corinthian church with a broad brush: "The church in Corinth is a divided church. This is seen not only in the party labels reported at 1:12 and treated in the first four chapters of the book, but also in a style of argumentation that pervades much of chapters 7–12."[66] After a greeting, Paul immediately addresses the "Corinthian slogans": "I am of Paul, and I of Apollos, and I of Cephas, and I of Christ" (1 Cor 1:12).[67] Even though it is difficult to confirm what

61. Hiigel, *Leadership in 1 Corinthians*, 15–16. Therefore, the term "church" (ἐκκλησία) in Paul's letters is used to designate, sometimes, the body of house churches as a whole, other times, the individual house church as a subgroup of the whole church.

62. Murphy-O'Connor, *St. Paul's Corinth*, 183.

63. Blue, "Acts and the House Church," 175. Writing to the Romans, Paul calls Gaius "my host and of the whole church" (Rom 16:23). According to Blue, Gaius is probably the praenomen of Titius Justus (Acts 18:7), a God-fearer who offered his house for Paul's missionary work in Corinth. The house may have been large enough for all Corinthian believers to come together.

64. Dunn, *Theology of Paul*, 541. Studying the implication of 1 Cor 14:23 ("the whole church"; ἡ ἐκκλησία ὅλη) in relation to 16:19 ("the church at their house"; ἡ κατ' οἶκον αὐτῶν ἐκκλησίᾳ), he acknowledges the "significance of the house churches within Pauline ecclesiology."

65. For example, Hurd argues that "these divisions were not parties, but simply reflected a general Corinthian tendency toward factiousness" (*Origin of 1 Corinthians*, 269). Conzelmann suggests that "the word σχίσματα, 'divisions,' implies in itself merely a neutral statement of the existence of divisions. It does not mean the existence of different systems of doctrine" (*1 Corinthians*, 32). Meanwhile, Fee presents quite a different viewpoint that, rather than a dissension within the community, "the greater problem of 'division' was between Paul and some in the community" (*First Corinthians*, 6).

66. Carson, *Showing the Spirit*, 17.

67. Three analogous expressions are made by Paul (1 Cor 1:12; 3:4–9, 22). It is hardly conceivable that Paul, Apollos, or Peter gave rise to the factions. In fact, Paul

was behind the Corinthian slogans, it surely reflects some factions, or at least factionalism, among the Corinthian believers.

The division might have something to do with the makeup of the Corinthian church. As indicated in the previous section, "the church at one's house" consisted mainly of one's household, and its leadership naturally falls to the patronal householder. On this typical constitution of the house churches, Murphy-O'Connor comments that "while such subgroups [house churches] would have tended to foster an intimate family-type atmosphere at the liturgical celebrations, they would also have tended to promote divisions within the wider city community."[68] The Corinthian slogans may be saying that one house group has more attachment to Paul, and another group favors Apollos over Paul. The church at Corinth, composed of several distinct house groups with their own leaders, may have been susceptible to internal tension and division.

That being said, however, it is to be noted that the division in the church did not mean a lack of relationship among the believers or among the house groups. The presence of disunity is rather an indication of vigorous actions and interactions taking place in the Corinthian church. Paul's saying, "there are contentions among you" (1 Cor 1:11), connotes that there existed unaffected communication and contact among the believers. If the "Corinthian slogans" exactly represented the church's situation, it then means that the four parties in the church underwent a tension in relationship, not a separation.

Discussing "the whole church" and "the church at one's house," Blue argues that "many of the problems arose because the individual house gatherings met under one roof."[69] This is true of the Corinthian situation that Paul particularly criticizes: "When you come together as a church (ἐν ἐκκλησίᾳ), I hear divisions among you (σχίσματα ἐν ὑμῖν)" (1 Cor 11:18). Paul refers to the occasion when house groups gather together to celebrate the Lord's Supper along with the common meal.[70] It is well

---

gives no hint of disagreement or resentment against a particular person of influence (cf. 1 Cor 3:6–9).

68. Murphy-O'Connor, *St. Paul's Corinth*, 183.

69. Blue, "Acts and the House Church," 174.

70. Linton explains that "1 Corinthians 11:17–34 describes the Lord's Supper as consisting of eating a full meal and not just nibbling bits of bread and sipping juice from a cup. Twice the word δεῖπνον (*deipnon*, "feast, banquet") is used to describe the meal. . . . Lord's Supper was celebrated in the context of a common meal through the fourth century" ("House Church Meetings," 240–41).

known that the common meal in the Greco-Roman society symbolized a fellowship and unity among the participants.[71] Even though "divisions" (σχίσματα) arose in the gathering of house groups, the community meal itself represented goodwill and real fellowship among the Corinthian believers. They preserved inter-church (house churches) relationships and communal activities.

When describing the Corinthian church as "the body of Christ and members of it individually" (1 Cor 12:27), Paul should have in mind the individual house churches at Corinth, that is, their patronal leaders and all believers in Christ. In the following discourse, Paul repeatedly emphasizes one body of Christ, using the word "build up" or "edify" (οἰκοδομέω) for unity.[72] It is not feasible to determine how the Corinthians, household leaders and lay believers, responded to the exhortation of Paul to be united in love. Still, the internal tension of the church itself reflects the intensity of relationships among the house churches in Corinth. Paul's coworkers, such as Crispus, Stephanas, Gaius, etc., were at the center of those relationships and communal activities.

Ephesus and the Lycus Valley

In Acts 19:10, Luke makes a concise statement about the outcome of Paul's missions in Ephesus: "all who dwelt in Asia heard the word of the Lord Jesus, both Jews and Greeks." Allowing for the hyperbolic language, Luke's account still indicates the prevalence of the gospel and the growth of Christian communities throughout the area. When Paul writes "the churches of Asia greet you" (1 Cor 16:19), the apostle refers to "all the brothers" (1 Cor 16:20) in Asia beyond those in the house of Aquila and Priscilla. Although there exists not much biblical data, one can easily conceive of the vigor and expansion of the gospel ministry in Asia Minor.

Before Paul began his ministry in Ephesus, Christian communities had already been founded in the city probably through the work of Paul's coworkers such as Priscilla and Aquila (Acts 18:19, 26; 1 Cor 16:19) and Apollos (Acts 18:24; 1 Cor 16:12). In addition, there were "some disciples,"

71. Banks affirms that "The most visible and profound way in which the community gives physical expression to its fellowship is the common meal" (*Paul's Idea of Community*, 80). For more discussion, see Smith, *From Symposium to Eucharist*, 1–12.

72. This term frequently occurs, particularly in chapter 14 (verses 3, 4, 5, 12, 17, 26). The theme of edification in unity "controls the thought of the entire chapter." Fee, *First Corinthians*, 657.

a group of followers of John the Baptist (Acts 19:1–3). Luke's narrative in Acts 19:17–20 suggests that a great number of people at Ephesus came to Christian faith. Hence, given the large number of converts, it may well be that the new believers met for worship in multiple places, forming several house churches.[73]

Paul invited the Ephesian church elders to Miletus on his way to Jerusalem. It is most probable that the elders represented the house churches in Ephesus (Acts 20:17, 28).[74] In his speech to them, Paul recapitulates his work in Ephesus as "teaching you publicly and from house to house" (Acts 20:20). If "teaching publicly" refers to the open lectures in the hall of Tyrannus, "teaching from house to house" implies Paul's itinerant teaching in the house churches scattered around the city. Ephesus was "the capital of the province of Asia and the leading city of Asia Minor, where the church grew very rapidly."[75] Naturally, a number of house churches were thriving in the area.

Epaphras, having heard of Paul presumably in the lecture hall of Tyrannus, became a disciple and brought the gospel to his hometown, Colossae (Col 1:7), and probably to Laodicea and Hierapolis in the Lycus valley (Col 4:13). Paul's designation of him as "a faithful servant/minister (διάκονος) of Christ on our behalf" (Col 1:7) signifies that Epaphras also worked as a minister representing Paul and his missions.[76] His ministry

73. Luke records that there arose a multitude of believers not only in Ephesus but also in almost all the cities along the course of Paul's journeys. It is only natural to expect multiple house churches in those cities. 13:43 (at Pisidian Antioch) "Many of the Jews and of the God-fearing proselytes followed." 14:1 (at Iconium) "A great multitude of Jews and Greeks believed." 14:21 (at Derbe) "[Paul and Barnabas] made many disciples." 17:4 (at Thessalonica) "A large number of God-fearing Greeks and quite a few prominent women joined." 17:12 (at Berea) "Many of them believed." 18:10 (at Corinth) "There are many people belonging to me in this city." 19:18 (at Ephesus) "Many of those who had believed came."

74. Paul's farewell admonition shows that the Holy Spirit made each of them an "overseer" to take care of the flock, the church of God (Acts 20:28). Although the leadership structure of the Ephesian church is not known, most scholars agree that the church comprised several house churches and that the elders were, formally or informally, the leading figures of the house churches.

75. Trebilco, *Early Christians in Ephesus*, 1.

76. A textual variant is explained in the NET note on Col 1:7: "Judging by the superior witnesses for the first-person pronoun ἡμῶν . . . vs. the second person pronoun ὑμῶν . . . ἡμῶν should be regarded as original." Thus, "on our behalf" is more plausible. See also Wilson, *Colossians and Philemon*, 95–96.

produced multiple churches in the Lycus valley.[77] Afterwards, Epaphras went to Rome to assist Paul but continued his prayer and toil (πόνος) for his home churches. His earnestness was conveyed to the churches in the Lycus valley through Paul's words (Col 4:12–13). It can be said that he was still playing an important role on behalf of the Christian community in the Lycus valley.

Discussing Col 4:12–13, Stenschke raises a meaningful question: "Is the Colossian Epaphras ('who is one of you') the human agent to unite these churches in the Lycus valley?"[78] He then points out that "Paul certainly lets the Colossians know that he sees them as part of a regional network (2:1; 4:13, 15–16), which includes the exchange of letters (4:16)."[79] Stenschke gives an affirmative answer to the question by referring to the regional network indebted to the ministry of Epaphras. As a founding minister, an itinerant teacher, and a praying partner, Epaphras must have contributed to the positive relationship of the local churches in the Lycus valley.

Nordling identifies five distinct house churches in the Lycus Valley, those at Colossae, Laodicea, Hierapolis, Nympha's house (Col 4:15), and Philemon's house (Phlm 2). Based on the fact that "none of which were more than fifteen miles removed from one of the others, and each congregation probably had been founded by Epaphras," he maintains that "there could only have been a considerable amount of give and take between the local Christians under such circumstances."[80] It is likely that Christians assembled as house churches and also as the church of the whole community. Although the New Testament does not say much about the activity of local house churches, it is highly plausible that Paul's coworkers in the local ministry played the leading roles in maintaining

77. Paul in Col 2:1 addresses three groups of believers: "I have struggle for you, for those at Laodicea, and for all who have not seen me personally." That is, at least three churches existed: the Colossians, the Laodiceans, and a group of believers whom Paul has not met (maybe those at Hierapolis; cf. 4:13). On the other hand, some believe that "all who have not seen me personally" does not refer to a third group but to those Colossians and Laodiceans who joined the churches after Paul left the area. See Barth and Blanke, *Colossians*, 273–75.

78. Stenschke, "Significance and Function," 199.

79. Stenschke, "Significance and Function," 199–200.

80. Nordling, "Philemon in the Context," 300. In addition, he cautiously argues for the role of Philemon's house in linking Paul to the Christians in Galatia: "a kind of 'pipeline' existed between Paul (wherever he was when he wrote Philemon), the Christians of the Lycus Valley discussed above, and possibly Christians still further removed that had been brought to faith in Christ as early as the first missionary journey conducted by Paul and Barnabas (cf. Acts 14: 21; 16:1, 18:23)."

the relationship of house churches and arranging communal activities in the local area.

Paul's Coworkers in the Trans-Local Ministry

It is notable that toward the end of 2 Timothy, Paul refers to at least eight major cities or provinces around the Roman Empire—Thessalonica, Galatia, and Dalmatia (4:10), Ephesus (4:12), Troas (4:13), Corinth and Miletus (4:20), and implicitly Rome (4:11, 21). Evidently, Paul's ministry outlook is very wide and international.[81] Behind this international ministry were Paul's coworkers. As the text shows, Paul refers to many different localities in connection with his coworkers who are visiting there or staying in the area.[82] This section examines the trans-local coworkers who moved from city to city as: (1) travel companions and messengers (e.g., Timothy, Titus, and Tychicus); (2) Paul's ministry associates from the local churches (e.g., Epaphras and Epaphroditus); and (3) messengers of the local churches to Paul (e.g., Stephanas and "messengers of the churches" in 2 Cor 8:23). Due to these trans-local coworkers, Paul could carry on his ministry in partnership with the churches near and far.

Paul's Travel Companions and Messengers

One of the major functions of Paul's coworkers was to convey the apostle's messages to the local churches in distant lands, often as the letter carriers. In the ancient world, the couriers functioned not only as the letter carriers but also as those who "expand on details within the letter, and even to expound and reinforce the primary message of the letter in oral communication."[83] Moreover, Paul's messengers were not the mere conveyors of news and information; they were Paul's "co-workers" who

81. Also, take notice of Paul's own statement concerning his ministry scope: "from Jerusalem and round about as far as Illyricum I have fully preached the gospel of Christ" (Rom 15:19).

82. Within this passage appear fifteen names of coworkers, each related to different cities: Demas, Crescens, Titus, Luke, Mark, Tychicus, Carpus, Priscilla and Aquila, Erastus, Trophimus, Eubulus, Pudens, Linus, Claudia, and "all the brothers" [in Rome].

83. Head, "Named Letter-Carriers," 297. Examining approximately 40 letters with identifiable carrier name(s) in the 68 volumes of the *Oxyrhynchus Papyri*, Head concludes that the ancient letter-carriers frequently supplemented the written contents of the letter with some oral communication.

were commissioned and devoted to the gospel presentation and church edification. They were the key players who helped to build up communication networks around Paul and the trans-local churches. This subsection examines three of those coworkers—Timothy, Titus, and Tychicus.[84]

Timothy

Timothy was converted by Paul probably during the apostle's missionary work in Lystra (Acts 14:6–20).[85] Afterwards, he joined Paul and Silas in their so-called second missionary journey (Acts 16:3).[86] After missionary works at Philippi, Thessalonica, and Berea, Paul's missionary band moved to Athens. Then, Timothy was sent back to Thessalonica to encourage and equip the new church in the city (1 Thess 3:2, 5). Paul's own words indicate the urgent need of communication for strengthening the faith of the Thessalonians: "When I could stand it no longer, I sent to find out about your faith" (1 Thess 3:5). Although undocumented, it is likely that Timothy not only delivered Paul's message to the Thessalonians but also taught and edified them as the apostle's delegate.

Timothy returned to Paul with positive news about the Thessalonian church (1 Thess 3:6). The seemingly redundant phrase "to us from you" (πρὸς ἡμᾶς ἀφ' ὑμῶν) carries the tone of sending an envoy, implying that the Thessalonians now sent Timothy to Paul. The ministry of Timothy was not unilateral but bilateral. It reveals the mutual nature of the relationship between the Thessalonian congregation and Paul's community in Corinth.[87] Subsequent words of Paul are emphatic and emotionally charged in disclosing the close and reciprocal nature of their relationship: "longing to see us as we also long to see you" (v. 6). Then, at the good news brought by Timothy, Paul at last became relieved. He confesses his

84. They are selected for discussion since their activities were more prominent than others' according to the biblical data in the book of Acts and Paul's letters.

85. That Timothy was one of Paul's own coverts is implied in Paul's description: "my beloved and faithful child in the Lord" (1 Cor 4:17); "true child in faith" (1 Tim 1:2); and "Timothy, (my) beloved child" (2 Tim 1:2).

86. In the present volume, "the second missionary journey" and "the Aegean mission" are used interchangeably. For the validity of these phrases, see Dunn, *Beginning from Jerusalem*, 660–62.

87. Paul must have written this letter (1 Thessalonians) in Corinth. According to Acts 18:5, Timothy and Silas came from Macedonia (Thessalonica) and were reunited with Paul at Corinth.

sense of security in various expressions: "we were comforted . . . by your faith" (v. 7); "for now we live, if you stand in the Lord" (v. 8); "How can we thank God . . . for all the joy we rejoice because of you" (v. 9). Communication has been made and turned out to be beneficial for Paul and his associates as well as for the Thessalonian believers.

Toward the end of the Ephesian mission, Paul purposed to go to Jerusalem via Macedonia and Achaia. He sent Timothy ahead to Macedonia and probably down to Corinth (Acts 19:22, 1 Cor 16:10).[88] The first letter to the Corinthians discloses that Timothy as Paul's representative was to remind the Corinthian congregation of what the apostle had taught everywhere in every church (1 Cor 4:17). Concerning the return of Timothy, Paul requests, "Send him on his way in peace, that he may come to me" (1 Cor 16:11). Similar to 1 Thess 3:6, "to us from you" (πρὸς ἡμᾶς ἀφ' ὑμῶν), Paul's word here suggests a reciprocity in ministry between Paul and the believers in Ephesus on the one hand, and the believers in Corinth on the other. Timothy played an important role in the process of Paul's communication and relationship with the Corinthians.

For later periods of Paul's ministry, it is difficult to trace the journeys made by the apostle or by his coworkers. According to Phil 2:19, Paul hoped to send Timothy to Philippi as soon as circumstances permitted. Sometime later, Timothy was left in Ephesus lest certain teachers should preach wrong doctrines (1 Tim 1:3). Biblical data shows that Timothy visited many cities in the short term (e.g., Thessalonica) or long term (e.g., Corinth and Ephesus) throughout his ministry with Paul. As Paul's associate, the young evangelist himself must have had a personal relationship with the local congregations in different areas. He had "a genuine concern about the welfare" of the local churches he visited (Phil 2:20). That Timothy was a frequent co-sender of Paul's letters reflects his close relationship and familiarity with various local churches. It may well be that Timothy, as a messenger of Paul and of the local churches on return, played a crucial role for Paul's partnership ministry with the local churches.

88. Barrett suggests the possibility that the journey of Acts 19:22 is the same journey referred to in 1 Cor 16:10. Erastus was not mentioned in 1 Corinthians for he himself was a Corinthian (Rom 16:23) and "was not visiting Corinth but simply returning home" (*First Epistle to the Corinthians*, 390).

Titus

Titus seems to have been with Paul and Barnabas in Antioch. He accompanied the two apostles on the trip to Jerusalem for the delivery of relief fund (Gal 2:1).[89] Although the name of Titus does not appear in the book of Acts, 2 Corinthians shows that during Paul's so-called third missionary journey he was with Paul and Timothy at Ephesus. From there, Titus was sent to Corinth probably as the courier of the "severe letter" (2 Cor 2:4; 7:8) in order to straighten up some problems in the church.

Titus's mission was fruitful. The church of Corinth received Paul's messenger and message "with fear and trembling" (2 Cor 7:15) and "were made sorry to repentance" (2 Cor 7:9). In turn, Paul was relieved over the good news Titus brought back from the Corinthians. Paul had been restless in Troas for missing Titus (2 Cor 2:13), but now was at rest over the coming of Titus to Macedonia (2 Cor 7:6). Titus worked as a messenger of reconciliation, contributing to the renewed relationship between Paul and the Corinthian congregation. He must have been in a good relationship with the Corinthian church, thereby functioning as "a key reason the congregation accepted Paul's correction."[90] Titus, like Timothy, was a "means by which Paul sought to establish close ties among these churches."[91]

It is noteworthy that the description of Titus's return from Corinth (2 Cor 7:5–7) bears considerable resemblance to 1 Thess 3:5–7, which describes the return of Timothy from Thessalonica. Mitchell does a comparative study of 1 Thessalonians 3 and 2 Corinthians 7 and finds that Paul worked "within some established conventions about envoys and their role in maintaining and reaffirming relationships between separated partners."[92] Titus and Timothy did carry out the important task of renewing relationships. Moreover, from the two analogous expressions of Paul, one can see how significant the role of envoys was to Paul himself. Until meeting his envoy, Paul was in "conflicts without, fears within" (2 Cor 7:5) and "no longer forbearing" (1 Thess 3:5). When the envoy came, Paul confesses, "God . . . comforted us" (2 Cor 7:6) and "we were comforted concerning you" (1 Thess 3:7). This pattern of restlessness and then rest depending on his envoys suggests the importance of messengers

89. In this volume, it is posited that the relief visit of Acts 11:29–30 corresponds to the Jerusalem meeting of Gal 2:1–10.

90. Willis, "Networking of the Pauline Churches," 75.

91. Willis, "Networking of the Pauline Churches," 75.

92. Mitchell, "New Testament Envoys," 661–62.

in Paul's life and work. It becomes more crucial "when there has been a rift of some kind between Paul and the church which requires third-party assistance to bring about the reconciliation of the relationship."[93] Titus successfully played the role of "third-party assistance."

Tychicus

Tychicus first appears in Acts 20:4, where he is said to have been from Asia and one of the church envoys who accompanied Paul on the trip to Jerusalem with the "collection" money. Tychicus might have been converted during Paul's mission to Ephesus (the so-called third missionary journey), since he appears only in the later days of Paul's ministry and mostly in relation with the churches in Asia, his home country. The importance of Tychicus lies in the role of letter-courier during Paul's first imprisonment in Rome. Most scholars agree that Tychicus carried Paul's letters to the Ephesians, to the Colossians, and to Philemon at the same time.[94] Besides the letters to the Ephesians and the Colossians, Tychicus is mentioned in Titus 3:12, where Paul plans to send either him or Artemas to replace Titus on Crete, and in 2 Tim 4:12, which reveals he has been sent to Ephesus. From these references in the New Testament, Tychicus seems to have been "one of Paul's regular emissaries" who traveled many cities conveying written and verbal messages of Paul.[95]

In the letter to the Ephesian church, Paul writes, "Tychicus . . . will make all things known to you, whom I am sending to you for this very purpose, that you may know the things about us and that he may comfort your hearts" (Eph 6:21–22). In almost identical words, Paul writes to the Colossians: "All the things about me, Tychicus . . . will make known to you, whom I am sending to you for this very purpose, that you may know the things about us and that he may comfort your hearts." (Col 4:7–8). The repeated use of the phrase "for this very thing" (εἰς αὐτὸ τοῦτο) emphasizes the purpose of sending envoys, which is "that you may know the things about us" (ἵνα γνῶτε τὰ περὶ ἡμῶν). The purpose of the letters to the Ephesians and to the Colossians was that Tychicus would bring

93. Mitchell, "New Testament Envoys," 643.

94. Moo presents three reasons for this view: (1) Tychicus plays the same role in Ephesus (Eph 6:21) as in Colossae (Col 4:7); (2) Tychicus is accompanied by Onesimus (Col 4:9); and (3) Ephesus and Colossae are no more than 120 miles apart (*Colossians and to Philemon*, 334).

95. Wilson, *Colossians and Philemon*, 296–97.

the news about Paul's situation in Rome to the churches in Asia. It was a crucial matter for Paul to communicate with the local churches, and Paul's envoys took the crucial part of mutual communication.

According to KJV, whose translation is based on other manuscripts, the purpose somewhat differs: it reads "he might know your estate and comfort your hearts."[96] Tychicus is said to have been sent to inquire about the churches in Asia rather than to inform them about the state of Paul in Rome. At any rate, both readings show that Tychicus contributed to the communication between Paul in Rome and the churches in Asia. The tradition of textual variance itself suggests the two-way direction of communication, flowing from Rome to Asia and vice versa. Moreover, it is to be noted that the communication was not made between Paul and the local churches only. Since Paul's ministry was carried out in the context of the local churches, "relationships among congregations—not only between Paul and the congregations—were created and maintained."[97]

In the letter to the Colossians, Paul mentions Tychicus and Onesimus: "They will make known to you all things that are here" (πάντα ὑμῖν γνωρίσουσιν τὰ ὧδε) (Col 4:9). The two envoys were to deliver Paul's letters to the local churches in Asia and tell them about what was going on with Paul. What does the phrase "all things . . . here" (πάντα . . . τὰ ὧδε) mean? English versions read, "the whole situation here" (NASB), "all things which are done here" (KJV), or "all things which are happening here" (NKJV). "Here" indicates Rome, where Paul was writing the letter under house arrest (cf. Acts 28; Col 4:3, 10). "All things" might refer to various issues: the legal situation concerning Paul's imprisonment and appeal to Caesar, the mission of Paul and his coworkers in Rome, and the overall ministry of house churches in Rome. Although there is no way of knowing exactly, the phrase "all things . . . here" at least relates to the ministry context of Paul, i.e., the community of believers around the apostle and their evangelistic activities in Rome.

In the letters to the Ephesians and the Colossians themselves, Paul does not disclose any specific circumstances of himself or the local

96. Manuscripts such as P46 and D1 offer ἵνα γνῶ τὰ περὶ ὑμῶν ("that he may know the things about you"). This reading, however, is "unlikely to be original" (Moo, *Colossians*, 335) and "seems at variance with the preceding εἰς αὐτὸ τοῦτο" (Wilson, *Colossians and Philemon*, 297). For further comments, see Metzger, *Textual Commentary*, 559.

97. Kloha, "Trans-Congregational Church," 181.

churches. There are only a few of general and brief descriptions.[98] It is to be noted that the delivery of concrete news about Paul in prison and the local churches in Rome, i.e., "all things . . . here," was left to the role of envoys. Further, the ending phrase, "that he may comfort your hearts" (Eph 6:22; Col 4:8), implies that the envoys would be able to expound the letter and strengthen the recipients. Theses coworkers—Paul's travel companions and messengers—were indispensable to the partnership ministry of Paul in trans-local networking and collaboration among the New Testament churches.

Ministry Associates from the Local Churches

Whereas Paul's travel companions (e.g., Timothy, Titus, Tychicus) worked mostly in accordance with the apostle's direction, some coworkers had their ministry base connected to their home churches. Through these coworkers, the local churches supplied financial and human resources for Paul's ministry. Since they ministered to their home churches and also served other churches along with Paul, their trans-local activities entailed mutual contacts and communication between the churches involved. This subsection traces the evidence of the inter-church relationship mediated by those coworkers, particularly by Epaphroditus of Philippi and Epaphras of Colossae.

Epaphroditus

Epaphroditus was the messenger (ἀπόστολος) of the Philippian church and the minister (λειτουργός) to Paul during his first Roman imprisonment (Phil 2:25). From its beginning, the Philippian church had financially supported Paul for his missions to other cities such as Thessalonica (Phil 4:15–16) and Corinth (2 Cor 11:9). Hearing of Paul's imprisonment in Rome, the Philippians resumed their support for the apostle by sending Epaphroditus and a financial gift with him (Phil 4:18). Epaphroditus labored in missionary works so intensely that he became sick, "close to

98. Paul's statements about himself include "Paul, the prisoner of Christ Jesus" (Eph 3:1), "a prisoner for the Lord" (Eph 4:1), "an ambassador in chains" (Eph 6:19), "for which I am in chains" (Col 4:3), "my fellow prisoner Aristarchus" (Col 4:10), and "Remember my chains" (Col 4:18).

death for the work of Christ" (Phil 2:30). Therefore, Paul sent him back to Philippi with the letter to the Philippians.

In Phil 2:25, Paul calls Epaphroditus my "brother" (ἀδελφός), "co-worker" (συνεργός), and "fellow-soldier" (συστρατιώτης). Also, in relation to the Philippian church, he is described as its "messenger" (ἀπόστολος) and "minister" (λειτουργός). From these designations, it is clear that Epaphroditus was not only a church messenger but also an evangelist who devoted himself to missionary works in his hometown Philippi and in Rome alongside Paul.

Concerning the travel of Epaphroditus, Dickson raises a question: why did the Philippians send their own missionary to Paul? As stated in Phil 1:5 ("your participation in the gospel") and 4:18 ("having received from Epaphroditus the things from you"), the immediate reason was to deliver financial assistance to Paul. However, Dickson finds another significant reason from the historical context of the word "rather" (μᾶλλον) in the opening statement of the letter (1:12). He argues that the Philippian church had been "under the impression that Paul's imprisonment would hinder the work of the gospel" and then sent out Epaphroditus, who "would be able to (and probably had done in Philippi years before) assist Paul in the preaching task."[99] The Philippian church had concern not only for Paul's financial need but also for the gospel ministry after Paul's imprisonment. That is why, according to Dickson, Paul quickly responded to the Philippians' concern: "what has happened to me has *rather* (μᾶλλον) turned out for the progress of the gospel" (Phil 1:12).[100]

Regardless of the main reason for dispatching Epaphroditus to Paul, the Philippians' action is significant in that the church in Philippi was interested and involved in Paul's ministry in Rome. As Paul designated, Epaphroditus served as Philippians' "apostle" (ἀπόστολος), i.e., "one sent on behalf of the congregation to perform a given task."[101] Epaphroditus thus carried out the task of ministering to Paul and participating in the evangelical work in Rome as a representative of the Philippian church. Paul states that Epaphroditus risked his life so as to "fill up the lack of your [the Philippians'] service to me" (Phil 2:30). Paul is not criticizing them but complimenting them for their support through their apostle, Epaphroditus. Although the church could not be along with Paul in

99. Dickson, *Mission-Commitment*, 316–17. See also O'Brien, *Philippians*, 90.

100. Dickson, *Mission-Commitment*, 316–17.

101. Fee, *Philippians*, 276.

prison, "the presence of their messenger, Epaphroditus, made up for their absence: the one filled the gap for the many."[102] The church at Philippi joined Paul and Paul's mission in Rome through her apostle/messenger.

Epaphroditus's activity in Rome is not known in detail except his role as the assistant and coworker of Paul; however, it can hardly be doubted that the evangelist from Philippi carried out missionary work in conjunction with other coworkers and the local believers in Rome. For example, it is quite conceivable that Epaphroditus associated himself and worked together with some of those "brothers who, trusting the Lord in my imprisonment, even more dare to speak the word without fear" (Phil 1:14). Furthermore, Epaphroditus's stay in Rome must have advanced the mutual awareness and relationship between the two Christian communities, as "the brothers with me [Paul]" and "all the saints, especially those of Caesar's house" sent greetings to the Philippian congregation (Phil 4:21–22). Hence, the aphoristic phrase "partnership in the gospel" (κοινωνία εἰς τὸ εὐαγγέλιον) (Phil 1:5) signifies not only the financial contribution of the Philippian church but also "the community's involvement in the preaching of the gospel *through* their apostle, Epaphroditus."[103] To sum up, the Philippian church collaborated in missions with the churches in Rome through the ministry of Paul and his coworkers.

Epaphras

Epaphras was a leading member of the Colossian church (Col 4:12). In fact, the Colossian church had started as a result of his mission in the city (Col 1:7). Probably, his work also brought forth other Christian communities in the Lycus valley: "he is working hard for you [the Colossians] and for those at Laodicea and Hierapolis" (Col 4:13). Afterwards, he moved to Rome and joined Paul's ministry there as the apostle's assistant. For part of the time, he was a "fellow prisoner" (συναιχμάλωτος), imprisoned together with Paul (Phlm 23).

In Col 1:7, Paul describes Epaphras as a "faithful servant of Christ on our/your behalf" (πιστὸς ὑπὲρ ἡμῶν/ὑμῶν διάκονος τοῦ Χριστοῦ).[104] The textual variation allows for a range of interpretations for the role

102. Hansen, *Philippians*, 210.

103. Dickson, *Mission-Commitment*, 317.

104. The reading "on your behalf" is taken by AV, NRSV, HCSB, and NLT, whereas "on our behalf" is adopted by NASB, NIV, RSV, and NET.

of Epaphras in relation to Paul as well as to the Colossian church. Most commentators posit that Epaphras was converted by Paul during the Ephesian ministry and sent to his hometown, Colossae, for missionary works there. In this sense, the first person (ὑπὲρ ἡμῶν) stands coherent, denoting that "Epaphras in his ministry has been acting on Paul's behalf, as his representative."[105] Paul therefore recommends Epaphras to the Colossians as "*our* beloved fellow servant" and confirms his faithfulness in Christ (Col 1:7).

On the other hand, the second-person reading (ὑπὲρ ὑμῶν) would signify "services rendered to Paul by Epaphras, acting on behalf of the Colossians."[106] Given the status and role of Epaphras in the Colossian church, it is likely that he visited Paul in Rome as a representative of the church and possibly of the other churches in the Lycus valley as well.[107] Col 1:4 intimates the emissary role of Epaphras: "we have heard of your faith in Christ Jesus and of the love for all the saints." Paul, his coworkers, and fellow Christians in Rome heard the news about the Colossian congregation most likely from Epaphras. Col 1:8 is more clearly saying that "he [Epaphras] also made known to us your love in the Spirit." (Col 1:8). The Colossian believers sent one of their leaders to Paul to deliver the good news of their love and the progress of the gospel in their neighborhood. Concerning this "our/your" variation, Moo succinctly explains that "if verse 7 is primarily about Epaphras's faithfulness as a minister to the Colossians on behalf of Paul, verse 8 is about his reliability as a messenger to Paul on behalf of the Colossians."[108] In any case, Epaphras connected two groups of Christians—Paul and the believers in Rome on the one hand, and the Colossians and their neighboring Christians on the other.

In reference to Epaphras's visit to Paul, it should also be noted that "probably the main reason for his visit was to seek advice from Paul as to how to deal with the false teaching which had arisen in Colossae. . . . Paul's letter is then written as a response to this urgent need."[109] The Colossian believers were to fight against certain heresies that threatened the

105. Wilson, *Colossians and Philemon*, 96.

106. Wilson, *Colossians and Philemon*, 96.

107. See Col 4:12–13: "Epaphras, who is one of you, . . . always laboring fervently for you in prayers, . . . has a great zeal for you, and those who are in Laodicea, and those in Hierapolis" (NKJV).

108. Moo, *Colossians and to Philemon*, 91.

109. O'Brien, *Colossians-Philemon*, xxx.

unity and truth of the church. Epaphras, the founder and probably the minister of the church, traveled to Rome to report on the worrisome situation. His pastoral concern is well attested in Paul's account: "[Epaphras] always laboring earnestly for you in his prayers that you may stand perfect and fully assured in all the will of God" (Col 4:12). It can be inferred that Epaphras's earnest prayers for the Colossian church were not only witnessed but also joined by Paul and the Roman Christians. In fact, Paul mentions the prayer for the Colossian believers: "since we heard [through Epaphras] about you, we have not stopped praying for you" (Col 1:9). Paul and the believers in Rome prayed for the church in Colossae, which was also a substantial example of trans-local collaboration between the churches.

Envoys from the Local Churches

The book of Acts and Paul's letters refer to the coworkers who were sent to Paul as the envoys of local churches. Unlike Paul's travel companions (e.g., Timothy and Titus) or ministry associates from the local churches (e.g., Epaphroditus and Epaphras) who ministered along with Paul for a considerable amount of time, these coworkers are recorded as having served for a limited time and for a particular mission. Still, their trans-local activities contributed to the communication and collaboration of partnership ministry.

Stephanas

Stephanas was a Corinthian Christian who had been baptized by Paul (1 Cor 1:16). Since Paul regards his household as "the first fruit of Achaia" (1 Cor 16:15), Stephanas was probably one of those won to Christ during Paul's first mission to Corinth (Acts 18:1–11). Converted, he and his household "devoted themselves (ἔταξαν ἑαυτούς) to ministry for the saints" (1 Cor 16:15).[110] In Garland's words, "they set themselves aside for

110. Even though the verb τάσσω "has more to do with appointing or assigning to a task, office, or position than *have devoted themselves* (NRSV, REB, NIV, NJB) might seem to suggest," the rendering *appointed themselves* carries a tone of "very self-centered forwardness" that might have made Paul uneasy. Therefore, the phrase is better understood in light of the "self-imposed duty" for the work of service and ministry. Thiselton, *First Epistle to the Corinthians*, 1338–39.

service to other Christians."[111] Paul's repeated mention of "the household of Stephanas" (1 Cor 1:16 and 16:15) clearly indicates that Stephanas was the head of a household. Also, given that Paul urged the Corinthians to "submit to such as these" (1 Cor 16:16), it is likely that Stephanas and his household played a leadership role in the ministry of the Corinthian church. One important role was to communicate the message of the church to Paul in Ephesus.

In 1 Cor 16:17, Paul rejoices over the coming of Stephanas, Fortunatus, and Achaicus from Corinth. Most commentators agree that Fortunatus and Achaicus were Stephanas's "slaves or freedmen, and thus a part of his household."[112] Due to some issues and conflicts in the church, the Corinthians might have sent Stephanas and his household members to Paul as "the couriers for the Corinthians' letter."[113] Fee thus says, "the three together would become a kind of 'official delegation' from the church."[114]

Paul confesses that their arrival made him glad "because they filled up the lack of yours" (1 Cor 16:17). Here, "the lack of yours" (τό ὑμέτερον ὑστέρμα) is not to be taken as a pejorative language that criticizes the Corinthians for certain shortcomings. The word ὑστέρμα is to be understood in terms of "*absence, deficiency, lack,* left by the distance between Paul and the Corinthian church itself," so the phrase rather reflects Paul's "*affection* for the Corinthian church with *appreciation* for their three representatives."[115]

The visitation of Stephanas and others to Ephesus made up for Paul's absence from the Corinthians, and vice versa. As Paul confesses "they refreshed my spirit and yours" (1 Cor 16:18), their coming (and probably their returning home) strengthened the relationship between Paul and the Corinthian believers. It is most probable that Paul wrote 1 Corinthians in reply to the Corinthians' letter and that the three men were now the couriers of the letter to the Corinthians. Stephanas's case exemplifies

111. Garland, *1 Corinthians*, 768.

112. Clarke, "Refresh the Hearts of the Saints," 287. See also Meeks, *First Urban Christians*, 56.

113. Ciampa and Rosner, *First Letter to the Corinthians*, 859.

114. Fee, *First Corinthians*, 832. In contrast, Garland has a different view: "We need not interpret this visit to be some kind of special delegation to Ephesus. The three travelers may have arrived on business and naturally made contact with their apostle" (*1 Corinthians*, 770). However, Fee continues to insist that even if they traveled to Ephesus on business, "the church would have asked them to carry their letter to Paul."

115. Thiselton, *First Epistle to the Corinthians*, 1340.

the trans-local communication and interrelationship executed by Paul's coworkers who are engaged mainly in local ministry.

"Messengers of the Churches" (2 Cor 8:23)

Paul wrote 2 Corinthians when he was staying in Macedonia prior to his final visit to Corinth. Along with the letter, he sent in advance his coworkers to Corinth: Titus (2 Cor 8:17); "the brother whose praise in the gospel is throughout all the churches" (2 Cor 8:18); and "our brother whom we often proved diligent in many things" (2 Cor 8:22). Whereas Titus is called "my partner and fellow worker among you," the other two brothers are addressed as "messengers of the churches" (ἀπόστολοι ἐκκλησιῶν) (2 Cor 8:23). The brother of verse 18 was appointed by the churches to travel with Paul to ensure the delivery of the relief fund to Jerusalem (2 Cor 8:19–20). Although the task of the other brother (2 Cor 8:22) was not explicitly explained, it is certain that he was also appointed by the churches to join the collection project.[116]

Regarding the brother of verse 18, Dickson argues that the phrase containing ἐν τῷ εὐαγγελίῳ denotes "the brother's *proclamation* of the gospel throughout the Pauline communities (of Macedonia)" and so the brother appears to have been an evangelist who had "responsibility for continuing the mission of Paul in parts of Macedonia."[117] More significant is the fact that the brother was highly spoken of "by all the churches" and that he was "appointed by the churches" (χειροτονηθεὶς ὑπὸ τῶν ἐκκλησιῶν) to support Paul's mission. As Paul and Barnabas "appointed" (χειροτονήσαντες) elders in every assembly in Galatia (Acts 14:23), the term χειροτονέω often conveys a tone of official designation. It is here used to signify "to choose, elect by raising a hand to signify a vote"[118] or "to elect or choose someone for definite offices or tasks."[119] The election was probably "a comparatively formal process" as was the normal practice of democratic procedures in Greco-Roman society.[120]

116. According to Barnett, *Second Epistle to the Corinthians*, 421, the two brothers were chosen to "go all the way to Jerusalem with the collection, representing the believers of Macedonia." For various attempts to identify "the brothers," see Martin, *2 Corinthians*, 274–75.

117. Dickson, *Mission-Commitment*, 134–35.

118. *Analytical Lexicon of the Greek New Testament*, s.v. "χειροτονέω."

119. BDAG, s.v. "χειροτονέω."

120. Thrall, *Second Epistle of the Corinthians*, 549.

Most probably, the brother was from the local community of Macedonia.[121] All the churches in the area or at least their leaders convened together and chose by vote (χειροτονέω) the brother, who had already been an acclaimed evangelist throughout the area. This brief passage (2 Cor 8:18–19) indicates how the local churches cooperated in selecting an emissary to Paul and how the coworkers participated in Paul's missions. The joint commission of envoys reflects "the unity of the trans-congregational church."[122]

Paul's Coworkers Related with non-Pauline Churches

This section studies Paul's coworkers who were engaged in ministry beyond the boundary of Pauline missions. They were significant partners of Paul for missionary campaigns or pastoral works. On the other hand, they also worked independently of Paul's missions. Those coworkers sometimes had a close relationship with other non-Pauline Christian communities, such as the churches at Jerusalem, Antioch, and Rome. Such dual relationship functioned as a bridge between Pauline and non-Pauline churches.

Apollos

Apollos was a Jew of Alexandria, who was "eloquent" and "mighty in the Scriptures" (Acts 18:24). He came to Ephesus and proclaimed Jesus in the synagogue boldly (Acts 18:25), though he knew "only the baptism of John" (Acts 18:25). After hearing from Priscilla and Aquila about "the way of God" more accurately (Acts 18:26), Apollos moved to Achaia and contributed to the growth of the Corinthian congregation subsequent to Paul's initial ministry in the city (Acts 18:27). By the time Paul wrote 1 Corinthians, Apollos was back in Ephesus (1 Cor 16:12). Later, in Titus

121. The brother was praised "by all the churches" (v. 18) and appointed "by the churches" (v. 19). What scope of "churches" does Paul mean? Barnett lists the options: "(1) all the churches everywhere, (2) all the churches of Judaea (so Nickle), (3) all the churches raised up by his mission in Macedonia, Achaia, and Asia, or (4) all the churches in Macedonia." Most commentators vie for option 4, because "both the antecedent reference (v. 1) and the succeeding (v. 19) reference to 'churches' are in regard to Macedonia—the former explicit, the latter implicit." Barnett, *Second Epistle to the Corinthians*, 420.

122. Kloha, "Trans-Congregational Church," 183.

3:13, Paul directs "help Zenas the lawyer and Apollos on their way." If this Apollos is the one under discussion, then he must have continued a close relationship with Paul for a lengthy period of time.[123]

It is to be noted that Apollos's mission to Achaia was not an undertaking of his own. Luke records, "when he [Apollos] wanted to cross to Achaia, the brothers encouraged, wrote to the disciples [in Corinth] to welcome him" (Acts 18:27). The believers in Ephesus encouraged Apollos and wrote for him a letter of recommendation to the Corinthian believers.[124] However, if the omitted object of "encouraged" is "them" (the disciples in Corinth) rather than "him" (Apollos), the relationship between the two Christian communities becomes more intimate with the text meaning "the brothers [in Ephesus] encouraged them [the disciples in Corinth] and wrote to the disciples [in Corinth] to welcome him [Apollos]."[125]

Another textual matter is worthy of consideration. The Western text D reads: "in Ephesus, the Corinthians who were visiting and hearing him [Apollos] encouraged him to go with them to their home country [Corinth]."[126] Some Corinthian believers were visiting Ephesus and heard Apollos's sermon. When they were traveling back to Corinth, they asked Apollos to come with them. He agreed and the Ephesian brothers supported their plan with a commendation letter to the Corinthian church. In this variant text, "the initiative is taken not by Apollos but by Corinthians who happen to be resident in Ephesus."[127] This Western reading sheds light on the mutual contact and cooperation between the churches across

123. Most commentators accept that this Apollos is the same person referred to in Acts 18:24–28 and 1 Cor 16:12. For example, Quinn comments, "All of these notices [concerning "Apollos"] refer to the same person, a Jewish Christian of Alexandrian origin with notable skills in interpreting the OT and communicating what he learned." Quinn, *Letter to Titus*, 257.

124. The letter of recommendation was a common practice of communication in Greco-Roman society. Early churches also practiced this type of letter-writing to introduce their envoys to other churches and ask for help for their journeys. In the present case, Priscilla and Aquila probably best fit as the authors of the recommendation letter, since the couple had been in Corinth with the believers (Acts 18:1–3) and were now in friendship with Apollos in Ephesus.

125. Most English Bibles, with the exception of KJV, NKJV, and HCSB, regard the hidden object as "him" (Apollos). However, there is no way of excluding the rendering of "them" (the Corinthian believers). Both translations are equally plausible in the verb's grammatical and semantic context.

126. The variant text of D reads: ἐν δὲ τῇ Ἐφέσῳ ἐπιδημοῦντές τινες Κορίνθιοι καὶ ἀκούσαντες αὐτοῦ παρεκάλουν διελθεῖν σὺν αὐτοῖς εἰς τὴν πατρίδα αὐτῶν.

127. Barrett, *Acts of the Apostles*, 890–91.

the Aegean Sea. Afterwards, Apollos's work in Corinth, particularly the demonstration of the gospel truth by affirming Jesus from the Scriptures, turned out to be of great help to the believers in Achaia (Acts 18:28). The story of Apollos reflects the early stage of inter-church relationships and collaborations for the cause of the gospel ministry.

Most scholars view the prepositional phrase περὶ δέ ("now concerning"), which occurs throughout 1 Corinthians (7:1, 25; 8:1; 12:1; 16:1, 12), as signaling Paul's reply to certain issues raised by the Corinthian congregation.[128] Hurd thus argues, "each of the passages thus introduced in 1 Corinthians appears to consist of an answer to a question or questions asked Paul by the Corinthians."[129] Fee says, "Almost certainly these pick up subsequent items in their letter to Paul."[130] On this understanding, the phrase περὶ δὲ Ἀπολῶ ("Now concerning Apollos") (1 Cor 16:12) suggests that the Corinthians had asked Paul and the Ephesian congregation to send Apollos to them again.[131] Paul then urged him to come to Corinth, but Apollos refused the request, probably for fear of worsening the factions among the Corinthian believers. Meanwhile, Paul's earnest encouragement shows "the strength of Paul's character and his absolute commitment to partnership in ministry."[132] The Corinthians' request for a teaching minister from Ephesus demonstrates the sharing of human resources among the early churches. The attitudes and actions taken by Apollos, Paul, and the two Christian communities together demonstrate a body of believers closely linked to one another in their common faith and ministry.

128. Because its first occurrence (1 Cor 7:1) reads "περὶ δὲ ὧν ἐγράψατε" ("Now concerning the things that you wrote"), most scholars interpret the phrase as the indicator which shows a literary movement to a new subject inquired by the Corinthians. However, this traditional view has been challenged by Margaret Mitchell. After examining the use of the phrase in a wide range of ancient Greek texts, she concludes that "the formula περὶ δέ is commonly used in papyrus letters which make no mention of a previous letter, so it is clearly not always an 'answering formula'" (Mitchell, "Concerning Περὶ δέ," 245). Although this prepositional phrase does not necessarily signal an answer to a question, Mitchell still admits that it does serve as "a topic marker introducing a readily-known subject" (251). At any rate, it is certain that the formula περὶ δέ provides a significant key to the understanding of the Corinthian issues.

129. Hurd, *Origin of 1 Corinthians*, 64.

130. Fee, *First Corinthians*, 274.

131. Hartin, *Apollos*, 64. On the contrary, Garland argues, "It may be the case that they made no inquiry about Apollos in their letter, and Paul simply anticipates their disappointment that Apollos had not returned and averts any suspicion that somehow he had prevented him from returning" (*1 Corinthians*, 761).

132. Taylor, *1 Corinthians*, 426.

Aquila and Priscilla

This couple is mentioned repeatedly in the book of Acts and Paul's letters.[133] They were among those who were forced to leave Rome by the edict of Claudius, which ordered the expulsion of all Jews from the city around 49 AD.[134] Taking refuge in Corinth, the couple met Paul who was on the Aegean mission to the city (Acts 18:2–3). When Paul left for Asia Minor, Aquila and Priscilla accompanied him to Ephesus and remained there whereas Paul traveled on to Jerusalem (Acts 18:19). On Paul's return from Syria, the couple might have stayed with him for a while (cf. 1 Cor 16:19) before they moved to Rome. According to Paul's letter to Timothy, the missionary couple were back in Ephesus, serving the Ephesian church (2 Tim 4:19).

It may well be that Priscilla and Aquila had been Christians when they met Paul in Corinth. Paul does not include their names in the list of those who were baptized by him (1 Cor 1:14–16). They are not called as "the first fruit of Achaia" as the household of Stephanas (1 Cor 16:15). It is not likely "for a Judean who had been expelled because of Christ to associate with anyone who is a Christ believer, for example Paul, unless that person is already a Christian."[135] In this sense, Keller argues, "their readiness to offer hospitality to Paul . . . is but a continuation of what they had already done in Rome before they were banished."[136] Priscilla and Aquila were instrumental in building up the Christian community in Rome from the outset.

Because the couple and Paul were in the same trade, Acts 18:2–3 says that Paul "came to them" and "stayed with them." Luke's account suggests that the couple opened a tent-making shop in Corinth, and Paul "presumably took advantage of this natural setting consisting of Aquila's colleagues and customers to develop evangelistic contacts."[137]

133. Acts 18:1–3, 18–19, 26; 1 Cor 16:19; Rom 16:3–5; 2 Tim 4:19.

134. Suetonius wrote that "Because the Jews constantly made trouble, which was instigated by Chrestus, he expelled them from the City" (*The Twelve Caesars*, 5.25). "Jews" here denotes the Christians who were mostly Jews in the beginning of the Christian movement. "Chrestus" seems to be a mistaken word for the Jewish title *christus*. See Evans, *Ancient Texts*, 289–99.

135. Nguyen, "Migrants as Missionaries," 70.

136. Keller, *Priscilla and Aquila*, 13. Keller suggests that Aquila and Priscilla might have received the gospel during the Pentecost event (Acts 2) and brought it to Rome.

137. Gehring, *House Church and Mission*, 134–35. For more detailed discussion, see Davis, "Business Secrets," 229.

Regarding the role of Priscilla and Aquila in founding the Corinthian church, the book of Acts is rather silent. However, most scholars agree with Murphy-O'Connor's argument that "at Corinth Prisca and Aquila did what they subsequently did at Ephesus and at Rome, where we hear of 'a church in their house' (1 Cor 16:19; Rom 16:5)."[138] The first Christian group in Corinth might have assembled in the couple's house, "in the living room above Prisca and Aquila's shop."[139]

Aquila and Priscilla came to Ephesus along with Paul. Luke's narrative, in which the couple took Apollos aside and taught about "the way of God more accurately" (Acts 18:26), indicates the significant role of the missionary couple in leading the Ephesian church. When Apollos wanted to extend his mission to Corinth, the Ephesian congregation wrote a letter of recommendation to the Corinthian believers. In all probability, Priscilla and Aquila were primarily responsible for writing the letter because the couple themselves had lived and worked in Corinth for many years. The missionary couple played a crucial role in founding the Ephesian church and then in developing the church's relationship with other Christian communities.

When the edict of Claudius, which had expelled Priscilla and Aquila from Rome, ceased to have effect, they probably moved back home and joined the Christian community there, again hosting the believers in their house. Concluding his letter to the Romans, Paul writes, "Greet Priscilla and Aquila, my fellow workers in Christ Jesus, . . . and the church in their house" (Rom 16:3–5). When Paul had not much to do with the formation of the Christian community at Rome, Aquila and Priscilla must have provided a channel for Paul and other churches to have connections with the believers in the capital city.

The couple's residence and mission in "three of the most important centers of early Christianity"—i.e., chronologically, in Rome, Corinth, Ephesus, Rome, and Ephesus—"underline their importance in the history of early Christianity."[140] The phrase "all the churches of the Gentiles [give thanks to Aquila and Priscilla]" (Rom 16:4) signifies "the very widespread nature of their influence, of whatever kind it was."[141] Also, it could be inferred that their ministries in multiple cities naturally brought forth

138. Murphy-O'Connor, "Prisca and Aquila," 49.

139. Murphy-O'Connor, "Prisca and Aquila," 48.

140. Murphy-O'Connor, "Prisca and Aquila," 40.

141. Dunn, *Romans 9–16*, 893.

the occasion of inter-church communications and contacts. The couple was "a significant means of connecting the churches."[142]

Barnabas

Although there had previously been evangelism to gentiles, the large scale of gentile conversion at Antioch was unheard of. It started with some unknown men of Cyprus and Cyrene, the Hellenistic Jews (Acts 11:20).[143] Instead of reaching their fellow Jews, they "took a momentous step forward" and began to preach the Lord Jesus to the Greeks.[144] A great number of the gentiles believed and turned to the Lord (Acts 11:21). Concerning the phenomenon, the Jerusalem church needed to send someone to Antioch to look into "the novelty of the situation," and the fact of the matter was that "much—far more than they could have realized—depended on their choice of a delegate."[145]

No one was better fit for the job than Barnabas. He was "a good man, full of the Holy Spirit and of faith" (Acts 11:24). That he was called "Barnabas" ("Son of Encouragement") suggests that he was held in high regard among the leaders of the Jerusalem church. Furthermore, Barnabas himself was "a Levite, a native of Cyprus" (Acts 4:36) like the Hellenistic Jews who first preached the gospel to the Greeks in Antioch. He was a man of God well versed in Hellenistic culture as well as in the Jewish traditions and laws. Barnabas, along with Paul, taught the new congregation, and the congregation grew larger. The Jerusalem church, by sending Barnabas to Antioch, played a substantial part for the settlement and growth of the Antioch church.

When the great famine took place in the days of Claudius, the Antioch Christians decided to send a contribution for the relief of the believers in Judea (Acts 11:28–30).[146] Barnabas, together with Paul, was

142. Willis, "Networking of the Pauline Churches," 76.

143. The definition of "Hellenistic" Judaism or "Hellenistic" Jews is difficult to establish. Here, the term is used in connection with the Greek language, the Greek Bible, and Greek synagogue worship. Many diasporan Jews returned home and settled in Jerusalem. Their descendants continued the Hellenistic language and culture, constituting the community of "Hellenistic" Jews. For more discussion, see Hengel, *Between Jesus and Paul*, 4–13.

144. Bruce, *Acts*, 225.

145. Bruce, *Acts*, 226.

146. This subject will be treated in detail in chapter 3, section "Financial Collaboration for the Jerusalem Church."

commissioned by the church to deliver the contribution to the Jerusalem elders. Besides the charitable purpose, the sending of gift might be "an important expression of solidarity across social and cultural boundaries," which had developed between the two Christian communities.[147] Barnabas, who had previously come to Antioch as a representative of the Jerusalem church, was sent back to Jerusalem, now representing the Antioch church.

As Antioch surfaced as the most important center of Christianity after Jerusalem, there emerged a cultural and theological difference between the two leading churches. Certain Jewish Christians from Jerusalem arrived at Antioch and taught that "Unless you are circumcised according to the custom of Moses, you cannot be saved" (Acts 15:1). After dispute, the Antioch church decided to send Barnabas and Paul to Jerusalem to discuss the matter. The whole narrative of Acts 15:1–35 records the challenge and solution for "maintaining harmony between these two missions."[148] A resolution was made generally in favor of the position of the gentile Christians at Antioch.

During the process of reconciliation, it can hardly be doubted that Barnabas, with strong ties with the Jerusalem community, greatly contributed to the communication and mediation between the two Christian communities. Barnabas must have endeavored "to maintain good relations with the church in Jerusalem . . . but also accepted and defended with all his authority the non-circumcision practice of the Gentile Mission."[149] Murphy studies the role of Barnabas in the book of Acts, examining six scenes of Barnabas's ministry through "a narrative-critical lens."[150] He makes a conclusive statement for his study: "A key depiction of Barnabas in the narrative is as an intermediary, as a relational bridge builder."[151] Barnabas was influential in building the bridge between the Jerusalem church and the Antioch church.

147. Peterson, *Acts*, 359.

148. Peterson, *Acts*, 356.

149. Holmberg, *Paul and Power*, 63.

150. Murphy, "Role of Barnabas," 319–41. He examines scene 1 (Acts 4:36–37), scene 2 (Acts 9:1–30), scene 3 (Acts 11:19–30), scene 4 (Acts 13:1—14:28), scene 5 (Acts 15:1–35), and scene 6 (Acts 15:36–41).

151. Murphy, "Role of Barnabas," 341.

Silas

Silas in the book of Acts is generally identified with the Silvanus appearing in the letters of Paul and Peter (1 and 2 Thess 1:1; 2 Cor 1:19; 1 Pet 5:12). After meeting, the Jerusalem Council appointed Silas and Judas Barsabas to convey the letter of resolution to Antioch along with Paul and Barnabas. Besides carrying the letter, they were commissioned to "report themselves the same things by word of mouth" (Acts 15:27). That Silas and Judas were dispatched to Antioch as the official delegates of the Jerusalem Council attests to their repute and character in the Jerusalem community. Luke describes them as "leading men among the brethren" at Jerusalem (Acts 15:22). Concerning the position of the Jerusalem congregation, Peterson is correct in saying that "Choosing *some of their own men* to accompany Barnabas and Paul, they hoped for a clear explanation of their intentions in writing the letter (v. 27) and a healing of any strained relationship between the churches."[152]

Arriving at Antioch, the delegates gathered the entire congregation, delivered the letter, and exhorted the believers (Acts 15:30–32). The Antioch congregation rejoiced over the encouraging words, and the mission of the Jerusalem delegates was successfully completed. Luke continues to write that "they were let go in peace from the brothers to those who had sent them" (Acts 15:33). The phrase "in peace" (μετ' εἰρήνης) unmistakably denotes the cordial feeling of their departure, signifying the reinforced relationship between Antioch and Jerusalem. Whereas Barnabas and Paul remained and ministered in Antioch, Silas and Judas, being the emissaries of the Jerusalem church, came back and must have reported to the Jerusalem church.[153] Silas and Judas played an important role in confirming the rapprochement between the two churches.[154]

152. Peterson, *Acts*, 437.

153. KJV and NKJV insert verse 34, "it seemed good for Silas to remain there," adopting the Textus Receptus that is based on the later Greek text and most probably unoriginal. The interpolation might have been made to give a more plausible explanation for verse 40, "Paul chose Silas and set out." In fact, Luke's account falls short of explaining how and when Silas returned to Antioch from Jerusalem to join Paul's Aegean mission. For further discussion, see Keener, *Acts*, 2295–96.

154. It is notable that they were "prophets themselves" (καὶ αὐτοὶ προφῆται) (Acts 15:32). The emphatic description of Judas and Silas as "prophets" is significant since "it suggests that prophetic ministry involved explanation and application of apostolic teaching, such as was found in the letter, and not simply prediction, as in the case of Agabus (13:28; 21:10–11)." Peterson, *Acts*, 441.

Afterwards, Barnabas left Paul (Acts 15:39); instead, Silas joined Paul in the Aegean mission. The two missionaries departed, "being committed to the grace of the Lord by the brethren" (Acts 15:40). Luke does not mention the commendation of the other missionary team, Barnabas and Mark, by the Antioch church; however, in all probability, they were also committed to the Lord by the church as they left for Cyprus. Likewise, despite Luke's silence on the Jerusalem church, it may well be that the Jerusalem community endorsed and prayed for Silas as he left for Antioch to join the Aegean mission with Paul. Jerusalem's approval of Silas for the mission to the gentile world is saying in other words that "one of the 'chief men' from Jerusalem was involved in the mission," and "the Jerusalem 'pedigree' of Silas would lend added authority to the mission and maybe even serve to remind the church back in Jerusalem that world evangelization was their responsibility too."[155] It is remarkable that Paul's so-called second missionary journey was not only commissioned by the Antioch church but also supported by the Jerusalem church through Silas.

Paul and Silas departed for the churches in Syria and Cilicia that had been planted during Paul's previous missions (Acts 15:41). Luke adds that, "as they were passing through the cities, they were delivering to them the decrees to keep, which had been decided by the apostles and elders in Jerusalem" (Acts 16:4). This account of the Jerusalem Council resolution is significant because it suggests that "in Luke's mind this is a journey which owes its origin to the Jerusalem Council."[156] In a similar vein, Marshall argues that during the second missionary journey, particularly in its initial stage, Paul might have "felt that he was the emissary of both the Antioch and the Jerusalem churches."[157] In sum, Silas's missionary journey with Paul is to be construed as a venture of Jerusalem-Antioch collaboration.

After the Aegean mission, Silas's whereabouts remain unknown except for the mention in 1 Pet 5:12. Peter addresses him as a "faithful brother," signifying that Silas was "not only a Christian believer, but a

155. Thomas, "Silas," 306.

156. Kaye, "Acts' Portrait of Silas," 17. The Jerusalem Council sent out its representatives to inform the gentile churches of the Council resolution. Thus, Kaye continues to argue that "the departure of Paul from Antioch is, in Luke's presentation, a continuation of the visit to Antioch from the Council in Jerusalem, and Silas is again the Jerusalem companion for Paul in a visit to churches addressed in the Council's letter" ("Acts' Portrait of Silas," 26).

157. Marshall, "Luke's Portrait," 106. He adds, "In any case, at the end of the campaign Paul goes up and visits 'the church' [the Jerusalem church]."

valued co-worker as well."[158] Peter also says that the letter was written "through Silvanus" (διὰ Σιλουανοῦ). Most scholars take this phrase as meaning Silas's role of letter-courier rather than his direct involvement in the letter-writing. Whatever tasks he performed, it is certain that Silas was Peter's important fellow worker. It is noteworthy that "Silas was associated with the two major figures of the early church, working very closely with both Paul and Peter."[159] The sharing of a coworker reflects that Paul and Peter—Pauline mission and Petrine mission—retained a shared view of gospel mission and maintained certain level of partnership ministry for the mission.

As he had formerly conveyed the letter of the Jerusalem church to Antioch, Silas now served as the letter courier of Peter in Rome. Also, in addition to delivering the letter, he probably served "as representative of the community sending the letter" and "would also gather information from his journey that could then be shared with the community in Rome."[160] Elliott rightly says: "On the whole, he would thus play a vital role in strengthening the personal ties uniting the brotherhood in Asia Minor and the brotherhood in Rome."[161]

Mark

Mark, the surname of John, was the cousin of Barnabas (Col 4:10), one of the prominent leaders in the Jerusalem church. His mother was Mary in whose house the early Jerusalem believers met (Acts 12:12). The apostle Peter called him "my son" (ὁ υἱός μου), which may imply that Mark had been converted and influenced by the apostle (1 Pet 5:13). All these factors lead to the idea that Mark was a young man rooted in the tradition of the Jerusalem church. He was chosen to accompany Barnabas and Saul, who were returning to Antioch after the delivery of relief fund to the Jerusalem church (Acts 12:25). Furthermore, he joined the two apostles as their assistant in the so-called first missionary journey (Acts 13:5). In addition to Barnabas, the Jerusalem church shared another core member, Mark, with the Antioch church.

158. Michaels, *1 Peter*, 307.

159. Thomas, "Silas," 306.

160. Elliott, *1 Peter*, 875–76.

161. Elliott, *1 Peter*, 876.

Mark abandoned the missionary journey at Perga in Pamphylia and returned to Jerusalem (Acts 13:13). Therefore, when Paul and Barnabas were discussing another mission project subsequent to the Jerusalem Council, Paul and Barnabas sharply disagreed over the issue of including Mark in the mission team. They separated from each other: Paul took Silas and went to Cilicia, and Barnabas headed for Cyprus along with Mark (Acts 15:36–41).

After thirteen or fourteen years, Mark again appears in Paul's writings. According to Philemon 24, Paul was with Mark in his first Roman imprisonment and called him "my fellow worker" (συνεργός μου).[162] Evidently, the breach caused by Mark's defection was repaired by then. Also, in the letter to the Colossians, Paul conveys Mark's greeting and adds, "about whom you received instructions: if he comes to you, welcome him" (Col 4:10). The instructions, as many commentators surmise, might have come "from Peter and/or Barnabas, who had already requested that the Colossians 'reinstate' Mark."[163] Paul was simply adding his personal confirmation of the instructions made by the other apostles. This short statement reveals good rapport and cooperation among Paul, Mark, Barnabas, and Peter. Paul's demand in 2 Tim 4:11 is emphatic: "Having taken Mark, bring him with you, for he is helpful to me for service."[164] Mark was an indispensable coworker towards the end of Paul's ministry at Rome.

Peter in his letter to the churches in Asia refers to Mark while greeting the believers in Asia Minor (1 Pet 5:13). Here, Peter's description of Mark, "my son" (ὁ υἱός μου), represents the same idea of intimacy and importance as indicated by Paul when he calls Timothy "my son" (1 Cor 4:17; 1 Tim 1:2, 18; 2 Tim 1:2; 2:1). As to the ministry relations among Peter, Silas, and Mark, Elliott gives a succinct statement:

162. Paul uses the same term in addressing Philemon (Phlm 1). "Whenever Paul wished to express his fellowship with his co-workers, he noted this especially through additions such as "my" or "our" (Phlm 1). Co-workers were not helpers of the apostle drawn in for his personal service. Rather, they were commissioned by God for the task of missionary preaching." O'Brien, *Colossians-Philemon*, 272–73.

163. Moo, *Colossians and to Philemon*, 339. See also O'Brien, *Colossians-Philemon*, 250–51.

164. When Paul was writing Colossians and Philemon, Mark was with the apostle in the Roman prison (Col 4:10; Phlm 24). At the time of writing 2 Timothy, however, it is unknown where Mark was. He might have been with Timothy at Ephesus, or "in a place that Timothy would pass through on his way to Paul." Marshall, *Pastoral Epistles*, 818.

> All three persons had early contacts in Jerusalem . . . and now all three were together once again in Rome. Along with Peter, Silvanus and Mark represented leading figures of the early Jerusalem community through whom the Palestinian Christian tradition of Jesus' teaching, suffering, death, and resurrection was transmitted from Jerusalem to Rome. All three thus represent in their personal careers the spread of the gospel from Jerusalem (Acts 12:1–17; 15:1–29) and Antioch (Acts 15:36–41; Gal 2:11–14) to Asia Minor (Acts 13–14; 16:1—18:22; cf. Acts 2:9–19) and eventually to Rome.[165]

It is noteworthy that the progress of their missions corresponds to that of Paul's missions, too. More strikingly, Mark and Silas who were Peter's inner-circle coworkers also played significant roles as Paul's companions and associates. This overlapping of ministry fields reflects the presence of positive relationships across Pauline Christianity and Petrine Christianity. Mark served as "a personal link between Paul and Peter."[166]

Conclusion

The present chapter examined Paul's coworkers as to how their activities contributed to Paul's partnership ministry, thereby strengthening the relationship of the New Testament churches in both local and trans-local dimensions. In the introductory section, Paul's coworkers were explored in terms of their functions, categorization, and relationship with the local churches. This section also discussed the Greco-Roman household and the household churches in Paul's ministry. The second section determined the nature of local church relationships by investigating the ministry of Paul's coworkers in local area such as Philippi, Corinth, and Ephesus and the Lycus valley. The third section concerned the trans-local coworkers whose missions encompassed multiple Christian communities around the Mediterranean world. Due to their extensive ministry scope, they could enhance trans-local communications and collaborations among the churches. The fourth section also discussed trans-local coworkers,

165. Elliott, *1 Peter*, 889.

166. Bird, "Mark," 31. He continues, "Thus the Markan Gospel would represent the literary deposit of a figure who was personally involved with two of the most influential personalities of the pre-70 CE church . . . the Gospel of Mark points to an early synthesis of Peter and Paul: Petrine testimony shaped into an evangelical narrative conducive to Pauline proclamation."

but those who worked not only with Paul but also with other apostles and in partnership with non-Pauline churches. Their ministry implicated wide and diverse church relationships, including various Christian communities in Jerusalem, Antioch, Ephesus, Corinth, Rome, etc.

Overall, this chapter showed that Paul's coworkers played a central role in the partnership ministry of Paul. Their missions—as house church leaders, messengers to and from local churches, ministry associates, or evangelists—greatly contributed not only to the expansion of Christian communities but also to the establishment of inter-community relationships, local or trans-local, Pauline or non-Pauline. In other words, Paul's coworkers functioned, locally, as the hub of house church networks, and trans-locally, as the nexus of inter-church networks across the Mediterranean world.

3

Collaboration through Financial Assistance

It is true that the apostle Paul "wrote more about money than he did about the Lord's Supper, or about baptism, or about the status of women."[1] Paul's frequent reference to finance indicates that his ministry often implicated financial activities in one way or another. Although Paul was primarily a self-supporting evangelist, he sometimes requested and received financial support from local churches. One of his major ministry projects was to raise a relief fund for "the poor among the saints in Jerusalem" (Rom 15:26). These financial activities were to link his churches into a network of economic collaboration. Therefore, a study of financial matters in Paul's ministry will reveal certain features of early church relationships.

Chapter 3 focuses on the cooperative nature of Paul's churches by examining various occasions of financial assistance among the churches. Related to the issue of poverty, charity, and money, this chapter also discusses the socio-economic background of early Christianity. The first section surveys the economic situation of the New Testament churches in the first-century Hellenistic and Jewish contexts. The second section explores various biblical data to find out how local believers responded to one another's financial needs, thereby promoting relationship and unity among the local house churches. The third section concerns the financial

1. Friesen, "Paul and Economics," 28.

aspect of Paul's missions. It investigates how Paul's missions were financially supported, particularly, by local churches. The last section deals with the "collection" for the Jerusalem church, first by the Antioch church and then by Paul's churches. It seeks to understand the overall collaboration of Paul's churches rendered through financial assistance.

Greco-Roman and Jewish Contexts

This section surveys the socio-economic settings of early Christianity. First, it briefly reviews the reality of ancient poverty, particularly in the land of Judea, to understand the economic condition that brought about financial assistance among the first-century Christians. Second, it discusses financial activities of the Greco-Roman "voluntary associations."[2] It will shed some light on the present study, since the first-century churches developed and functioned quite similarly to the contemporary voluntary associations.[3] Lastly, this section also surveys the financial support system of Jewish communities in the Diaspora. The understanding of Jewish communities will help explain the first-century Christian communities, for the early church was influenced and shaped, most of all, by Jewish traditions.

Economic Situation of the New Testament Churches

Along with most ancient historians and New Testament scholars, N. Morley argues that "virtually everyone in antiquity was vulnerable to periodic food crises" on account of the capricious weather of the Mediterranean basin as well as the continuing political disturbances and wars.[4] Harris explains the severity and pervasiveness of Roman poverty in relation to

2. The term "voluntary associations" has recently become a scholarly parlance owing to the seminar of the Canadian Society of Biblical Studies (1988–1993). See Wilson, "Voluntary Associations," 1–2. A concise definition of the Greco-Roman voluntary associations could be made as "relatively small (often 15–30 members), unofficial groups that met together regularly to engage in a variety of social and banqueting activities which, inextricably, were also aimed at honouring gods and goddesses." Instone-Brewer and Harland, "Jewish Associations," 202.

3. It is natural and most probable that Pauline communities, along with the diaspora Jews, adopted various organizational structures and functional forms from their environment, the first-century Greco-Roman society. Accordingly, it is true that "both synagogues and churches were viewed in antiquity as 'associations.'" Richardson, "Building an Association," 36.

4. Morley, "Poor in the City," 33.

the structure of the labor market, the social pattern of inheritance, and the lack of imperial measures to relieve the problem.[5] It is a general consensus that the great majority of ancient people in the Greco-Roman world lived a life of near subsistence level while only a small elite enjoyed economic privileges.

The problem of poverty was acute in times of famine, which was also a common phenomenon in the first century world. In *The Natural History*, Pliny mentioned the flood of the Nile river: "The greatest increase known, up to the present time, is that of eighteen cubits, which took place in the time of the Emperor Claudius."[6] Probably, the author was referring to the "record flooding and the subsequent famine which followed in the mid-forties."[7] Likewise, Josephus recorded: "when Claudius was emperor of the Romans, and Ismael was our high priest, and when so great a famine was come upon us, that one-tenth deal [of wheat] was sold for four drachmae, . . . even while so great a distress was upon the land."[8] Widespread evidence demonstrates the prevalence of famine and food shortage during the New Testament period.[9] Among them is Luke's account of Agabus and a great famine (Acts 11:28).

The hardship of famine was felt more severe in the land of Judea, particularly in Jerusalem. Located in the upland of hillsides and mountains, Jerusalem was recurrently short of water and grain supplies. Without sufficient provisions, the city suffered extreme deprivation, and a great part of its population lived "chiefly or entirely on charity or relief."[10] Queen Helena of Adiabene once visited Jerusalem and saw "many people died for want of what was necessary to procure food."[11] Hence, the queen sent her servants to Alexandria to buy corn and to Cyprus to obtain dried figs and distributed them to the Jerusalemites in need.[12]

5. Harris, "Poverty and Destitution," 27–54.

6. Pliny the Elder, *Nat.* 5.10.

7. Winter, "Acts and Food Shortages," 63.

8. Josephus, *Ant.* 3.15.3.

9. Winter, "Acts and Food Shortages," 62–65. He surveys the evidence of grain shortages throughout the Empire during much of the Claudian reign.

10. Jeremias, *Jerusalem*, 111–12.

11. Josephus, *Ant.* 20.2.5.

12. Queen Helena was the mother of Izates I, the king of Adiabene, a semi-independent kingdom extended over the upper region of the Tigris River in the first century. For more information see Gottheil, "Adiabene."

The economic condition of the Jerusalem church must have been similar to that of the general population of the Holy City. Jewish Christians in Palestine were sometimes called "Ebionites," a term derived from the Hebrew word for "the poor" or "poor ones." The title may suggest their ethical emphasis on the state of living poorly and austerely. More importantly, it seems to be "a conscious reminiscence of a very early term ["the poor"] which is attested by St. Paul's letters as an almost technical name for the Christians in Jerusalem and Judaea."[13]

Impoverishment among the Jerusalem believers can be inferred also from Paul's description of his churches. Paul states that the churches of Macedonia made a generous donation in the midst of their "deep poverty" (2 Cor 8:2). Later, he mentions "your [the Corinthians'] surplus for their [the Jerusalem church's] lack" (2 Cor 8:14), denoting the relative wealth of the Corinthian believers in comparison with "the poor" in Jerusalem. Although the Macedonian churches are not directly mentioned in this comment, Paul's narrative suggests that the economic situation of the Jerusalem church was much worse than that of the Greek churches including the Macedonians who were themselves in "deep poverty." It is no wonder that one of the major tasks for Paul and his churches was to provide financial aid to the poor believers in Jerusalem.

It was not until recent years that New Testament scholars paid due attention to the issue of poverty and the poor in Pauline studies.[14] For most of the twentieth century, scholars held the view that "the constituency of early Christianity, the Pauline congregations included, came from the poor and dispossessed of the Roman provinces."[15] This consensus seemed plausible, considering the tone of Paul's description of the Corinthian church, "not many wise according to the flesh, not many mighty, not many noble" (1 Cor 1:26). Since the 1970's, however, the view of the 'poor church' has receded into the background, as a number of influential scholars have begun to espouse a new understanding of the social

13. Chadwick, *Early Church*, 23. In Paul's letters, he observes those phrases: "the poor saints in Jerusalem" (Rom 15:26); "to remember the poor" (Gal 2:10); and possibly, "alms for my [poor] people" (Act 24:17).

14. Ogereau, "Jerusalem Collection as Κοινωνία," 363.

15. Meeks, *First Urban Christians*, 52. In general, along with Meeks, Adolf Deissmann is credited as the proponent of this long-held view. However, Friesen regards Deissmann differently: "it is an inaccurate description of Deissmann's position. Deissmann actually agreed with Judge, Theissen, Malherbe and Meeks that Paul's assemblies included a cross-section of society" ("Poverty in Pauline Studies," 324–25).

status of the early Christians.[16] This so-called "new consensus" claims that early Christian communities represented, not just a poor class of the society, but "a greater degree of social diversity than had previously been acknowledged, with some members coming from the ranks of the well-to-do."[17]

It is interesting that in more recent years the "new consensus" has been seriously challenged even to the extent that the old view seems to be re-emerging. One of the most significant works behind the shift is Meggitt's *Paul, Poverty, and Survival* published in 1998. Based on more rigorous socio-economic analysis of the Greco-Roman world, Meggitt maintains that all the Pauline congregations belonged to the stratum of the poor and marginalized in the contemporary society.[18] His study has brought up a renewed interest in the poverty level of the first Christians.

It is to be noted that the pendulum swing between the old and the new consensus seems to be "one primarily of focus."[19] Namely, the 'old consensus' underscored the lower-class while recognizing the middle-class in the church, and the 'new consensus' focused on the modest and middle level while acknowledging the lower class in the church. Friesen, therefore, makes an observant statement about the financial status of Paul's churches that there is no old or new consensus, but simply twentieth-century consensus, which says that "the members of these assemblies represented a cross-section of society, coming mostly from the middle and lower sectors of society, with some members from the higher sectors."[20]

New Testament churches consisted not only of have-nots but also of some men and women of means—e.g., Joseph, called Barnabas (Acts 4:36–37), Sergius Paulus (Acts 13:6–12), Lydia (Acts 16:14–15), Jason (Acts 17:5–9), Philemon (Philemon 1), Erastus (Rom 16:23), and so on. The gap in the economic condition of believers—especially between those in Jerusalem and those in other cities abroad—supplied the earliest

16. For example, see Malherbe, *Social Aspects of Early Christianity*, ch. 2, "Social Level and Literary Culture"; Theissen, *Social Setting of Pauline Christianity*, ch. 2, "Social Stratification in the Corinthian Community"; and Meeks, *First Urban Christians*, ch. 2, "The Social Level of Pauline Christians."

17. Horrell, "Domestic Space," 357.

18. Meggitt, *Paul, Poverty and Survival*. His argument was further developed by a number of scholars, including Longenecker, *Remember the Poor* and Friesen, "Poverty in Pauline Studies," 323–61. For critiques of this position, see Barclay, "Poverty in Pauline Studies: A Response to Steven Friesen," 363–66, and Horrell, *Social Ethos*, 91–101.

19. Russell, "Idle in 2 Thess 3:6–12," 110.

20. Friesen, "Poverty in Pauline Studies," 325.

churches with the responsibility and opportunity to reach out to their needy members, thereby reinforcing inter-church relationships through financial cooperation.

Financial Assistance in Voluntary Associations

A large portion of the people in Greco-Roman cities and towns were affiliated with a certain voluntary association, a social club or guild organized for communal activities and support. Scholars agree that the associations pervaded the ancient world and functioned as a social fabric of the Greco-Roman society.[21] The voluntary associations could be classified according to "their respective membership bases" into three groups: "those associated with a household, those formed around a common trade (and civic locale), and those formed around the cult of a deity."[22] The membership number of an association was usually between thirty and forty but rarely beyond one hundred.[23] Their meetings took place often at private homes, linked to the traditional household conventions and influenced by patron-client relationships.[24]

In metropolitan areas such as Rome, Alexandria, and Ephesus, a number of voluntary associations had some connections with one another according to their likeness in occupation, neighborhood, worship, or hometown. Although they did not establish a highly structured organization, the associations functioned like an organizational body of social groups. For instance, each association had a leader—called πατήρ, ματήρ,

21. Evidence is widespread and obvious from numerous inscriptions, papyri, and literary texts. In Ephesus, for example, the existence of voluntary associations is attested by "some 3,500 inscriptions relating to all manner of associations." Billings, "From House Church to Tenement Church," 554. For overall evidence materials, see Ascough, Harland, and Kloppenborg, *Associations in the Greco-Roman World.*

22. Kloppenborg, "Collegia and *Thiasoi*," 26. A different classification is also possible on the basis of their functions, e.g., professional guilds, funerary societies, religious sects, and philosophical schools.

23. McCready, "*Ekklēsia* and Voluntary Associations," 61. Similarly, Craffert says that "there could be any number between ten and a hundred, the average presumably being 10–35 members" ("Pauline Household Communities," 314).

24. Craffert, "Pauline Household Communities," 315. Kinship language was common: the association members were called "brothers" or "friends," and the leaders and patrons, "fathers" or "mothers." The group itself was often designated as "*koinon*" and its cognates, representing the nature of mutual support and companionship between the members or between the associations.

ἄρχων, or προστάτις—and these leaders "would convene and chair meetings, oversee the rites, arrange for banquets and funerals, and enforce the regulations and decrees of the associations."[25] Relationships among local associations developed, and one of the most significant outcomes of the relationships was financial assistance among the association members as well as among the local associations.

Most associations kept a common fund or a treasury for the administration of their fund.[26] Harland argues that the existence of such a fund is "implied in many inscriptions from Asia Minor simply in connection with the members paying for something . . . 'from their own resources' (ἐκ τῶν ἰδίων)."[27] Gaius, a Roman jurist, wrote: "When persons are allowed to form a partnership (*corpus*) under the title of an association (*collegium*), society (*societas*), or some other name, they are, like a municipality (*res publica*), entitled to hold property in common, have a common treasury (*arca*), and have an agent or advocate (*syndicus*)."[28]

The common fund would pay for those events such as banquets, burial of members, erection of monuments, etc. More important and relevant to the present study is the fact that the common fund was often used to help members or associations in need. Examining the widespread evidence of financial assistance, particularly in the form of loans, Harland affirms that the offering of loans was "an accepted practice in a Greek cultural context over a significant span of time," and "the role of associations or association members in providing loans can be understood within the broader context of 'mutual support' or reciprocity among members."[29] The Greco-Roman voluntary associations were cooperatively related with one another through financial assistance.

It has been widely agreed that there were disparities between the voluntary associations on the one hand, and the Jewish communities in the Diaspora and the Pauline Christian communities on the other.[30] Most

25. Ascough, "Greco-Roman Philosophic," 14–15.

26. Harland, "Associations and the Economics," 15. As resources for the common fund, Harland lists the contribution of benefactors/patrons, fees and fines paid by members, and a collection of funds or materials for a special project.

27. Harland, "Associations and the Economics," 15–16.

28. *Digest*, 3.4.1. See Ascough, Harland, and Kloppenborg, *Associations in the Greco-Roman World*, 270.

29. Harland, "Associations and the Economics," 29.

30. Harland, *Associations, Synagogues, and Congregations*, 180. He lists four main points of the scholars who maintain distinction between voluntary associations and

of all, the former has been viewed as "a self-contained local phenomenon" whereas the latter has been considered to encompass trans-local and international linkages.[31] More recently, however, Ascough and some others have proposed a contentious view that "there were in fact stronger translocal links between some associations than is often admitted" and that such trans-local links are found mostly in the groups of "foreigners" scattered throughout the Mediterranean world.[32] Exploring numerous inscriptions, Ascough provides substantial evidence that demonstrates "the maintenance of contact with the place of origin of the association and/or its members, as well as contact between associations in various locales."[33]

A good example is the inscription of Puteoli (the port city of Rome), which reveals a dynamic relationship among the trans-local groups of Tyrian merchants.[34] An association of Tyrian merchants in Puteoli wrote to their homeland, the city of Tyre, asking for financial assistance in paying the expenses of the association. In response to the request, the Tyrian council asked another Tyrian association in Rome to help the association at Puteoli. Afterwards, the Tyrian settlers in Rome "have always had the custom of furnishing the 250 denarii for those in Puteoli."[35] Locally and sometimes trans-locally, the Greco-Roman associations collaborated with one another by means of offering loans and collecting money for fellow associations in need.

Financial Assistance in Jewish Communities

As mentioned above, the immigrants of the Greco-Roman world often organized themselves into a community of local and trans-local

groups of Jews or Christians: (1) Christian/Jewish groups were inclusive and varied in social composition while the associations were mostly homogenous; (2) Christian/Jewish groups used different titles and terminology for their organization and leaders; (3) Associations lacked extra-local relations; and (4) Christian/Jewish groups were largely sectarian while associations were not.

31. Meeks, *First Urban Christians*, 80.

32. Ascough, *Paul's Macedonian Associations*, 93.

33. Ascough, *Paul's Macedonian Associations*, 100.

34. *CIG* 5853. See Ascough, Harland, and Kloppenborg, *Associations in the Greco-Roman World*, 204–5. In conjunction with this sourcebook, Harland provides a useful database website, Associations in the Greco-Roman World: An Expanding Collection of Inscriptions, Papyri, and Other Sources in Translation, at http://philipharland. com/greco-roman-associations/.

35. Associations in the Greco-Roman World, "Puteoli."

connections for their own socio-economical and religious benefits. The most conspicuous and permanent among them were the Judeans.[36] They founded a number of ethnic settlements nearly all over the Roman imperium.[37] Almost all the cities of the Greco-Roman world had a group or groups of Jews usually gathered around the *synagogue*.[38] This institution played a pivotal role in both consolidating the local Jews and building the international networks of Jewish communities in the Diaspora.

The Jewish synagogue was more than a place of worship. As most scholars agree, it may best be viewed as "a kind of community center," which carried out various functions such as communal worship, banquet and meals, civil government and jurisdiction, financial aid, etc.[39] Particularly, according to Rosenfeld and Menirav, the first-century synagogue functioned as "the heart of material and economic affairs and sometimes even served as a catalyst for economic activity in the ancient world."[40] As a functionary of economic affairs, one of the most prominent activities of the Jewish synagogue was to provide financial assistance for its needy members.

Given the Judaic tradition of charity and the economic hardship of the immigrants in the first-century world, it was quite natural and necessary for any Jewish communities in the Diaspora to maintain some programs of communal aid. Since the Jewish community usually assembled

36. Rives emphasizes that "by far the most important example of permanent immigrants who formed associations for the worship of an ancestral deity were the Judaeans" (*Religion in the Roman Empire*, 122–23).

37. According to Philo, the Jews were so populous that "no one country can hold them, and therefore they settle in very many of the most prosperous countries in Europe and Asia both in the islands and on the mainland, and while they hold the Holy City where stands the sacred Temple of the most high God to be their mother city." Philo, *Flaccus*, 327–29. Generally speaking, there were over five million Jews living in the diaspora and about 2 to 3 million, in Palestine during the first century CE.

38. It is likely that "at least one synagogue stood in every town of Palestine, even in the smaller places. In the larger cities their number was considerable, as for example in Jerusalem, Alexandria and Rome." Schürer, *History of the Jewish People*, 445. For the location of the Jewish communities, see Feldman, "Diaspora Synagogues," 49. Feldman lists some sixty-six Diaspora "prayer groups or synagogues" scattered around the Mediterranean world. The term *proseuche* was favored in diasporan Jewish communities, whereas *synagogue* was dominantly used in Judaea. Also see Levine, *Ancient Synagogue*, 127.

39. Claussen, "Meeting, Community, Synagogue," 148. According to Claussen, it is hardly possible "to make a clear distinction between their religious and their communal activities."

40. Rosenfeld and Menirav, "Ancient Synagogue as an Economic Center," 276.

in the synagogue, the plan and allocation of the charity were made in the synagogue, and thus "the synagogue became synonymous with the place for giving charity, or more precisely, for announcing the giving of charity."[41] The scope of charitable acts was not limited to the boundary of local communities; it often included multiple synagogues in a metropolitan area and even the trans-local communities in distant lands.

A substantial number of epigraphic and documentary evidences demonstrate how Jewish communities worked together to support their members in need. At Ostia and Delos, for instance, the famous inscription from Aphrodisias of Asia Minor bears witness to the Jewish "clannishness" of close community life and mutual aid.[42] Particularly, the inscription shows the term πάτελλα, which indicates "the distribution station for charity food—i.e. a community soup-kitchen."[43] In this connection, Jeremias summarizes two distinct forms of charity that were practiced in the first-century Jewish communities: "The *tamhūy* ('poor bowl') was distributed daily among wandering paupers, and consisted of food. . . . The *quppāah* ('poor basket') was a weekly dole to the poor of the city."[44] Operation of the food bank continued on a regular basis with the fund supported by community-wide donors such as Jews, proselytes, and 'God-fearers' in the area.[45] The arrangement of financial assistance—a

41. Safrai, "Communal Functions of the Synagogue," 191–92. He continues to argue that Jesus' saying—"So when you give to the poor, do not sound a trumpet before you, as the hypocrites do in the συναγογυες and in the streets" (Matt 6:2)—insinuates "the accepted custom of giving charity publicly in the synagogue."

42. Reynolds and Tannenbaum, *Jews and God-fearers*, 87. Aphrodisias was an ancient city in Asia Minor, about 90 miles east of Ephesus. From the construction site of the city museum, a third-century inscription was fortuitously found in 1976. It consists of two contiguous faces of a 9-foot-high marble stone.

43. Reynolds and Tannenbaum, *Jews and God-fearers*, 27. Reynolds and Tannenbaum make this argument based on the assumption that "the Mishnaic Hebrew word for 'dish' (*tamḥui*) is used in the Mishnah and Tosephta and in both Talmudim as the name of a charitable institution."

44. Jeremias, *Jerusalem*, 131. Jeremias provides mostly second- and third-century Rabbinic sources, which can also be applied to the time of Jesus. Besides, Schürer also makes the same distinction "between the weekly money-chest (*cupa*), from which the local poor were supported regularly once a week, and the 'plate'(*tamḥui*), from which any needy person (especially strangers) could obtain a daily portion" (*History of the Jewish People*, 437).

45. Feldman, "Diaspora Synagogues," 62. On the contrary, "Greek cities had no permanent arrangements for feeding the poor; at best such distributions occurred at festivals or on special occasions."

communal fund and food distribution—"clearly bound local Jewish communities together."[46]

Another form of social support in the Jewish community was the freeing of slaves. In and around the ancient city of Panticapaeum on the eastern shore of Crimea, a good number of Jewish manumission inscriptions have been found, and most of them attest that the process of manumission was accomplished by the communal effort of the whole Jewish community. For example, one of the inscriptions, discovered in 1989 and dating to 51 AD, ends with the passage: "freedom to be guaranteed by the guardianship of the Jewish community [συναγωγῆ τῶν Ἰουδαίων]."[47] The freeing of slaves was a process of financial redemption, which was made possible through a collective action of the entire Jewish community. Observing the characteristic formula and the recurrence of the manumission language, Overman maintains that "the procedure was fairly standard within these Bosporus diaspora communities."[48] The widespread evidence of Jewish manumissions surely reveals "a network of closely related diaspora Jewish communities" in the northeast corner of the Bosporus.[49] Such network of financial collaboration is evident in nearly all of the Jewish communities in the Greco-Roman world.

Financial Collaboration in Local Churches

This section examines the financial assistance of New Testament churches practiced mainly for their own communities. That is, local activities are in view, trans-local activities being left for a later discussion. As observed in the previous chapter, most New Testament churches in major Roman cities were composed of multiple house assemblies or house churches. Accordingly, the activity of New Testament churches, e.g., the church at Jerusalem or at Corinth, represents the collective activity of the local house churches in Jerusalem or in Corinth. The church activity must have occurred in the context of mutual relationships and interactions among the house churches in the area. The purpose of this section is to highlight the collaborative relationship of the churches/house churches by studying their communal activities, particularly, through financial assistance.

46. Barclay, "Money and Meetings," 118.

47. MacLennan, "In Search of the Jewish Diaspora," 46.

48. Overman, "Jews, Slaves, and the Synagogue," 153.

49. Overman, "Jews, Slaves, and the Synagogue," 157.

"Community of Goods" in Jerusalem

Financial assistance in New Testament churches occurred as soon as the first Christian community formed at Jerusalem. In Acts 2:42–47 and 4:32–35, Luke unmistakably describes the Jerusalem church as a "community of goods": "they were selling the property and possessions and sharing them to all as anyone had need" (2:45). Since the common ownership of properties seems incongruent with other accounts of Luke (e.g., 5:4, 6:1), and unseen anywhere else in the New Testament, Conzelmann argues that Luke's portrayal "should not be taken as historical" and "it is meant as an illustration of the uniqueness of the ideal earliest days of the movement."[50] On the contrary, many others believe that the earliest "community of goods" is a "historically verifiable aspect"[51] and that the event was portrayed with "the language of Greek philosophizing about the ideal society."[52] The accounts of Acts 2:42–47 and 4:32–35 represent the social reality that the earliest believers responded to their needy members "in the Jerusalem house-churches by means of their pervasive acts of sharing which Luke believed had indeed happened."[53]

During the days subsequent to the Ascension, the group of Jesus followers was quite small and might have stayed together in one place, the Upper Room.[54] When the group grew to one hundred and twenty, they still managed to gather in the place. After Pentecost, however, the whole situation dramatically changed. When Peter preached the gospel to the crowd in Jerusalem, about three thousand people were added to the number of believers (Acts 2:41). Furthermore, Luke says, "the Lord was adding those being saved to the church every day" (Acts 2:47). The Christian community at Jerusalem grew larger and larger.

50. Conzelmann, *Acts of the Apostle*, 24.

51. Capper, "Palestinian Cultural Context," 356.

52. Capper, "Palestinian Cultural Context," 324. Capper suggests the language of Greco-Roman friendship traditions. Two of well-known Greek proverbs are noted: "friends have all things in common" (κοινᾶ τᾶ [τῶν] φίλων) and "friends are one soul" (μία ψυχή). These phrases are remarkably similar to Luke's account. For further study of the friendship traditions, see Mitchell, "Social Function of Friendship," 255–72.

53. Bartchy, "Community of Goods in Acts," 317–18.

54. Luke records "when they had entered [Jerusalem], they went up to the upper room, *where they were staying*" (Acts 1:13). The imperfect periphrastic ἦσαν καταμένοντες, which emphasizes a continued action, reveals that the disciples were staying together in the Upper Room even from before the Ascension. The list of the eleven names indicates that only the eleven disciples were staying there together, and others frequently visited the place to join in prayers and fellowship.

Besides the great number of new believers, another development was that "all those who had believed were at the same place (ἐπὶ τὸ αὐτό)" (Acts 2:44). The phrase ἐπὶ τὸ αὐτό usually denotes the physical sense of "being together." When Luke uses the phrase in the book of Acts, therefore, he conveys the idea of togetherness, "being in the same place at the same time."[55] Paul writes the same words to describe the whole congregation of the Corinthian believers assembled in one place (1 Cor 11:20).[56]

Given the meaning of ἐπὶ τὸ αὐτό and the large number of Jerusalem believers, Luke's account of "all those who had believed were together" needs to be understood in its context. It is improbable that one building or one place at Jerusalem could accommodate thousands of people who would meet together (ἐπὶ τὸ αὐτό), particularly, for the table fellowship. Meanwhile, most scholars agree that the first Christians of Jerusalem did not form themselves into a community living as the Qumran community did.[57] The point is that the Jerusalem believers assembled primarily in small numbers in the settings of individual houses.[58] The breaking of bread "from house to house" (κατ'οἶκον) (Acts 2:46) reveals the common way of Christian gatherings at private homes.

Depending on their social connections—e.g., family, friends, business associates, or neighborhoods—the new believers in Jerusalem must have set up many household groups to continue their faith and faith community. Such form of small group gatherings was quite natural because

55. The phrase appears five times in Acts: 1:15; 2:1, 44, 47; 4:26. In 2:1, the adverb ὁμοῦ ("together") is added before ἐπὶ τὸ αὐτὸ, enhancing the idea of togetherness. The one in 2:47 is, unlike others, best rendered as "to the assembly" or "to their own number."

56. The first half of the verse συνερχομένων οὖν ὑμῶν ἐπὶ τὸ αὐτὸ is rendered as "when ye come together therefore into one place" (KJV), "therefore when you meet together" (NASV), or "now when you come together at the same place" (NET).

57. Walton summarizes the "community of goods" at Jerusalem: "the life of the earliest believers in Jerusalem was marked by a remarkable level of economic sharing which fell short, however, of the common ownership found at Qumran" ("Primitive Communism," 109).

58. Acts 2:46 reads "continuing with one mind in the temple" (προσκαρτεροῦντες ὁμοθυμαδὸν ἐν τῷ ἱερῷ). The believers seem to have gathered in the Solomon's colonnade. Luke writes that "all the people ran together to them in the porch called Solomon's" (Acts 3:11), and "they were all with one mind in the porch of Solomon" (Acts 5:12). Solomon's Portico ran along the east side of the Court of the Gentiles. Even though Luke says that the believers in Jerusalem habitually gathered in the temple courts, it is not certain that he was confirming the presence of the whole Christian community in that spot every day. It is rather probable that while a large number of people convened in Solomon's Portico to hear the preaching of the apostles, more meetings took place in much smaller numbers at homes.

the first believers, most of whom were Jews, followed the contemporary model of *haburah* or *chaburah*, a voluntary type of Jewish association.[59] The phrase "all those who had believed were together" (Acts 2:44) should then be understood in light of multiple house groups, many of which would have developed into more established house churches.

Luke gives a brief statement about the characteristics of the first Christian community, one of which is "fellowship" (2:42).[60] Its Greek term κοινωνία basically means "close association involving mutual interests and sharing, association, communion, fellowship, close relationship" among the people.[61] Beyond the relationship itself, the term also means "to share with someone in something" and "to give someone a share in something," indicating the sharing of material resources.[62] The word κοινωνία, particularly in the present text, carries the meaning of financial sharing, as Peterson argues that "[it] could simply refer to material blessings, as described in Acts 2:44–45, where we are told that the believers had everything in *common* (*koina*)."[63] There is no doubt that the κοινωνία of the Jerusalem community manifested itself through the sharing of food and goods among the believers.

Luke recounts in Acts 4:34–35 an interesting practice of the Jerusalem church: the believers sold their properties and "laid the proceeds at the apostles' feet."[64] Individual believers or household groups did not manage their financial contributions on their own. They brought the price of what was sold to the apostles, and the apostles administered the common fund

59. *Haburah* or *Chaburah* ("friend") was "a group of friends formed for religious purposes" in the Jewish society, but it also served "a wider social purpose as a common weekly meal, usually on the eves of sabbaths or holy days." Bruce, *Acts*, 81.

60. Receiving the gospel of Christ, the believers devoted themselves to meeting together and soon began to form a distinctive group, which was characterized by the teaching of the apostles, fellowship, breaking of bread, and prayer (Acts 2:42).

61. BDAG, s.v. "κοινωνία." The Greek term is also used to refer to the fellowship of believers with Christ (1 Cor 1:9, 1 John 1:3) or with the Holy Spirit (2 Cor 13:13, Phil 2:1).

62. Hauck, "κοινός," 808. He further explains that "The sense 'to give a share,' which is rare in secular Greek, is more common in the NT, especially in Paul."

63. Peterson, *Acts*, 159–60. He concludes that it may be most right "to give *koinōnia* its widest interpretation in 2:42, including within its scope 'contributions, table fellowship, and the general friendship and unity which characterized the community.'"

64. Scholars do not regard the description as indicating a form of communism operating upon the common ownership of property. Acts 5:4 clearly shows that any property belonged to its owner, and the use of its proceeds in case of selling the property was subject to the owner's decision. The sharing of possessions occurred voluntarily.

according to the need of individual believers or households. It is noteworthy that all the indicative verbs of Acts 4:34–35 (ἦν, ὑπῆρχον, ἔφερον, ἐτίθουν, διεδίδετο, εἶχεν) are in the imperfect tense, and all the participles (πωλοῦντες, πιπρασκομένων), the present tense. This combination of imperfect verb and present participle suggests "a gradual liquidation of assets, not selling everything all at once."[65] Or, more importantly, it implies that the sharing of property was "a regular occurrence and happened over a period of time."[66] One of the most distinctive features of the first Christians was to take care of their needy members on a regular basis.

As discussed above, the Jerusalem believers assembled primarily as household groups, and the household groups, in all probability, may have varied in their social and economic backgrounds.[67] Some household groups would be more well-to-do than others, and financial resources would flow accordingly.[68] The sharing of goods was done not only on a personal level but also on the level of household groups and even larger people groups of the community. Acts 6:1 reports the complaint of the Hellenistic Jews against the Hebrews since the Hellenistic widows were being overlooked in the distribution of food. This suggests that the allotment was carried out according to the different social groups in the Jerusalem community.

The Jerusalem church as a community of goods demonstrates that the earliest believers were engaged in financial assistance for their needy members. Reference to the common fund administered by the apostles (Acts 4:34–35, 37; 5:2) denotes their authority over the use of the fund until the new arrangement of Acts 6:2–6. Such governance of the apostles also implies a centralized and concerted work of the church. It would be fair to say that the household assemblies in Jerusalem, under the guidance of the apostles and deacons, participated in the sharing of food and goods as givers or receivers of the gift. It was the first pattern of local church relationships and communal activities.

65. Bock, *Acts*, 215.

66. Schnabel, *Acts*, 272. Given the account of 4:36–37 and 5:1–11, it may be that "as needs arose," people of means sold their lands and houses to meet those needs.

67. The Jerusalem church was pluralistic, socially and economically. Reflecting the diversity of the Holy City, the church "contained the fabulously rich as well as the unbearably poor." Fiensy, "Composition of the Jerusalem Church," 214.

68. A typical example would be the household of Barnabas, who had sold land and brought the proceeds to the apostles (Acts 4:36–37). Also, his sister was the mother of Mark, who owned property ("the Upper Room") in the city of Jerusalem.

"Brotherly Love" in Macedonia

In 1 Thess 4:9–10, Paul compliments the Thessalonians for their "brotherly love" (φιλαδελφία) for all the believers in Macedonia.[69] What does Paul exactly mean by "brotherly love"? The Greek word denotes, originally, love "in the literal sense of love for blood brothers or sisters," and figuratively, love "in the transferred sense of affection for a fellow Christian."[70] When Greek authors used the word, they usually emphasized the meaning of "collaboration, solidarity, and harmony or concord" between siblings.[71] In the New Testament, the same word is used to signify the loving relationship of the believers, reflecting an intimate and genuine love of kinship.[72]

F. F. Bruce argues that the Greek term φιλαδελφία (1 Thess 4:9) is "more restricted" than the word ἀγάπη in its semantic scope, as nuanced in the preceding text of 1 Thess 3:12.[73] Likewise, the list of Christian virtues in 2 Pet 1:5–7 ("add . . . to φιλαδελφία, ἀγάπη") alludes to the relatively particular meaning of φιλαδελφία and the all-inclusive meaning of ἀγάπη. Granted, the "brotherly love" of the Thessalonians has to do more with a specific behavior than with an emotive disposition. Also, it is to be noted that concerning "brotherly love," Paul says ποιεῖτε αὐτὸ ("you do it") (1 Thess 4:10). The term ποιέω refers to a range of activity, such as "bringing something into being, bringing something to pass" and it also signifies "to produce something material, make, manufacture, produce."[74] In short, "brotherly love" represents the good works that the Thessalonians did in love for fellow Christians.

69. The verse starts with "now concerning" (περὶ δέ), an epistolary formula Paul commonly uses in order to reply to a question raised by the letter-recipients or to introduce a new subject already known to them (e.g., 1 Cor 7:1; 8:1; 12:1; 16:1; 1 Thess 5:1). With no evidence for any letters sent from the Thessalonians to Paul, the phrase seems to introduce Paul's general response to the "good news of faith and love" delivered by Timothy (1 Thess 3:6).

70. BDAG, s.v. "φιλαδελφία."

71. Green, *Thessalonians*, 204.

72. Paul uses the word once more in Rom 12:10: "Be devoted to one another in brotherly love." With similar meaning, it is used in Heb 13:1, 1 Pet 1:22; 3:8, and 2 Pet 1:7.

73. Bruce, *1 and 2 Thessalonians*, 89. Paul employs ἀγάπη along with "for one another" and "for all men," implying a general character of love toward many unspecified people.

74. BDAG, s.v. "ποιέω."

From the statement "you do it toward all the brothers in all Macedonia," it is evident that the Thessalonian Christians extended the "brotherly love" to those outside the boundary of their city. How was the "brotherly love" practiced to all the believers in the province? Both Green and Weima propose three ways of extending the love.[75] First, the believers in Thessalonica, the major seaport and commercial center in the Roman province, provided hospitality for travelers coming from the churches in other cities. Second, the Thessalonians supported the evangelistic activities taking place in other areas just as the Philippians did for Paul's missions at Corinth (2 Cor 11:9). Third, the Thessalonian church provided financial assistance to the poor in other cities as well as in their own community.

While these three modes are all possible in demonstrating brotherly love, the last one seems to be most relevant to the context of the Thessalonian church.[76] Green comments on the passage that "most likely, Paul is reflecting on the way the Thessalonian church lent economic aid to needy believers in other parts of the province."[77] The Thessalonians' practice of love suggests not only the presence of "the lines of communication which linked their city with other places in the province"[78] but also "the evidence of the emerging solidarity between congregations in distinct localities."[79]

In 2 Thess 3:10, Paul cautions against those who are idle (ἀτάκτως) and not working for their own food, recalling his charge, "If anyone is not willing to work, neither let him eat." According to Meggitt, Paul's word suggests that "the members of the Thessalonian church were practicing a form of economic mutualism" and "the idlers were, in fact, being supplied with food by other church members," abusing the church's brotherly love.[80] Such "economic mutualism" could not be limited to the church of Thessalonica; it may have been practiced in other churches as well.[81]

75. Green, *Thessalonians*, 206–7. Weima, *1–2 Thessalonians*, 290–91.

76. Paul's letters to the Thessalonians do not mention any occasions of the church receiving traveling Christians or supporting evangelistic missions. On the contrary, the letters frequently relate to such topics as Christian attitudes toward work, diligence, financial responsibility for fellow believers, and so on. See, particularly, 1 Thess 4:11–12 and 2 Thess 3:6–12.

77. Green, *Thessalonians*, 205. Also, see Weima, *1–2 Thessalonians*, 290–91.

78. Bruce, *1 and 2 Thessalonians*, 90.

79. Green, *Thessalonians*, 207.

80. Meggitt, *Paul, Poverty and Survival*, 162.

81. Meggitt, *Paul, Poverty and Survival*, 163.

Paul's letters to the Thessalonians reveal the cooperative relationships among the churches in the province of Macedonia as well as among the house churches in the city of Thessalonica.

In practicing brotherly love, the Thessalonians may have offered financial aid to believers in various places: probably Philippi and Berea where Paul had launched Christian missions; possibly Amphipolis and Apollonia on the way from Philippi to Thessalonica (Acts 17:1); and probably the places "where the evangelistic activity of the Thessalonians has resulted in the formation of new churches (1 Thess 1:8)."[82] Although little record survives to confirm the activities of other churches, it is conceivable that some other churches shared financial resources following the Thessalonian church, since Paul writes "you became examples to all in Macedonia and Achaia who believe" (1 Thess 1:7–8). For instance, there is no reason to doubt that the church at Philippi, which had financially participated in Paul's ministry, may have practiced the same "brotherly love" toward its own members and toward the believers in other Macedonian cities. Paul's churches/house churches in Macedonia collaborated with one another by means of providing financial assistance to the needy members in their communities.

"Ministry to the Saints" in Achaia

At the end of 1 Corinthians, Paul refers to the household of Stephanas: "they were the first fruits of Achaia and they set themselves to the ministry for the saints" (1 Cor 16:15). Since the meaning of the Greek verb *τάσσω* is "to appoint someone to a position/task," Paul's purport in the phrase, ἔταξαν ἑαυτούς, seems stronger than "to devote themselves," the rendering of most English Bibles.[83] Completely determined, Stephanas and his household members assigned themselves to the ministry for

82. Weima, *1–2 Thessalonians*, 290. Paul writes, "the word of the Lord has sounded forth from you [the Thessalonians], not only in Macedonia and Achaia, but also in every place." Without doubt, the Thessalonians played a significant role in spreading the gospel in the area.

83. Hence, Thiselton comments that "*Devoted themselves* must be understood in the sense of *set themselves aside* for this work" (*Corinthians*, 1338). In a similar sense, Robertson and Plummer point out the use of the reflexive pronoun ("appointing themselves") and explain the ministry of Stephanas as "a self-imposed duty" (*Corinthians*, 395).

the saints in the community. What was represented by "the ministry (διακονία) for the saints"?

In the New Testament, διακονία is used in several meanings: (1) "waiting on tables" and in its wider sense "supervision of the common meals" (Luke 10:40, Acts 6:1); (2) "any discharge of service" in Christian love (1 Cor 12:4–11, Eph 4:11–12); (3) "the discharge of certain obligations in the community" (Acts 1:17, Rom 11:13, 2 Cor 4:1); and (4) "the collection for the Jerusalem saints" (Acts 11:29, 2 Cor 9:1).[84] It is clear from the context that the present ministry of Stephanas and his household was done for the saints in their own community, not to the saints in Jerusalem. Also, it was most likely a voluntary service rather than an obligatory one. Therefore, the ministry of Stephanas had to do with the first and the second of the above list.

Διακονία as "waiting on tables" presumably led to the ministry of food for the poor. As Capper argues, the communal care for the poor in the church was "always associated with table-fellowship in early Christianity."[85] Concerning the usage of the word διακονία in Paul's ministry, Weiser gives a succinct explanation: "In the life of Paul's churches, what is considered διακονία is esp. charitable care for the needy, either in the respective churches themselves (Rom 12:7; 1 Cor 16:15) or for the Jerusalem Church in the form of a collection (Rom 15:25, 31; 2 Cor 8:4, 19f; 9:1, 12)."[86] Harris further argues, "However that be, διακονία seems to have become a technical term in the early church for charitable financial relief within congregations (Acts 6:1) and between them (Acts 11:29; 12:25; Rom 15:31)."[87] According to this semantic understanding, the ministry of Stephanas and his household may have been to help and serve those in need.

There is substantial evidence that three grain shortages afflicted Corinth during the early days of the church.[88] Paul's reference to "the present distress" (1 Cor 7:26) may denote the famines that the Corinthian believers were suffering from.[89] It is no doubt that at the time of

84. Beyer, "διακονέω, διακονία, διάκονος," 87–88.

85. Capper, "Palestinian Cultural Context," 351.

86. Weiser, "διακονία," 303.

87. Harris, *Second Epistle to the Corinthians*, 567.

88. Winter, *After Paul Left Corinth*, 6.

89. Winter comments, "the language which Paul used seems to suggest that Corinth experienced some difficulties, and literary and nonliterary evidence points to yet another famine with the attendant social dislocation and anxiety that it caused" (*After Paul Left Corinth*, 224).

famine, the urgent ministry of the church was to share food with the famine-stricken people. In this connection, Garland suggests that "the service of Stephanas to the saints involved the distribution of food."[90] While commending the Stephanases' faithful "ministry to the saints" (1 Cor 16:15), Paul probably thought of their commitment and devotion, particularly, to the charitable service for the poor.

As confirmed by Paul, the household of Stephanas was a leading family known for their caring ministry to the saints. Besides Stephanas's household, however, there might also have been other households who were engaged in the similar service. Paul depicts the household of Stephanas as "the first fruits of Achaia." What does Paul mean by this figurative language? It may mean that Stephanas's household was the first one converted by Paul's mission in Achaia.[91] Or it may be that Stephanas and his household had been converted before Paul arrived at Corinth. More probably, however, as Thiselton suggests, the significance of "the first fruits" does not come from "being *first* in a sequential sense, but *first* in the sense of constituting a *sample, pledge,* or *promise of* more to come."[92] In this light, more households might have arisen in the community and followed the model of Stephanas's household.

After the mention of Stephanas's household, Paul urges the Corinthians to submit to Stephanas and to "everyone who works together and toils" (1 Cor 16:16). Paul's language here reveals the existence of church leaders who worked together in line with Stephanas's ministry. In Corinth, there might be six or more house churches, called altogether "the church of God in Corinth" (1 Cor 1:2).[93] They met regularly as house churches scattered around the city and occasionally as a whole at one place. Accordingly, the Corinthians' financial assistance might be rendered on two levels, within the individual house churches and between the house churches in Corinth and its vicinity. Through "the ministry to the saints," the Corinthians took care of their needy members particularly

90. Garland, *1 Corinthians*, 769.

91. There is a problem with this interpretation. Paul had had some converts even before he preached in Corinth. Acts 17:34 reads, "some men joined him [Paul] and believed, among whom were Dionysius the Areopagite and a woman named Damaris and others with them."

92. Thiselton, *First Epistle to the Corinthians*, 1338.

93. They met probably at the houses of the church leaders who were also Paul's coworkers—Aquila and Priscilla (Acts 18:2–3), Titius Justus (Acts 18:7), Crispus (Acts 18:8), Chloe (1 Cor 1:11), Stephanas (1 Cor 1:16; 16:15), Gaius (Rom 16:23), and Phoebe (Rom 16:1–2) at Cenchrea (the eastern port of Corinth).

with economic aid. Furthermore, working together for the ministry, the house churches in Achaia enhanced their relationship and collaboration with one another.

Financial Collaboration for Paul's Missions

This section seeks to find out how Paul and his coworkers met their financial needs in missionary works, and how Christian communities financially supported Paul's missions. The first subsection presents Paul's financing policy of self-support and explains its reason and motive. The second and third subsections discuss Paul's financial relationship with the Philippian church and with other churches, respectively. Although there are only a few biblical accounts of inter-church relations in financial matters,[94] Paul's ministry must have induced a number of occasions for the churches to work together for the spread of the gospel. Local and trans-local financial collaborations occurred in connection with Paul's missionary works.

Paul's Self-support

It is evident that Paul believed in the right of evangelists and ministers to receive financial compensation from those who are ministered. In 1 Corinthians 9, Paul elaborates the legitimacy for compensation, employing the analogy of the earnings of soldiers, farmers, and shepherds (9:7), expositing on the Law of Moses (9:9–10), defending the material reward for spiritual labor (9:11), and referring to the allotment for those who serve in the Temple (9:13). Also, he writes to the Galatians: "let the one who is taught the word share all good things with him who teaches" (Gal 6:6). Paul himself thankfully received financial gifts from the Philippian church, not just once but a number of times.[95] He even asked the local

94. Explicit church-to-church financial actions are recorded only in relation to the Jerusalem church. Acts 11:29–30 describes the financial support of the Antioch church for the Jerusalem church: "each of them [the Antiochenes] determined to send a contribution for the relief of the brethren living in Judea." Also, several passages in Paul's letters (1 Cor 16:1–2; 2 Cor 8:1—9:15; Rom 15:25–27) refer to the financial assistance of Paul's churches for the Jerusalem church.

95. During the so-called second missionary journey, the Philippians "sent a gift more than once" to Paul who was working in Thessalonica (Phil 4:16). While staying in Corinth, Paul did not depend on the Corinthians since "the brothers came from

churches to provide financial assistance for his coworkers who were visiting the area.[96]

Although Paul espoused the financial compensation for Christian workers and did accept financial gifts, "Paul's general missionary policy was that he maintained financial independence."[97] It is apparent from his saying to the Thessalonians: "For you remember, brethren, our labor and hardship that we proclaimed to you the gospel of God, working night and day so as not to be a burden to any of you" (1 Thess 2:9). T. D. Still makes a conclusive statement on this issue: "Even if he occasionally received material assistance from given congregations and persons, it was Paul's stated missionary policy and practice to be fiscally independent (see esp. 1 Cor 9:12, 15, 18)."[98] To keep the policy of financial autonomy, Paul's way of living was "to do manual labor to support himself."[99]

Why did Paul keep the policy of self-support for his missionary works? In the time of Jesus, it was quite customary for Jewish rabbis or scribes to engage in a secular calling as well as their work of teaching.[100] It may be that Paul, accustomed to the Jewish religion and tradition, might have adopted the common practice of Jewish teachers, that is, to teach the Scriptures and work for a living. According to Peerbolte, however, the closest parallel to Paul's missions was the teaching of the traveling philosophers in the Greco-Roman world.[101] He thus suggests that Paul's financial logistics were analogous to those of Cynic philosophers, who often labored with their own hands to stay financially independent.[102]

Macedonia and supplied my [Paul's] need" (2 Cor 11:9). Later, Paul confessed that he was fully supplied even in imprisonment, "having received from Epaphroditus what you [the Philippians] have sent" (Phil 4:18).

96. For example, Paul recommended Phoebe, the deaconess (διάκονος) of the Cenchrean church, to the believers at Rome and asked for hospitality and financial help for her (Rom 16:1–2). Also, the apostle told Titus and the church at Crete to "help Zenas the lawyer and Apollos on the way and see that they have everything they need" (Titus 3:13). Paul asked the churches for financial assistance on behalf of his coworkers.

97. Walton, "Paul, Patronage and Pay," 221.

98. Still, "Did Paul Loathe Manual Labor?," 782.

99. Friesen, "Poverty in Pauline Studies," 350. For the detailed discussion of Paul's manual labor, see Hock, *Social Context of Paul's Ministry*. His volume has been influential on the study of Paul's secular profession, tentmaking.

100. Jeremias, *Jerusalem*, 113.

101. Peerbolte, *Paul the Missionary*, 227.

102. Paul, according to Peerbolte, modelled the practice of the Greek philosophers: "Paul worked as an artisan, thereby creating his own financial independence as well as the opportunity to proclaim the gospel." Peerbolte, *Paul the Missionary*, 227.

In contrast to this association with traveling rabbis or Greek philosophers, S. Walton proposes three reasons for Paul's financial independence.[103] First, Paul sought to differentiate himself from those traveling teachers who "peddle the word of God" for material gains (2 Cor 2:17). Secondly, Paul made himself the model for "working hard not to be a burden to anyone" (2 Thess 3:7–9). Thirdly, Paul presented the gospel of Christ without charge since he was under order to do so. God entrusted him with the evangelistic task (1 Cor 9:16–17). Walton's explanation, based on Paul's own writings, seems more evidential and persuasive than the assumption that equates Paul's missions with the teaching of traveling rabbis or Cynic philosophers.

Paul's labor had to do with his ministry situation of the time. When he started evangelistic works in a place where the gospel had never been preached, the apostle would not accept financial assistance from the local people, unbelievers who first needed to receive the gospel.[104] Even after the establishment of a Christian community, Paul avoided becoming a financial burden to the community for fear that his works might be ruined because of his opponents. While staying in Corinth, therefore, Paul refused to receive financial compensation from the Corinthians lest there might be any obstacles to the progress of the gospel of Christ (1 Cor 9:12, 2 Cor 11:9).

When Silas and Timothy, who had been left in Berea (Acts 17:10–15), arrived at Corinth, Paul "became wholly absorbed with proclaiming the word, testifying to the Jews that Jesus was the Christ" (Acts 18:5 NET). It is noteworthy that the coming of Silas and Timothy brought about a change in the pattern of Paul's ministry.[105] Previously, he had worked along with Aquila and Priscilla during the week (Acts 18:3) and argued for the gospel in the synagogue each Sabbath (Acts 18:4). Now, Paul devoted himself to the full-time ministry of the gospel. Possibly, Silas and Timothy brought financial gifts from Macedonia or worked themselves in order to support Paul financially. The point is that Paul

103. Walton, "Paul, Patronage and Pay," 224–25.

104. Schnabel, in *Early Christian Mission*, 1450, argues that Paul's financial dependence on the local patrons might induce the compromise of the gospel and hamper its progress in the area.

105. Peterson, *Acts*, 510. From the context, the imperfect verb συνείχετο is best taken inceptively, "began to be absorbed with" (NASB) or "became absorbed with" (NET). Most commentators recognize the change triggered by the coming of Silas and Timothy.

prioritized the preaching of the gospel. He decided whether or not to work on the grounds of the effectiveness of his gospel ministry.

Another notable text is Acts 20:34–35. On his final journey to Jerusalem, Paul dropped by Miletus, the outer port of Ephesus, and invited there the elders of the church for a farewell instruction. Adumbrating his Ephesian ministry in retrospect, the apostle says how he earned a living while preaching the gospel: "these hands ministered to my needs and to those who were with me" (Acts 20:34). Paul labored with his own hands to support his companions as well as himself. It is also probable that Paul's coworkers occasionally worked and supported Paul particularly when he was in prison.[106] Paul and his coworkers worked for one another's needs.

In the subsequent verse, he mentions the reason for his principle of financial independence: "I showed you that by working hard in this manner you must help the weak and remember the words of the Lord Jesus, that He Himself said, 'It is more blessed to give than to receive'" (Acts 20:35). Paul's testimony reveals the primary motive for his economic policy of self-support. That is, the purpose of "working hard" was not for his financial independence per se; it was to "help the weak" and "give" to others. Not only in receiving gifts from others but also in working with his own hands, the underlying concern of Paul was mutual support and cooperation based on Christ's love.

Financial Support from the Philippian Church

From the time Paul set foot in Europe on his second missionary journey, he had a close relationship with the Philippian church. When Paul first proclaimed the gospel at Philippi, a Christian assembly formed in the house of Lydia, a merchant of purple cloth from Thyatira.[107] Afterwards, Paul proceeded from Philippi to Thessalonica (1 Thess 2:2) and there received financial gifts from the Philippians more than once (Phil 4:16). It is conceivable that Lydia and the congregation at her house sent gifts to continue their support for Paul just as they had provided accommodations to Paul and his companions at Philippi.

106. Cassidy, *Paul in Chains*, 78, 222–24.

107. During the Philippian mission, Paul and Silas stayed at Lydia's house (Acts 16:15). The new believers also assembled at the house (Acts 16:40). It is probable that both the household of Lydia and the household of the Philippian jailer (Acts 16:33–34) developed into the house churches of Philippi.

The Philippians' assistance for Paul's ministry continued as he moved to Corinth. When Paul wrote to the Corinthians that "I robbed other churches by receiving wages to minister to you" and "the brothers from Macedonia supplied what I needed" (2 Cor 11:8–9), he must have thought of the gifts from the Philippian church. Thanks to the church's support, Paul was able to proclaim the gospel and minister to the Corinthians free of charge. Years later, the Philippian Christians resumed their support by sending another financial gift to Paul through Epaphroditus, demonstrating the "same generous spirit which had characterized their lives from the beginning."[108] Rightly, Paul attests to the church's special position in his ministry: "after I departed from Macedonia, no church shared with me in the matter of giving and receiving but you alone" (Phil 4:15).

Scholars have presented diverse views of the background to the financial relationship between Paul and the Philippians. Earlier, J. P. Sampley called attention to the concept of consensual *societas*, a Roman social construct, which was a "legally binding, reciprocal partnership of association, freely entered upon between one person and one or more other persons regarding a particular goal or shared concern."[109] Observing a number of financially-nuanced terms in the Philippian letter, Sampley posited that the important word κοινωνία (1:5; 4:14–15) represented the partnership of the Roman *societas*.[110] Recently, this view has been reinforced by Julien Ogereau, who intensively surveyed the use of κοινων-cognates and claimed that κοινωνία can "correspond to the legal and commercial Roman concept of *societas*."[111] Paul and the Philippian church, according to Ogereau, had entered into a financial agreement with a shared goal of proclaiming the gospel. However, there remains a question of whether Paul exactly meant the legal and commercial concept of *societas* when he mentioned the companionship and fellowship that he had enjoyed with the Philippians.

108. O'Brien, *Philippians*, 8.

109. Sampley, *Pauline Partnership in Christ*, 13. In the *societas*, a "shared goal" was essential—"partners agreed to use property or labor in common towards a particular goal that was beyond the property or labor itself."

110. Sampley, *Pauline Partnership in Christ*, 60–61. Emphasizing the commercial and technical sense of the word κοινωνία, he even argues that "the last section of the Letter to the Philippians is a formal receipt tendered by Paul to the Philippian Christians for their gift-payment in response to his need-request" (55).

111. Ogereau, *Paul's Koinonia with the Philippians*, 219.

Scholars such as Peter Marshall and G. W. Peterman understand the financial relationship between them in terms of the Greek concept of *friendship*.[112] Admittedly, Paul's language concerning the Philippian gift (Phil 4:15) carries a technical sense of financial matters.[113] Yet, while acknowledging the economic nuance of Paul's language, Marshall still suggests that "given the financial basis of the majority of friendships and the common use of commercial language and ideas in describing them," the phrase "in the matter of giving and receiving" (εἰς λόγον δόσεως καὶ λήμψεως) may be "an idiomatic expression indicating friendship."[114] Therefore, it signifies "a warm and lasting relationship" more than "a simple two-way transaction."[115] It seems that the relationship between Paul and the Philippian church bears a resemblance to the Greek notion of *friendship* rather than the financial contract of *societas*. Still, it is to be noted that their friendship formed because of their common faith in Christ and developed as a "partnership (κοινωνία) in the gospel from the first day" (Phil 1:5).

Acknowledging the universality of the patronage system in the Greco-Roman world, Steve Walton raises a key question as to whether Paul's ministry simply reflected the patronage system of the world or transformed the system "through a theological and Christological lens."[116] Based on his study of biblical texts, Walton concludes that Paul "re-drew the map of human relationships offered by the patronage system" by placing both himself and the Philippians in the place of client, and God in the place of patron.[117] Paul's relationship with the Philippians was not of the system of patron/client hierarchy, but of the equal standing of partnership. Schnabel describes it as the "committed fellowship of the church founder and the church members," that is, the fellowship of "Paul

112. Marshall, *Enmity in Corinth*, 25. In the Greco-Roman world, "friendship" could be defined as "any human relationship based upon conscious reciprocity (ἀντιφίλησις) of goodwill (εὔνοια)." See also Peterman, *Paul's Gift from Philippi*, 51–89.

113. For example, the phrase εἰς λόγον reflects the accounting concept of "to the account of," and the expression δόσεως καὶ λήμψεως ("giving and receiving") refers to "monetary transactions on two sides of a ledger." O'Brein, *Philippians*, 533–34.

114. Marshall, *Enmity in Corinth*, 163.

115. Marshall, *Enmity in Corinth*, 163.

116. Walton, "Paul, Patronage and Pay," 221.

117. Walton, "Paul, Patronage and Pay," 233. With God placed at the center, the relationship between Paul and the Philippians greatly differed from the patronage system of the Greco-Roman world.

through his missionary work that led to the establishment of the church, and the Philippians through their personal support of the gospel."[118]

Although financial activities of Paul and his churches can be better understood in the socio-economic context of the Greco-Roman world, the Philippians' financial assistance for Paul cannot be fully explained by referring to the Roman *societas*, the Greek ideal of *friendship*, or the patron/client system per se. Most fundamental to the bonding between Paul and the Philippians, according to Paul's own words, was the grace of God and the affection of Christ they all shared together in the gospel of Christ. In Phil 1:7–8, Paul confesses his earnestness toward the Philippians: "I have you in my heart . . . you all are partakers of grace with me . . . how I long for you all with the affection of Christ Jesus." Properly, the spiritual bond in Christ manifested itself through financial gifts, establishing a partnership (κοινωνία) in the gospel between Paul and the Philippian church.

One notable fact is that the financial gift sent to Paul was an outcome of communal agreement. Namely, the house churches in Philippi most likely joined together in funding Paul's missions. In the early stage of his Corinthian ministry, at least two households—those of Lydia and the Philippian jailer—might have participated in the financial project. As for the recent gift delivered by Epaphroditus (Phil 4:10, 18), some more house churches—possibly, the household of Euodia and the household of Syntyche—might have joined the contribution. Paul's ministry was indebted to the financial collaboration of the house churches in Philippi. In other words, Paul's partnership with the Philippians presupposed the communal partnership among the Philippian house churches, as they were exhorted "to stand firm in one spirit, with one soul, striving together for the faith of the gospel" (Phil 1:27).

Paul affirms to the Corinthians that "when I was with you and needed something, I was not a burden to anyone" (2 Cor 11:9). This was possible due to the gifts from Philippi. It means that the support of the Philippian church was meaningful not only to Paul himself but also, consequently, to the Corinthian church. In this sense, Johnson perceptively argues that "in effect, the Philippian church shared its possessions not only with Paul but with the Corinthian community."[119] The Philippian church provided financial assistance to the incipient church at Corinth

118. Schnabel, *Early Christian Mission*, 1448.

119. Johnson, "Making Connections," 165.

through Paul's ministry. The Philippians' financial assistance for Paul indicates the collaborative nature of early church relationships, both locally among the house churches in Philippi and trans-locally between the churches in different regions.

Financial Support from Other Churches

The Philippian church was not the only one that contributed to Paul's missions. While referring to the financial support from Macedonia for his ministry in Corinth, Paul hyperbolically says that "I robbed other churches, taking wages from them to minister to you" (2 Cor 11:8). The plural "other churches" suggests that the financial support did not come from just one church, but from several churches. Which, then, were these "other churches"? At first glance, this statement seems inconsistent with his own words to the Philippians: "in the beginning of the gospel, when I departed from Macedonia, no church shared with me concerning giving and receiving but you alone" (Phil 4:15).

If Paul had only the Philippian church in mind while speaking of "other churches," the plural ἐκκλησίας may have been used as a rhetorical expression for "other believers"[120] or referred to multiple house churches in Philippi.[121] Both of these arguments seem to be awkward and strained considering the normal use of the term ἐκκλησία. Harris presents a more reasonable explanation that although the Philippians alone had "a semi-formal partnership in the gospel" (Phil 1:5), the churches at Thessalonica and Berea may also have contributed to Paul "on occasion."[122] That is, the discrepancy between the two biblical accounts, 2 Cor 11:8 and Phil 4:15, represents the different types of relationship Paul had with his churches. The former denotes the communities who provided Paul with ad hoc support, and the latter, the Philippians' particular type of "partnership" in Pauline ministry.

Many commentators expound on Phil 4:15 along with Harris, paying much attention to the commercial aspect of "giving and receiving"

120. Barnet, *Second Epistle to the Corinthians*, 515–16n20.

121. Peterman, *Paul's Gift from Philippi*, 146n134.

122. Harris, *Second Epistle to the Corinthians*, 757–58. Paul came to Corinth from Philippi by way of Thessalonica, Berea, and Athens (Acts 16:11—17:15). It is probable that "when he left Macedonia for Achaia, the believers in Philippi and perhaps Thessalonica and Berea sent him on his way with the necessary provisions for his evangelistic effort in the south."

(δόσεως καὶ λήμψεως) and accepting the phrase "but you alone" (εἰ μὴ ὑμεῖς μόνοι) unconditionally. As a result, they tend to regard Paul's partnership with the Philippian church as a unique, commercially-charged one, which is quite different from the relationships Paul had with other churches.[123] However, although the phrase of partnership with the Philippian church carries a sense of commercial transactions, it certainly has "far more than a literal, financial meaning," creating "metaphors for spiritual transactions."[124] Therefore, a better interpretation of the phrase "giving and receiving" may well be that "material gifts passed from the church to the apostle, and spiritual blessings flowed the other way."[125] To be sure, such spiritual transactions were not limited to the Philippian church. Paul describes his reciprocal relationship with other churches as well: "if we sowed spiritual blessings among you, is it too much to reap material things from you?" (1 Cor 9:11); "if the Gentiles have shared in their spiritual things, they are indebted to minister to them also in material things" (Rom 15:27). On this understanding, Paul's partnership with the Philippians may not be so distinct from the partnership with the Corinthians or with other churches.

It is to be noted that in Phil 4:15 the verb "shared" (ἐκοινώνησεν) is modified by the adverbial clause of time: "no church shared with me *when I went out of Macedonia*" (ὅτε ἐξῆλθον ἀπὸ Μακεδονίας). That means that some churches might have shared with Paul *afterwards*. With the temporal clause, which is appositional to "in the beginning of the gospel," Paul emphasizes the long-lived, special friendship he has had with the Philippian church.[126] The emphasis becomes more specific in the subsequent verse: "for even in Thessalonica you sent a gift more than once for

123. For examples, Richard Melick says that "the other churches failed in their obligations to the gospel . . . Paul pointed out that others had received but not given" (*Philippians, Colossians, Philemon*, 156). Ralph P. Martin suggests that "the absence of this special feature of *giving and receiving* in Paul's later relations with his churches will mark out the Philippians as in a class apart" (*Philippians*, 185). According to Gerald F. Hawthorne, Paul thought that the Philippians were "uniquely his partners in his missionary endeavors," and the commercially nuanced words "invariably refer to financial transactions" (*Philippians*, 270).

124. Hansen, *Philippians*, 319.

125. Martin, *Philippians*, 185. But Hawthorne poses a widely different view: "these words refer to the financial gift of the Philippians on the one hand, and the receipt they received back from the apostle acknowledging its safe arrival, on the other hand" (*Philippians*, 270).

126. Paul's reference to the Philippians' longtime support is also found in Philippians 1:5, "your participation in the gospel *from the first day* until now."

my needs" (Phil 4:16). Paul's intention was to appreciate the Philippians' old-aged partnership in the gospel, not to differentiate her from other churches in the level of ministry relationship. It can hardly be doubted that not only the Philippian church but also many other churches were partners with Paul for the gospel of Christ. It was true even of the church from which Paul refused to accept financial compensation.

Paul's "free of charge" mission in Corinth (1 Cor 9:18, 2 Cor 11:9) should be counterbalanced by his remarks on ministry plans and expectations: "perhaps I shall stay with you, or even spend the winter, that you may send me forth (με προπέμψητε) wherever I may go" (1 Cor 16:6). Most scholars believe that the verb "send" (προπέμπω) bears a technical sense, "to assist someone in making a journey . . . with food, money, by arranging for companions, means of travel, etc."[127] After the days of self-support in Corinth, Paul now allowed and even asked the Corinthians "to assist him on his further journeys, so that in this way they, too, may have a share in his ministry."[128] Ciampa and Rosner make a more specific argument that Paul wanted to spend some extended time in Corinth (1 Cor 16:6–7) "so that they could help him on his journey . . . put funds together and make other arrangements as well."[129] Paul may have thought of "casting the vision for his work while among the Corinthians or possibly expanding his traveling ministry team with members from that church."[130] Although this argument is beyond verification, its point is indisputable: Paul and the Corinthians worked together in financial and ministerial partnership for the gospel of Christ. As the Philippians financially helped Paul in Corinth, the Corinthians were supposed to help Paul in other mission fields.

Unlike the churches in Macedonia and Achaia, the church at Rome was not founded by Paul. Although he had quite a number of acquaintances in Rome, Paul had not even visited the church when he wrote the letter to the Romans. Hence, the relationship of Paul with the Romans could not be the same as the relationship with the Corinthians who had been converted and ministered by Paul. Nevertheless, interestingly

127. BDAG, s.v. "προπέμπω." The phrase is rendered as "send me on my way" (NASB), "send me on my journey" (NKJV, NET), and "help me on my journey" (NIV). The verb appears again in verse 11 with regard to Timothy's travel. Additionally, it is found in Acts 15:3; Rom 15:24; Titus 3:13; and 3 John 6.

128. Fee, *First Corinthians*, 905.

129. Ciampa and Rosner, *First Letter to the Corinthians*, 847.

130. Ciampa and Rosner, *First Letter to the Corinthians*, 847.

enough, Paul discloses his missionary plans and expectations to the Roman Christians (Rom 15:24) in the same way he did to the Corinthians (1 Cor 16:6). Differing only in voice (active/passive), both statements relate the same content in the same mood.[131] According to Dickson, "the casual way Paul states his expectations" to the Corinthians may be an indication that the helping act of προπέμπω was "a shared assumption among Pauline communities."[132] Paul's words to the Romans are no less casual than the words to the Corinthians. If Dickson is right, which is highly probable, the financial cooperation through "προπέμπω" was a common phenomenon not only to Pauline communities but also to other communities such as the church at Rome.

Phoebe, the leader of the house church at Cenchrea, the eastern port of Corinth, is generally assumed to be the bearer of Paul's letter to the Romans. Jewett argues that the primary task of Phoebe was to "create the logistical base for the Spanish mission," that is, "to present the letter to the several house churches in Rome and discuss its contents and implications with church leaders."[133] Jewett continues that such mission support would require a "unification of the Roman house churches so that they would be able to cooperate in the support of the Spanish mission."[134] No document is existent to determine whether Roman house churches joined in financing Paul's mission to Spain, or whether Paul ever undertook the mission.[135] Even so, the fact that Paul sent Phoebe of Cenchrea to Rome (Rom 16:1–2) and requested the Romans' support for the Spanish mission (Rom 15:24) was a strong indication that Paul carried out his missionary works in cooperation with others—individuals, coworkers, and local

131. Both verses convey three elements: (1) Paul's stay with the recipients for some time, (2) "sending Paul on his journey" (προπέμπω), and (3) destination of Paul's journey.

1 Cor 16:6	Rom 15:24
perhaps I shall stay with you	when I have first enjoyed your company for a while
you may send me on my way	I hope to . . . be sent on my way by you
wherever I go	there (to Spain)

132. Dickson, *Mission-Commitment*, 197.

133. Jewett, "Paul, Phoebe, and the Spanish Mission," 151–52. In a similar vein, Stuhlmacher argues that one of the main reasons for writing the letter to the Romans was to pave the way for the establishment of the Spanish mission support among the Roman churches. See Stuhlmacher, "Purpose of Romans," 231–42.

134. Jewett, "Paul, Phoebe, and the Spanish Mission," 151–52.

135. The New Testament is silent about the outcome of the Spanish mission. However, a number of extra-biblical sources (e.g., Clement of Rome, *The Muratorian Canon*, Chrysostom, Jerome, etc.) confirm that Paul carried out the mission.

churches. Such partnership ministry of Paul must have entailed the network of collaboration, direct or indirect, among New Testament churches.

Financial Collaboration for the Jerusalem Church

This section investigates two financial projects for the Jerusalem church and explores the networking and collaboration among the churches involved in the projects. First, it explains the Temple tax system in the Diaspora to understand the Jewish background of financial collections. Second, it discusses a relief fund by the Antioch Christians for the Jerusalem church. Then, third, Paul's collection for Jerusalem is examined in terms of its motivations and effects on the church relationship. This section proves that the first-century churches, Jewish or gentile, Pauline or non-Pauline, communicated and cooperated together to minister to fellow Christians in need, particularly, those in Jerusalem and Judea.

The Jewish Temple Tax

Tellbe correctly states that besides the widely accepted Judaic triad—i.e., circumcision, Sabbath, and food laws—the Jewish Temple tax was also "a significant Jewish boundary marker defining Jewish identity in the Diaspora prior to 70 CE."[136] There were Jewish communities in almost all the cities of the Roman world in the first century AD.[137] All men over the age of twenty in the communities were required to "bring their first fruits to the temple," namely, to pay an annual half-shekel temple tax.[138] Furthermore, they took part in the contribution "with exceeding cheerfulness," since the contribution was looked upon as the fulfillment of their religious duties and the "ransom" for their freedom and safety.[139]

136. Tellbe, "Temple Tax," 19.

137. For centuries, Jews had been dispersed around the Greco-Roman world by compulsory expulsion or voluntary migration. By the time of the New Testament, they have established a great number of diasporan communities almost all over the Empire. Josephus mentions Antiochus the Great (242–187 BCE) who ordered the transportation of 2,000 Jewish families from Mesopotamia and Babylon to Lydia and Phrygia, providing them with the land for houses and farms and allowing them to live by their own laws (*Ant.* 12.3.4).

138. Philo, *Spec. Laws* 1.77. The origin of the Temple tax can be traced to the Torah commandments in Exod 30:11–16.

139. Philo, *Spec. Laws* 1.77.

Thus Josephus boasted about the riches of the Jerusalem Temple: "And let no one wonder that there was so much wealth in our temple; since all the Jews throughout the habitable earth, and those that worshipped God; nay, even those of Asia and Europe, sent their contributions to it; and this from very ancient times."[140]

Drawing on the inscriptional data of the Sardis synagogue in western Asia Minor, Bonz makes an interesting study about the distinctive approach to religious benefaction by the ancient Jewish communities. He credibly argues that whereas the pagan religion—the imperial cult or private associations—was mainly financed by wealthy families or individuals, the financing of Judaic religion, in comparison with the pagan counterparts, was accomplished by the majority of the Jews in the community.[141] Their religious benefaction may have thrived with "a flexible and broadly based revenue structure, consisting of large and small private donations and a well-supported common fund."[142] A typical practice of this Jewish tradition of religious benefaction was, most significantly, the Temple tax that was honored and paid by all the Jewish communities.

Although the tax was levied on each individual, it proceeded as a part of the community project, local and trans-local. First, the half-shekel money or its equivalent was collected and stored in a secure place within the local community. Philo records, "there is in almost every city a storehouse for the sacred things to which it is customary for the people to come and there to deposit their first fruits."[143] Depending on the geopolitical condition, the local collection may have been transported to a regional gathering point, before the sum of the collections was finally shipped to Jerusalem. While the Temple tax was locally collected at various times during the year, the large sum of the collections was brought to Jerusalem, normally, once a year.[144] To be sure, its transportation must

140. Josephus, *Ant.* 14.7.2.

141. Bonz, "Differing Approaches to Religious Benefaction," 148–50. Of course, there were some exceptions. For example, many burial societies of the pagan world were established and maintained by a good number of humble memberships rather than a few of the rich. Some wealthy Jews or proselytes made substantial donations for the benefit of the Jewish community.

142. Bonz, "Differing Approaches to Religious Benefaction," 152.

143. Philo, *Spec. Laws* 1.78. Also, Josephus refers to a city, Nisibis, in which the Jews deposited their collected half-shekel tax as well as other contributions to Jerusalem (*Ant.* 18.9.1).

144. Tellbe, "Temple Tax," 21. The shipment was made usually at Passover for the Palestinian Jews, at Pentecost for the Jews close to Palestine, and at the Feast of the Tabernacles for the diaspora Jews.

have been a serious concern for the Jewish communities because of the political and social opposition to the capital outflow and the risk of robbery on the road.[145]

The collection of annual half-shekel tax from all male Jews played a significant role in maintaining the worship and cultic system of the Jerusalem temple. However, a more significant role was that it connected all the Jewish communities in the Diaspora to one another and then to Jerusalem, the capital of the Jewish people. When the Temple tax was collected into the depository of a local community, it would have helped reinforce the individuals' sense of belonging to the local Jewish society. When the local collections were gathered to a regional place, the process "must have helped tie Diaspora communities together across geographical boundaries."[146] The safe delivery of the collections to Jerusalem was probably the deepest concern for all the Jewish communities in the Diaspora. The Temple tax, with its ethnic and religious implications, was instrumental in networking Jewish communities together locally and trans-locally.

Nickle highlights the fact that Paul's collection ministry was patterned after the collection of the Temple tax in the Diaspora. The parallels between them "are too numerous to have been coincidental":

> (1) Jerusalem was the place to which the money was delivered. . . . Jerusalem represented the centre of their respective interests. (2) Pentecost was an important date for the delivery. (3) Men were appointed in each of the local communities to accompany the funds to Jerusalem. In both instances, this was not just for the sake of security, but also in order that the one sent could represent the entire community in Jerusalem. (4) Central reception areas were established in which the contributions and representatives from the local communities were gathered together. (5) Advantageous use was made of the protection provided under the special concessions granted to Judaism by the Roman Government. (6) The prudent practice of regularly setting aside money for the contribution was encouraged. (7)

145. For example, Cicero writes that "it was the practice each year to send gold to Jerusalem on the Jews' account from Italy and all our provinces, but Flaccus [the governor of Asia Minor] issued an edict forbidding its export from Asia . . . At Apamea a little less than a hundred pounds of gold was seized as it was being exported . . . at Laodicea a little more than twenty pounds was seized . . . at Adramyttium, a hundred pounds . . . at Pergamum, not much" (*Flac.* 67–68).

146. Barclay, "Money and Meetings," 118–19.

> Special care was taken to ensure that no opportunity might be provided for the personal vilification of those directly connected with the funds. (8) The contributions manifested a tangible expression of unity and solidarity.[147]

Many scholars agree that Paul's collection project for the Jerusalem church reflected the Jewish custom of paying the half-shekel tax, externally in its organization and logistics, and internally in its theological significance of unity and charity.[148]

Antioch's Financial Aid to Jerusalem

Acts 11:27–30 relates the episode that the Antioch church sent Barnabas and Saul (Paul) to Jerusalem along with a famine relief.[149] This act of financial contribution for the Jerusalem church did not happen all of a sudden. There had been relations between the two churches that led to concerns and provisions for each other. With persecution arising, many believers in Jerusalem were scattered to Phoenicia, Cyprus, and Antioch (Acts 8:1; 11:19). When some men of Cyprus and Cyrene preached the gospel to the Greeks in Antioch, a great number of people believed and turned to the Lord (Acts 11:20–21). Having heard of the evangelistic movement in Antioch, the Jerusalem church sent out Barnabas to inquire into and lend support to the emerging community of faith (Acts 11:22).[150] Barnabas fetched Saul (Paul) from Tarsus, and they together taught a multitude of believers, who were first called "Christians" (Acts 11:25–26).

147. Nickle, *Collection*, 87–89.

148. However, some scholars deny the link between the "collection" and the Jewish Temple tax. For example, Barclay argues that since Paul's collection was not for the temple-cultus, but for the poor in the Jerusalem church, "it was parallel not to the Jewish temple tax but to the payments for foodstuffs for famine-struck Judaea organized by Helena and Izates (46/47 CE; Josephus, *Ant.* 20.2.5; cf. Acts 11.27–30)" ("Money and Meetings," 121).

149. Some scholars are dubious about this Lukan account because of the variance between Galatians and Acts in terms of Paul's visit to Jerusalem. For a detailed discussion, see chapter 4, section "Collaboration through Visitations."

150. Jerusalem's reaction to the news is parallel to that of Acts 8:14, where Peter and John were sent to Samaria to check out the revival movement there. Also, according to Marshall, Jerusalem's reaction to Antioch was hardly "motivated by suspicion, still less by hostility"; it was to "do something to placate a group of right-wing Jewish Christians in Jerusalem" (*Acts of the Apostles*, 213–14).

The dispatch of Barnabas was not the only contact Jerusalem had developed with Antioch: there were prophets coming and going between them.[151] Agabus, one of the prophets who had come down from Jerusalem, warned in prophecy that there would be a severe famine all over the world (Acts 11:27–28a). It came to pass in the time of Claudius,[152] and the Antiochene church sent a famine relief to Jerusalem by the hands of Barnabas and Paul (Acts 11:28–30). Barnabas acted as an intermediary in developing the relationship between the Jerusalem church and the new church at Antioch, and in bringing Paul back to the ministry in connection with the Jerusalem apostles (cf. Acts 9:27).

In Acts 11:29, Luke describes that the Antiochene collection was done "as each was prospering" (καθὼς εὐπορεῖτό τις). Καθώς is used "in the sense of measure," that is, "in proportion as any prospered."[153] Together with the subsequent phrase "each of them determined" (ὥρισαν ἕκαστος αὐτῶν), the passage gives the impression that "each disciple was free to decide what he should do with his profits."[154] The collection was made based on individuals and voluntary actions. Further, as Bruce comments, the members of the Antiochene church may "have set aside a fixed sum out of their property or income as a contribution to it."[155] Later, in Paul's own financial campaign for Jerusalem, reappear the individual and voluntary principle of the Antiochene collection (2 Cor 9:7) and the proper way of preparing the collection (1 Cor 16:2).[156]

151. Bock, *Acts*, 417. Similarly, Hengel and Schwemer suggest that "Luke has paradigmatically combined a number of visits into this one" (*Paul between Damascus and Antioch*, 239).

152. Claudius ruled the Empire from AD 41 to 54, during which a series of famines took place in various parts of the world—in Judea, in Rome, in Egypt, and in Greece (cf. Josephus, *Ant.* 3.15.3; 20.2.5; 20.5.2). It seems that the famine attacked the land of Judea during the procuratorship of Tiberius Alexander (AD 46–48), and Egyptian documents indicate a major famine there in AD 45–46. Therefore, the Judean famine has occurred, probably, around AD 46. For a helpful review of the famines during the reign of Claudius, see Winter, "Acts and Food Shortages," 59–78.

153. Barrett, *Acts*, 565. It could be rendered "as much as one is well-off," "in the proportion that any of the disciples had means" (NASB), "everyman according to his ability" (KJV), "each according to his ability" (NKJV, NIV), or "each in accordance with his financial ability" (NET).

154. Barrett, *Acts*, 565.

155. Bruce, *Acts*, 243.

156. Advising the Corinthians about the collection for Jerusalem, Paul uses expressions similar to Acts 11:29, "as each one has purposed in his heart" (2 Cor 9:7) and "let each one of you put aside, storing up as he may prosper" (1 Cor 16:2).

It is noteworthy that Luke uses the word διακονία to refer to the famine relief for Jerusalem (Acts 11:29; 12:25). The word appeared earlier in Acts 6:1 to denote the daily serving of food to the needy widows in Jerusalem. Luke may have viewed the Antiochene famine relief as an equivalent to or an outgrowth of the food ministry of the Jerusalem church. Also, Paul uses the same term to denote his own collection ministry (Rom 15:31). For Luke and Paul, to send a relief fund to Jerusalem was to "serve/help" (διακονέω) the poor in Jerusalem. It is interesting to see that the pattern of the Antiochene collection in Acts 11:29 is closely reflected in Paul's own collection ministry (1 Cor 16:2; 2 Cor 9:7; Rom 15:31). The act of financial assistance—performed in Jerusalem, in Antioch, and in Paul's churches—has been the backbone of Christian ministry since the birth of Christianity.

Because a multitude of people—Jews, proselytes, God-fearers, and Greeks—became Christians in Antioch, it is probable that "some of the wealthy homeowners made their homes available to the congregation as assembly places."[157] It is then also probable that the famine relief was carried out according to the household assemblies, that is, through their local networks and collaborations. Just as the Philippians' financial assistance for Paul's missions presupposed the communal agreement among the house churches in Philippi, the Antiochene support for the Jerusalem church must have involved prior actions on the part of the local house churches in Antioch.

In its beginning, the Antiochene church received spiritual support from the Jerusalem church (Acts 11:20–23). When the Jerusalem believers were struck by famines, the Antiochenes in turn sent relief funds to Jerusalem (Acts 11:27–30). In this material way, as Peterson comments, "they expressed their gratitude for receiving the gospel from Christians in Judea."[158] There developed a solid relationship between the two Christian communities, and their relationship was one of the reciprocal sharing, the essence of Christian fellowship. The key point of the Lukan narration is that the famine relief from Antioch to Jerusalem "embodies the unity between the mixed Jewish-Gentile community in Syria and the Jewish leadership in Judea."[159] Or it might have been "calculated to strengthen

157. Gehring, *House Church and Mission*, 111.

158. Peterson, *Acts*, 358.

159. Downs, "Paul's Collection," 56.

the bond between the totally Jewish-Christian church of Jerusalem and the mainly Gentile-Christian church of Antioch."[160]

Paul's "Collection" for the Jerusalem Church

Besides the preaching of the gospel, the major task of Paul was to raise relief fund for "the poor among the saints in Jerusalem" (Rom 15:26). From his early days of ministry, Paul engaged himself in caring for the poor. Responding to the Jerusalem apostles' request to "remember the poor," Paul confirmed that he had already been "eager/diligent to do it" (Gal 2:10).[161] The theme of the collection for Jerusalem appears in nearly all his major epistles (Rom 15:25–31; 1 Cor 16:1–4; 2 Cor 8–9; Gal 2:10). The longest exhortation Paul made to the Corinthians was to promote and guide the collection process (2 Cor 8–9). His last visit to Jerusalem was to deliver the contribution to the Jerusalem church (Rom 15:25). There is no doubt that Paul put a great amount of his time and energy over the years in the financial campaign for the poor believers in Jerusalem.

What inspired Paul to make such efforts for the Jerusalem church? What was the motivation behind the collection ministry? Scholars have generally identified "three perceptible directions of interest" in Paul's mind: (1) the anticipation of Christian eschatology, (2) the expression of Christian unity, and (3) the realization of Christian charity.[162] Paul yearned for the day when Israel would turn to Jesus Christ (Rom 9:1–5; 10:1) and believed that the conversion of the gentiles would ultimately turn out for the salvation of Israel (Rom 11:11–26). Munck construed the collection project in light of this eschatological fulfillment of salvation. Paul's final visit to Jerusalem along with the relief fund and the delegates from his gentile churches, according to Munck, represented the realization of the Old Testament prophecies that "all the nations will stream to

160. Bruce, *Acts*, 230.

161. Paul's statement in Gal 2:10 does not straightly indicate the collection project for the Jerusalem church. As this book posits, it represents the event of Acts 11:29–30 (Antioch's famine relief for Jerusalem), and the letter to the Galatians was written prior to the Jerusalem Council (Acts 15). Therefore, "remember the poor" in Gal 2:10 is to be understood as "a general principle," while Paul's collection project for Jerusalem is "a particular application of that principle." Longenecker, *Remember the Poor*, 339.

162. Nickle, *Collection*, 100. The arrangement is here reversed. Besides, Downs observes four significant implications in the collection project: (1) an eschatological event, (2) the gentiles' obligation toward the Jews, (3) an ecumenical offering, and (4) a charitable act of material relief. See Downs, *Offering of the Gentiles*, 3–26.

it [Jerusalem]" (Isa 2:2; Mic 4:1) and "the wealth of the nations will come to you" (Isa 60:5; Mic 4:13).[163] However, discussing the salvation of Israel and the gentiles in Romans 9–11, Paul makes no reference or allusion to his collection project or trip to Jerusalem. Neither does he mention, explicitly or implicitly, those Old Testament prophecies. Without evidence, it is hard to correlate Paul's collection project to the eschatological fulfillment of Old Testament prophecies.[164]

Referring to the collection, Paul employs the noun κοινωνία three times (2 Cor 8:4; 9:13; Rom 15:26) and the verb κοινωνέω once (Rom 15:27).[165] Given the frequent use of the term κοινωνία in connection with the collection, many scholars would agree with Downs's statement that the collection was a "a tangible expression of the mutual relationship shard by Jews and Gentiles through the gracious manifestation of the gospel of Jesus Christ."[166] Surveying the semantic range of the Greek term κοινωνία, Peterman questions even the rendering of κοινωνίαν τινὰ ποιήσασθαι (Rom 15:26) with "make a contribution," a common translation in all English Bibles, and prefers to take it as "establish a fellowship."[167] Along these lines, Paul's collection project may have been implemented mainly for the unity of Christian communities around the Mediterranean world. In fact, the collection demonstrated the presence of active relationship between Paul's churches in the Diaspora and the church at Jerusalem. This ecumenical concern is also apparent from Paul's request of the Romans to pray that "my service (διακονία) for Jerusalem may prove acceptable to the saints" (Rom 15:31).

While the term κοινωνία reflects social unity and solidarity, it also signifies a concrete manifestation of the social relationship, e.g., monetary assistance or financial partnership.[168] Cranfield thus regards the word κοινωνία as denoting "the concrete contribution collected" through

163. Munck, *Paul and the Salvation of Mankind*, 301.

164. For more arguments against the eschatological interpretation, see Downs, *Offering of the Gentiles*, 6–9.

165. The Greek term basically means "close association involving mutual interests and sharing, association, communion, fellowship, close relationship" among the people. BDAG, s.v. "κοινωνία."

166. Downs, *Offering of the Gentiles*, 15–16.

167. Peterman, "Romans 15:26," 457–60.

168. Besides the meaning of "close association" or "close relationship," the term also denotes "sign of fellowship, proof of brotherly unity, even gift, contribution." BDAG, s.v. "κοινωνία."

Paul's ministry.[169] On this understanding, Horrell proposes that the fundamental reason for the collection was "the desire to relieve the poverty of the poor among the saints in Jerusalem."[170] Proponents of this view usually put emphasis on the Jewish background of almsgiving for Paul's collection project. Watson argues that inadequate attention to the Jewish background has resulted in "an imbalanced and often overly politicized picture of the collection,"[171] and then seeks to understand the collection from the perspective of the Jewish traditions of caring for and giving to the poor.[172] To be sure, the collection project of Paul was deeply indebted to the long-established custom of Jewish communities, the act of charity for the poor. Particularly, the phrase εἰς τοὺς πτωχοὺς ("for the poor") with the partitive genitive τῶν ἁγίων ("among the saints") intimates that Paul was concerned especially for those who were destitute (Rom 15:26). Paul's collection ministry was done to relieve the poverty in the Jerusalem church.

It should be noted that the above "three perceptible directions of interest"—eschatological, ecumenical, and charitable—were not mutually exclusive; rather, "they were so welded together that each was presented as essentially involved in the other."[173] Paul's collection concomitantly symbolized the eschatological phenomena of the gentile piety and pilgrimage, attested to the unity of Jews and gentiles in Christ, and supplied material resources for the needy in Jerusalem. In a sense, deeply theological ideas and purely practical concerns are intertwined in the collection ministry. Thus, noticing the theological language of 2 Corinthians 8–9, Horrell perceptively argues that "an essentially material act—the giving of money—is of itself profoundly theological."[174]

Notably, Paul describes to the Corinthian believers, the donors, a prospective response of the Jerusalem believers, the recipients of the donation. After receiving the gift from the Corinthians, believers in

169. Cranfield, *Epistle to the Romans*, 772. See also Dunn, *Romans 9–16*, 874–75.

170. Horrell, "Paul's Collection," 75–76.

171. Watson, "Paul's Collection," 1–5.

172. Watson, "Paul's Collection," 123–29.

173. Nickle, *Collection*, 100.

174. Horrell, "Paul's Collection," 76–77. Horrell calls this concept "a materialist theology," by which he means "a theology which engages with social, economic and political realities, a theology which insists that the gospel has to do with the whole of life, including the material conditions and socio-economic relationships in which people are enmeshed" (79).

Jerusalem will be "in their prayers on your behalf, longing for you" (2 Cor 9:14). Longing in prayer must be sure evidence for a significant relationship between believers. Then, what would cause the prayerful longing in the Jerusalem church? Paul says, "because of the surpassing grace of God in you" (2 Cor 9:14). Considering the *inclusio* construction with 2 Cor 8:1 ("grace of God"), the "surpassing grace of God" denotes "God's gracious action in inspiring generous giving (cf. vv. 6–8) and in supplying the resources to give (vv. 8–11)."[175] Namely, on account of the generous collection from the Corinthians, the believers in Jerusalem will long for them in prayer. Paul's collection ministry represents a reciprocal, significant relationship between Paul's churches and the Jerusalem church or, in a way, between gentile Christians and Jewish Christians.

Besides the gentile-Jewish relationship, the collection project entailed a communal networking and collaboration among Paul's churches. For example, as discussed above, the local churches in Macedonia sent their emissaries to Paul to join the the apostle's collection ministry (2 Cor 8:23). They were "messengers of the churches" (ἀπόστολοι ἐκκλησιῶν). Who were "the churches" that have been represented by the messengers? Most commentators identify them as the local churches in Macedonia, the place where Paul was writing 2 Corinthians. Paul's financial project must have brought the churches/house churches in Macedonia together to collect contributions and to elect the messengers. Certainly, the collection for the Jerusalem church enhanced the relationship and unity of the local churches.

Thrall makes an elaborate and interesting argument: "It is more likely that the envoys were appointed either by the churches of Asia or by those of Macedonia, or, perhaps, by the two groups in combination, whereby the election took place in the Asian congregations and was then confirmed in the Macedonian churches."[176] If Thrall's reconstruction was what really happened in the selection of the envoys, it could reasonably be said that significant activities of cooperation took place not only among the local churches but also among the churches beyond the local area. The joint commission of local envoys unmistakably testifies the inter-church collaboration through collection ministry of Paul.

175. Harris, *Second Epistle to the Corinthians*, 658. In 2 Cor 8:1, the "Grace of God" denotes the grace given to the Macedonian church in connection with the collection for the Jerusalem church: "even in a great affliction, their abundance of joy and their deep poverty overflowed in the wealth of their generous giving" (2 Cor 8:2).

176. Thrall, *Second Epistle of the Corinthians*, 560–61.

The magnitude of the trans-congregational involvement in the project is well attested in the book of Acts and Paul's letters. From multiple provinces and cities, Paul had the following funds and/or delegates:

> from the Galatian region (1 Cor 16:1) we hear of Derbe (Acts 20:4) and Lystra (Acts 20:4); from Macedonia (2 Cor 8:1–5; 9:2, 4) we hear of Berea (Acts 20:4), Thessalonica (20:4) and Philippi (cf. Acts 16:16 and 20:6; an inference about the "we" sections of Acts; see Nickle, 68); from Achaia we hear of Corinth (Rom 15:26; 1 Cor 16:1–4); from Mysia and Lydia we hear of Ephesus (Acts 20:4) and perhaps Troas (Acts 20:5–6); it is possible that funds came from Tyre (Acts 21:3–4), Ptolemais (Acts 21:7), and from both Cyprus and Caesarea (Acts 21:16). It is even possible that funds were collected from Rome (cf. Rom 12:13; 15:26 with 2 Cor 8:4; 9:13; and Rom 1:13 with 2 Cor 9:6–10).[177]

Undoubtedly, Paul's collection for the Jerusalem church was an international ministry. Its whole process must have helped unite many New Testament churches across the Mediterranean world. It occasioned, first, communal actions among the house churches in many cities, second, trans-local collaborations among the Pauline churches in different regions, and lastly, the cooperation between Pauline churches and the Jerusalem church. The wide and substantial effect of Paul's collection ministry on New Testament church relationships cannot be overemphasized.

Conclusion

Chapter 3 examined Paul's partnership ministry through financial assistance, i.e., charity in local churches, financial aid for Paul's missions, and collection projects for the saints in Jerusalem. These economic activities among the earliest churches were not a novelty. Many of their features took inspiration from the social convention of the Greco-Roman world such as the financial practice of voluntary associations and, most importantly, from the long-established Jewish traditions of community and charity.

It was argued that the act of financial assistance was an embodiment of the church in communal relations and collaborations. That is, Paul's plan for the Spanish mission supposed a unitary and cooperative action of the churches/house churches in Rome. Paul requested for the

177. McKnight, "Collection for the Saints," 143–44.

Romans to help his way (προπέμπω) to Spain (Rom 15:24). It was like "a missionary of the church in Antioch applying for a grant from the church in Rome."[178] To be more specific, the Spanish mission project implicated not only a work of Paul's missionary team but also a trans-local collaboration of various Christian communities—the church at Corinth, where Paul was staying and writing the letter; the church at Cenchrea, where Phoebe set out from; the church at Rome, whose support Paul was asking for; and the church at Antioch, which originally commissioned Paul for missionary journeys.

As every act of charity "clarifies and reinforces its social boundary," financial assistance among the churches must have enhanced the consciousness of belonging to one body in Christ.[179] Conversely, the common faith in Christ and the body of Christ promoted charitable acts among fellow Christians. Either way, it is certain that the early churches' financial assistance for the poor and for Christian missions reveal the spirit of love and cooperation among the New Testament churches—Pauline and non-Pauline, gentile and Jewish.

178. Kloha, "Trans-Congregational Church," 183.

179. Barclay, "Money and Meetings," 121.

4

Collaboration through Communicative Activities

ALTHOUGH A COMMUNICATIVE ACTIVITY—e.g., letter-writing, visitation, or conference—is not an act of collaboration per se, it usually indicates the presence of some relationship between the parties involved. People communicate often to build up a constructive relationship, and an effective communication is able to accomplish the goal, mutual understanding and cooperation between the people. This was true of Paul's ministry, which included many occasions of communication with local churches, church leaders, and coworkers. The vigor of communication in Paul's ministry suggests that Paul's churches were in dynamic relationship with one another and with other non-Pauline churches as well. This chapter, therefore, explores the communicative activities of Paul and traces therein the cooperative nature of New Testament church relationship.

Communications and networks in Paul's ministry bore a great deal of resemblance to those of the first-century world. A review of social relations in antiquity will be helpful to understand how Paul and the earliest churches established their communal link and expanded their boundary of fellowship. After this contextual study, the subsequent sections investigate the relevant texts in Paul's letters and the book of Acts to ascertain early church networks through Paul's letters, visitations, and church conferences. They will determine the intensity of New Testament church relationship and partnership mediated by Paul's ministry.

Greco-Roman and Jewish Contexts

Early churches, in their expansion and networking across the Mediterranean, owed much to "the travel structures and communication mediums that were already in place in the first cent. CE."[1] Thus, this section surveys the first-century context in which the Christians communicated and associated with one another. The first subsection overviews the ancient travel and letter-writing in New Testament times. The second subsection briefly discusses the interrelationship of Greco-Roman voluntary associations. Most importantly, the final subsection reviews the social network of Jewish communities in the Diaspora.

Travel and Letters in the Greco-Roman World

Acts of the Apostles, the chronicle of early church missions, is "the record of the geographical spread of the Gospel message by land and by sea."[2] Accordingly, one of the most prominent aspects of Paul's ministry was that Paul and his coworkers were constantly on the road for their missionary works. Traveling was an indispensable element for their missions. It was not unique to Christian missions; traveling was a common phenomenon for the life and work of the first-century Mediterranean population. Casson summarily describes the extent of ancient travel: "The Mediterranean world of the first two centuries A.D., then, was bigger than it had ever been before. . . . The roads and sea ways were now thronged with traders in larger numbers than the Greek world had ever known, with armies, bureaucrats, couriers of the government post, and just plain tourists."[3] Scholars of antiquity agree that the mobility of Greco-Roman society was more intensive and widespread than has usually been thought.[4]

1. Blumell, "Travel and Communication," 652.

2. Rapske, "Acts, Travel and Shipwreck," 3. Acts 1:8 outlines the geographical spread of the gospel from Jerusalem and Judea (chapters 1–7), to Samaria (8:4–25), Caesarea (8:40; 10:1–48), Damascus (9:10–22), Antioch (11:19–26), and throughout the Mediterranean world to Rome (13:1—28:31).

3. Casson, *Travel in the Ancient World*, 127.

4. For example, Blumell argues that "it is becoming increasingly evident that people in NT times were more mobile and traveled more extensively than was once thought" ("Travel and Communication," 652). Also, Hezser claims that "mobility was therefore much more wide-spread than commonly assumed and had a significant impact on many aspects of ancient society" (*Jewish Travel in Antiquity*, 5).

The surge of travel and transportation owed much to the *Pax Romana* and the highly developed Roman road systems. Epictetus, a Greek philosopher from Hierapolis, Phrygia, once stated that "Caesar has obtained for us a profound peace. There are neither wars nor battles, nor great robberies nor piracies, but we may travel at all hours, and sail from east to west."[5] In line with this statement, a tombstone inscription in Hierapolis states that Flavius Zeuxis, a merchant of the city and a contemporary of Paul, traveled from Asia Minor to Italy as many as seventy-two times over the years of his business career.[6] Exceptional as it may be, his trip reveals the magnitude of inter-regional travel in the first-century Greco-Roman world.

According to the calculation of ORBIS, the Stanford Geospatial Network Model of the Roman World, the journey of Flavius Zeuxis from Lycus Valley via Cape Malea to Rome took 23 to 25 days, covering about 1,450 miles.[7] Thus, the total mileage traveled by the Hierapolis merchant amounts to more than 200,000 miles, considerably exceeding the travel of Paul who had been on "journeys frequently" (2 Cor 11:26).[8] By the time of the New Testament, the Romans had built "a vast network of roads which connected Roman Italy with its provinces."[9] That is, all the cities and provinces mentioned in the New Testament were connected together by a solid system of roads. The connection and mobility left a significant impact on the social network of people and religious groups in the first-century Mediterranean world.

Why did the ancient people travel? Casson suggests "five basic motives for travel: people left home on business, either their own or the

5. Epictetus, *Discourses* 3.13.9.

6. The inscription above the tomb entrance reads: Φλαούϊος Ζεῦξις ἐργαστὴς πλεύσας ὑπὲρ Μαλέαν εἰς Ἰταλίαν πλόας ἑβδομήκοντα δύο ("Flavius Zeuxis, merchant, who sailed seventy-two trips around Cape Malea to Italy"). See *CIG* 3920. Cape Malea is the southern tip of Peloponnesus peninsula of Greece.

7. ORBIS has been developed by the interdisciplinary project of Stanford University to reconstruct "the time cost and financial expense associated with a wide range of different types of travel in antiquity. The model is based on a simplified version of the giant network of cities, roads, rivers and sea lanes that framed movement across the Roman Empire." See ORBIS, http://orbis.stanford.edu/orbis2012/#.

8. In 2 Cor 11:26, Paul recalls that he had "journeys many times, [in] dangers of rivers, dangers from robbers, . . . dangers among false brothers." Schnabel offers a detailed itinerary of Paul's missionary journeys and calculates Paul's travel mileage to be at least 15,500 miles, about 8,700 miles of that by land. See Schnabel, *Early Christian Mission*, 1125–26, 1197–99, 1288.

9. Hezser, *Jewish Travel in Antiquity*, 4.

government's, for their health, to go on pilgrimage to an oracle or shrine, to be present at well-known festivals, and in a very few cases, to see the world."[10] Religious motives were prominent particularly for Jews and Christians.[11] In New Testament times, Jews of both Palestine and the Diaspora traveled to Jerusalem, particularly, on the three major festivals—Passover, Pentecost, and Tabernacles. Religious leaders such as patriarchs and rabbis occasionally made tours to various Jewish communities in Judea and in the Diaspora. As for Paul and his coworkers, travels were made mostly for the purpose of evangelistic and pastoral missions. In addition, they also made trips to Jerusalem to support those in financial need and to cooperate with the Jerusalem apostles in the gospel ministry.

In the Greco-Roman world "the most common form of long-distance correspondence was epistolary."[12] The importance of letters in ancient communication is attested simply by the great portion of epistolary writings in the New Testament. It is to be noted that the New Testament letters, notwithstanding their forms and styles, never moved via "a kind of sacred superhighway" as if they were separate from the letters of the Greco-Roman society.[13] New Testament epistles were part of the first-century social conventions. Most scholars agree that the New Testament and early Christian letters should be approached and understood from the perspective of the history of letter-writing in Greco-Roman antiquity. In his influential volume, *The New Testament in Its Literary Environment*, Aune identifies four major literary types in the New Testament—gospels, acts, letters, and apocalypse—and compares them to the ancient Greco-Roman literature—biographical, historical, epistolary, and apocalyptic writings.[14] Regarding letters, he argues that "early Christian letters have many formal similarities to the ancient papyrus letters recovered from Egypt . . . Yet while nearly all the papyrus letters are relatively brief, many early Christian letters are quite lengthy."[15]

10. Casson, *Travel in the Ancient World*, 147.

11. The religious motives were not limited to Jews and Christians. Those who worshiped Greek and Roman deities also traveled "regularly to particular shrines or temples to venerate and invoke certain gods and goddesses." Blumell, "Travel and Communication," 653.

12. Blumell, "Travel and Communication," 654.

13. Epp, "New Testament Papyrus Manuscripts," 38.

14. Aune, *New Testament in Its Literary Environment*, 13.

15. Aune, *New Testament in Its Literary Environment*, 160.

By the first century BC, rhetoric emerged as an important element for the Greco-Roman letter-writing, especially among the educated. Cicero, the great Roman orator a century before Paul, began to write *literary* letters: rhetorical expressions adorned the letters; topics such as philosophy and ethics were discussed; brief and simple letters grew longer and more sophisticated; and this type of letters were often intended to have several addressees or multiple readers.[16] Although Pauline epistles resemble the ancient common letters written on certain occasions, they are far from ordinary letters. Paul's letters seem to stand "in the middle of this stream of gradual transformation."[17] Written in response to various practical issues of his churches, Paul's letters teem with rhetorical skills and philosophical/theological thoughts of a cultured writer in the Hellenistic world. Rather than the letters of simple correspondence, Paul's letters were written with a view to giving some instructions and admonitions to Christian communities.

For the study of ancient letters, Stowers proposes a *functional* approach, that is, to understand the letters of antiquity as a means of performing different social functions in the contemporary context. He convincingly argues:

> When interpreters must rely solely on reconstructing a historical occasion for letters from clues within the letters themselves, they are caught in a vicious circle. The only basis for an interpretation of the letter is information derived from an interpretation of the letter. If, however, researchers can show through the comparative study of Greco-Roman letters that a New Testament letter follows or adapts certain conventions, is a certain type, or functions in a certain way, then the researcher has introduced an outside control over that vicious circle.[18]

In short, for a historical reconstruction, it is important to know the type/function of the ancient letter as much as to know its content information. Social types and contexts behind the letters matter the most in interpreting and understanding the ancient letters.

16. Capes et al., *Rediscovering Paul*, 55. The authors further say that Seneca, another famous Roman orator, followed and furthered the pattern of the literary epistle undertaken by Cicero, "blurring the lines between the bare everyday letter and the published rhetorical letters."

17. Capes et al., *Rediscovering Paul*, 55.

18. Stowers, *Letter Writing*, 25.

Three types of social relationships were prevalent in the Greco-Roman society: (1) between superiors and subordinates represented by client-patron relationship; (2) between equals/friends; and (3) among the household members.[19] In conjunction with these three social relationships, Stowers also presents six categories of ancient letters according to their functions: (1) letters of friendship; (2) family letters; (3) letters of praise and blame; (4) letters of exhortation; (5) letters of mediation or recommendation; and (6) accusing, apologetic, and accounting letters.[20] The three types of social relationship were important to the development of early Christian communities, and so "most Christian letter writing is understandable within these contexts."[21] Likewise, all of the above six functions of Hellenistic letters are observable, explicitly or implicitly, in the letters of Paul.

One important aspect of the ancient letters is the role of letter-carriers. Head examines the sixty-eight volumes of the *Oxyrhynchus Papyri*, focusing on the forty letters with identifiable carrier name(s). Concerning the role of letter-carriers, he concludes that "when named and identified within the letter, the letter-carrier frequently supplements the written communication with some oral supplement."[22] In addition, he also notices "letter-carriers bringing other goods or supplies alongside a letter."[23] This papyrological evidence fits well into the role of Paul's co-workers who acted not only as Paul's letter-carriers but also as his representatives to local Christian communities.

Socio-Religious Networks of Voluntary Associations

Voluntary associations represented the whole texture of the Greco-Roman society and culture. The evidence is widespread: numerous inscriptions are extant "from virtually every locale in the ancient world and from every period from the fourth century BCE to the later Roman Empire."[24] The

19. Stowers, *Letter Writing*, 27.

20. Under the category of letters of exhortation, he distinguishes subtypes: (1) paraenetic letters (exhortation and dissuasion); (2) letters of advice; (3) protreptic letters (exhortation to a way of life); (4) letters of admonition; (5) letters of rebuke; (6) letters of reproach; and (7) letters of consolation.

21. Stowers, *Letter Writing*, 31.

22. Head, "Named Letter-Carriers," 279.

23. Head, "Named Letter-Carriers," 297.

24. Kloppenborg, "Collegia and *Thiasoi*," 17.

majority of the inscriptions describe "the voting of honors for their members and the inscribing of membership lists," suggesting that "beyond cultic engagements and the pleasures of drinking and dining, associations afforded their members with a sense of belonging, honor, and achievement."[25] Certainly, the concern of voluntary associations was to increase the benefit of their members through communal actions and relations. The bond of intimacy is expressed in their use of language: "father" or "mother" was used to designate their leader or patron; "brothers" denoted the members; and the voluntary association was called *koinon* or its cognates.[26]

Trans-local links between associations are found typically in relation to immigrant societies. The first-century world saw innumerable people leaving their countries for various reasons and settling down in foreign lands. The foreign settlers usually kept connections with their homeland, continuing their native culture and religion. As introduced in the previous chapter, a Tyrian association in Puteoli (the port of Rome) asked the city of Tyre for financial assistance, and the Tyrian senate responded by having another Tyrian association in Rome send the necessary fund to Puteoli.[27] This event demonstrates the presence of translocal links between associations "not only of commercial, but of social, moral, and religious interest, involving mutual obligations."[28]

The cult of the Thracian goddess, Bendis, found in the island of Salamis reveals that there existed two Bendis associations in the area.[29] Being separate and distinctive, they had a relationship with each other. Both associations "assumed the responsibility for the conduct of the *Bendideia* [the festival of Bendis] in a remarkable display of cooperation between a citizen association in Athens and a metic association in the Piraeus."[30] An inscription from the sanctuary of Egyptian gods in Thessalonica introduces that Sarapis, an Egyptian god, appeared to Xenainetos in a dream and gave an order to establish the cult of Sarapis and Isis in Opus, a town on the Euboean Gulf.[31] It may be that the Egyptian cult started

25. Kloppenborg and Ascough, *Greco-Roman Associations*, 6.

26. Ascough, "Greco-Roman Philosophic," 16.

27. *CIG* 5853. See chapter 2, section "Greco-Roman and Jewish Contexts."

28. Ascough, "Translocal Relationships," 230.

29. One was based on the acropolis (Athens) and the other was at the harbor (Praeus). See *IG* II2 1317, 1317b and *SEG* 59.152, 155.

30. Kloppenborg and Ascough, *Greco-Roman Associations*, 10.

31. *IG* X/2 255. The Euboean Gulf is an arm of the Aegean Sea between the Greek mainland and the island of Euboea.

in Thessalonica, and later spread to Opus, where the story of Xenainetos's dream was inscribed, and a copy was taken back to Thessalonica to become a part of its local tradition.[32] Clearly, there were inter-community relationships between the two associations at Thessalonica and at Opus.

The cult of Dionysos was popular in the province of Asia. As the Asians migrated to Thrace, Macedonia, and Attica, the cult expanded to all over the Mediterranean world.[33] Particularly, the Dionysiac artists—musicians, poets, actors, etc.—formed "one of the longest standing religious associations," enlisting and uniting numerous members in the Roman Empire by means of their wide-ranging travels and contacts.[34] It was a common phenomenon in the Greco-Roman world that traveling troupes of artists moved from one Dionysiac center to another, offering their services.[35] Exploring the inscriptional data on the travel of the Dionysiac artists during the Hellenistic and Roman period, Sophia Aneziri gives a more elaborate argument: "in the Hellenistic period, travel is focused through a number of regional associations of artists, whereas in the Roman empire, . . . eminent artists are designated as belonging to the *oikoumenē* ('the inhabited world' within the boundaries of the Roman empire)."[36] With the changing world of expanding frontiers and the increase of international festivals and travels, the Imperial associations of Dionysus nurtured an awareness of the world-wide horizon, and then "achieved the status of an empire-wide network."[37] By the first century AD, "the local Dionysiac associations probably existed alongside the larger, 'world-wide' guild."[38]

32. Sellew, "Religious Propaganda in Antiquity," 15–20. See also Ascough, *Paul's Macedonian Associations*, 97; and Kloppenborg and Ascough, *Greco-Roman Associations*, 360–61. Commenting on this event, Koester argues that "the story is a typical example for the missionary style of the Egyptian religion, where the god himself initiates the movement of his cult to new areas." Koester, *Paul and His World*, 51.

33. Kloppenborg and Ascough, *Greco-Roman Associations*, 394–95.

34. Ascough, *Paul's Macedonian Associations*, 98. In those days, artists—such as poets, musicians, dancers, actors, etc.—were needed for the staging performances of drama and music in the setting of Greek festivals and games. Most of them organized themselves into certain associations, which were often called "Guilds of the Artists devoted to Dionysus" (Σύνοδοι τῶν περὶ Διόνυσον τὲνιτῶν). Aneziri, "World Travelers," 218.

35. Wilson, "Voluntary Associations," 3.

36. Aneziri, "World Travelers," 217.

37. Aneziri, "World Travelers," 217.

38. Wilson, "Voluntary Associations," 99.

Epicurus, among the many Greek philosophers, is considered to be the first who "intentionally set out to form a philosophical association."[39] DeWitt claims that Epicureanism was "the first missionary philosophy" and "the first world philosophy."[40] Epicurus established his school "the Garden" in Athens and placed much emphasis on communal life and friendship based on a kinship model. The Epicureans hence sought to practice the teaching of love and forgiveness for one another. As "missionary" associations, however, their activities were not confined to their school premises only; "every convert everywhere became a missionary," reaching out to places near and far.[41] Accordingly, Epicurean schools multiplied throughout the Mediterranean world with many adherents. Also, Epicurus and the Epicureans were busy in writing letters to new converts and to fellow associations in distant lands. The letters were written with a view to propagating the philosophy of Epicurus and strengthening the network of his followers around the Mediterranean basin, and the letters were probably read aloud at communal gatherings.[42] The Epicureans, at least apparently, bore a striking resemblance to the Christians. In this sense, "the first missionary philosophy," Epicureanism, may have been "a natural preparation for the first missionary religion," Christianity.[43]

Socio-Religious Networks of the Jewish Diaspora

According to Strabo, a Greek geographer and historian of the late first century BC, "it was not easy to discover a place in the entire world where Jews were not to be found."[44] Josephus similarly wrote, "Now these Jews are already gotten into all cities; and it is hard to find a place in the habitable earth that hath not admitted this tribe of men, and is not possessed by it."[45] Allowing for their hyperbolic and propagandistic nature, the statements still convey a truth about the demography of Jewish population. According to Claussen, by the first century AD, while 2.5 to 2.8 million Jews were in Palestine, more than twice the number (5 to 6 million)

39. Ascough, "Greco-Roman Philosophic," 7.
40. DeWitt, *Epicurus and His Philosophy*, 26.
41. DeWitt, *Epicurus and His Philosophy*, 28.
42. Glad, *Paul and Philodemus*, 175.
43. DeWitt, *Epicurus and His Philosophy*, 31.
44. Roscher, "Status of the Jews in the Middle Ages," 17.
45. Josephus, *Ant.* 14.7.2.

were living in the Diaspora, scattered all over the Roman Empire.[46] It is reasonable to assume the ubiquity of Jewish community throughout the first-century Greco-Roman world.

The ubiquitous Jewish community cannot be discussed apart from the 'synagogue,'[47] of which essence is well explained by S. Safrai:

> But the main factor in the significance of the synagogue was that it was regarded as the assembly of the local Jewish community, giving expression to the civic and communal spirit of the people. The word synagogue should not be taken as meaning just 'meeting-house.' It stands for the people, the community, the congregation and the place where they assembled.[48]

Accordingly, besides worship and prayer, various public and community meetings were held at the synagogue, including communal banquets, judicial proceedings, political meetings, conferences for decision-making, and so on.

Josephus tells of a community meeting that took place in the synagogue of Tiberius: "they all came into the Proseucha [προσευχή]. It was a large edifice; and capable of receiving a great number of people."[49] The meeting was convened to debate over the conflict with the Roman regime and continued for two days. Although there were some leading figures in the meeting, it proceeded quite democratically: "the multitude were not pleased with what was said . . . and had certainly gone into a tumult . . . put off their council till the next day."[50] In a word, the Jewish synagogue was "the rallying-point for community life in the towns and villages of the Land of Israel and the Diaspora."[51] It shaped the core of Jewish identity in antiquity.

Undoubtedly, there were multiple synagogues in a large Jewish community, and those synagogues usually constituted a centralized organization representing and governing the whole Jewish community of the city. The *Letter of Aristeas* records an event whereby the Jewish community of Alexandria approved the translation of the Hebrew Scriptures into the

46. Claussen, "Meeting, Community, Synagogue," 144.

47. In the first-century Greco-Roman world, the Jewish synagogue went under several names. Most prevalent and important of them were συναγωγή and προσευχή,.

48. Safrai, "Synagogue," 908.

49. Josephus, *Life* 54.

50. Josephus, *Life* 54.

51. Josephus, *Life* 909.

Greek Septuagint. Aristeas here designates the Jewish community in the ruling as "*politeuma*" (πολιτεύμα).[52] The Alexandrian *politeuma* was "a quasi-autonomous civic corporation . . . exercising administrative and judicial power over its own members independently of the municipal authorities of the city."[53] The *politeuma* was led by the "*gerousia*" (γερουσία), a classic term signifying the "council of elders."[54] The *gerousia* was composed of the "*archons*" (ἄρχων)—the leaders from various synagogues in the community—and entitled to direct the community's affairs as a "supra-synagogal council."[55]

Three Greek inscriptions found in Bernice of Cyrenaica corroborate the finding of the Alexandrian Jewish community.[56] The first inscription, dated to 8–6 BC, is a resolution passed by the Jews of Bernice in honor of a community benefactor.[57] It shows that the Jewish community was organized as a *politeuma* and led by *archons*, as with the case of Alexandria. The second inscription, dated to 24–25 AD, records a communal vote—casting white stones—to honor a Roman official in charge of the district.[58] Dating to 56 AD, the last one refers to a community resolution commemorating financial contributions made by nine members for the repair of the synagogue building.[59] These three inscriptions all show how the Jews of Bernice dealt with their community affairs collectively through the organized council of elders and its voting process by majority.

In Rome, there were about thirteen synagogues during the Augustan era, and at least five synagogues in the first century AD.[60] Granted, it

52. *Let. Aris.* 310. A parallel passage is found in *Ant.* 12.2.13. Josephus may have appropriated the story for his writing or may have used the same source used by the author of *the Letter of Aristeas.*

53. Smallwood, "Diaspora in the Roman Period," 177.

54. Philo, in *Flaccus* 10, employs this term to represent the "council of elders". Flaccus is alleged to have arrested and killed thirty-eight members of the Jewish *gerousia*, "council of elders."

55. Williams, *Jews in a Graeco-Roman Environment*, 111. See also White, *Building God's House*, 91.

56. See Cohen, *From the Maccabees to the Mishnah*, 104–5; Applebaum, *Jews and Greeks*, 160–67; and Levine, *Ancient Synagogue*, 96–104. For their Greek texts and comments, See Runesson, Binder, and Olsson, *Ancient Synagogue from its Origins*, 163–70.

57. *CIG* 3:5362.

58. *CIG* 3:5361.

59. *CJZ* 72.

60. See Richardson, "Augustan-Era Synagogues," 19–23; Levine, *Ancient Synagogue*, 105–6; and Leon, *Jews of Ancient Rome*, 135–66.

is unusual that among the numerous inscriptions of Jewish catacombs in Rome there is no mention of a centralized organization for those synagogues. It has therefore been a near consensus that the synagogues in Rome were "independent units and only loosely connected with one another" in contrast to the synagogues in Alexandria or in Bernice, where the multiple synagogues constituted one political body, the *politeuma*.[61] On the other hand, however, Philo seems to suggest a communal body of synagogues by using the term *politeia* (πολιτεία) in reference to the Jews in Rome.[62] Josephus always refers to the Jews in Rome as "a single community, acting in a united manner."[63] The Apostle Paul, having arrived at Rome, called together "the leading men of the Jews" (Acts 28:17). Presumably, although not equal to the Alexandrian *politeuma*, "some kind of supra-synagogal structure" might have operated to deal with the issues and challenges common to all Jews residing in Rome.[64]

While the synagogue was a rallying-point of the Jews in the local level, the Temple of Jerusalem was a focal point for all the Jewish communities in the world. The significance of the Temple in the life of the Jews is well attested by their observance of the Jewish law such as Temple tax and pilgrimage to Jerusalem. The half-shekel tax not only provided useful funds for the Temple cultus but also preserved a psychological link with Jerusalem for the Jews in the Diaspora. More importantly, Jerusalem truly turned into the center of the Jewish world each year: Philo states, "thousands of men from thousands of cities streamed to the Temple at every festival, some by land and some by sea, some from the east and the west, some from the north and the south."[65] This Jerusalem event

61. Lampe, "Early Christians," 21.

62. Philo, *Embassy* 157. In this regard, Applebaum argues that Philo appears to convey a notion of the *politeuma* in Alexandria by the term πολιτεία ("Organization of the Jewish Communities," 499).

63. Williams, *Jews in a Graeco-Roman Environment*, 119.

64. Williams, *Jews in a Graeco-Roman Environment*, 119.

65. Philo, *Spec. Laws* 1.69. In similar words, Josephus describes the scene: "an immense multitude ran [to Jerusalem] together, out of Galilee, and Idumea, and Jericho, and Perea, that was beyond Jordan" (*J.W.* 2.3.1). Luke's account in Acts 2 is more specific about the places from which the pilgrims came: "there were Jews dwelling in Jerusalem, devout men, from every nation . . . Parthians and Medes and Elamites, and residents of Mesopotamia, Judea and Cappadocia, Pontus and Asia, Phrygia and Pamphylia, Egypt and the districts of Libya around Cyrene, and visitors from Rome, both Jews and proselytes, Cretans and Arabs—we hear them in our own tongues speaking of the mighty deeds of God" (Acts 2:5–11).

was characteristic of the Jews: "such mass international pilgrimage is not attested for any other cult in the Roman empire."[66]

When the pilgrims gathered in Jerusalem, they had opportunities to have fellowship and celebration with one another from various parts of the world. Both Josephus and Philo proudly comment on the friendly atmosphere of the Jerusalem festivals.[67] An inscription from a pre-70 AD synagogue in Jerusalem shows that the synagogue provided traveling Jews with accommodation and food: "Theodotus . . . built this synagogue for the reading of the law and the teaching of commandments, as well as the guest house and the rooms and the water supplies, as a lodging for those coming from abroad."[68] The local synagogues in Jerusalem served as centers of hospitality where the pilgrim travelers could stay comfortably and exchange various information and advice. The synagogue functioned as "a kind of liaison office between a certain community in the Diaspora and the local community in Jerusalem."[69]

The socio-religious bond between Jerusalem and the Diaspora was further demonstrated in the jurisdiction of Jerusalem authority over the synagogues scattered over the Empire. One of the most important and common rulings was the proclamation of the New Moon and the month of intercalation, which took place in the court of the Jerusalem Temple.[70]

66. Goodman, "Pilgrimage Economy of Jerusalem," 61. It was unique because "only Jews insisted (at least in theory) both that only one Temple was a valid place for sacrifices and that all adult male devotees of the cult were duty bound to make regular obeisance there."

67. Josephus records that "let them . . . maintain a friendly correspondence with one another by such meetings and feastings together . . . acquaintance will be maintained . . . by seeing and talking with one another, and so renewing the memorials of this union" (*Ant.* 4.8.7). Philo describes the events as "forming a friendship with those hitherto unknown, but now initiated by boldness and a desire to honor God, and forming a combination of actions and a union of dispositions so as to join in sacrifices and libations to the most complete confirmation of mutual good will" (*Spec. Laws* 1.69–70).

68. *CIJ* 2.1404.

69. Rosenfeld and Menirav, "Ancient Synagogue as an Economic Center," 262–63.

70. Every two or three years, the court determined that a month should be added to correct for the difference between the lunar calendar of 354 days and the solar year of 365 days. Also, month by month, the decision of the New Moon was made in the court and transmitted to all the Jewish communities around the world. According to the decision, then, the Jews were able to observe their feast-days and read the right portion of the Torah. See Safrai, "Relations between the Diaspora and the Land of Israel," 206–7.

The decision was communicated to all the major Jewish communities by sending envoys and letters. The rabbinic literature contains many stories of such envoys, who visited Jewish communities and supervised the implementation of the laws and decrees.[71] Acts 9:2 records that Paul was sent to the synagogues at Damascus as an envoy of the Jerusalem court in order to arrest the "heretical" followers of Jesus in the city. Justin Martyr, criticizing the Jews, reports that "you [the Jews] selected and sent out from Jerusalem chosen men through all the land to tell that the godless heresy of the Christians had sprung up."[72] Jerusalem exerted great religious influence on the Jews of the Diaspora; as such, intensive links were maintained between the diasporan Jews and their homeland. The social and religious links of the Jews had much bearing on the earliest church, which emerged in the context of Jews and Judaism. In a much similar fashion, Paul and others were sent out to "the Gentile believers in Antioch, Syria, and Cilicia" as the envoys and letter-carriers of the Jerusalem church (Acts 15:23).

Collaboration through Letters

One of the most common methods of communication in Greco-Roman society was letter-writing. Likewise, writing letters was a significant means of communication in Paul's ministry. He frequently engaged himself in writing letters to his coworkers and churches. In this section, several features of Paul's letters will be discussed in light of their contributions to the building of Christian networks and communities. First, the prevalence and importance of letters in Paul's ministry are discussed. Second, the inclusion of co-senders in his letters is examined to shed light on the reality of partnership ministry. Third, the practice of greetings to or from multiple persons is investigated to understand its effect on interchurch relationships. Fourth, the implication of frequent references to other churches is explored.

71. Although the rabbinic texts (Mishnah, Tosefta, Talmud, etc.) date after the third century AD, most scholars agree that the traditions therein are "a faithful reflection of the idea and practices of rabbinic Judaism before 70 CE." Instone-Brewer, *Traditions of the Rabbis*, 1–2.

72. Justin Martyr, *Dial.* 17.

Paul's Letter-Writing

Eusebius wrote that "there flourished many learned men in the Church at that time, whose letters to each other have been preserved and are easily accessible. . . . We have been able to gather from that library material for our present work."[73] It seems that there was plenty of letter-writing in the days of early church. The importance of letter-writing is apparent from the fact that twenty-one of the twenty-seven New Testament writings take the form of letters. Two of the others, Acts of the Apostles and Revelation, include a number of letters within themselves. It is not too much to say that the New Testament consists of ancient letters. Among the twenty-one epistolary writings, as many as thirteen are ascribed to Paul. However, besides the thirteen, Paul certainly wrote more letters, which are no longer extant.

Paul preached the gospel in Corinth during his second missionary journey (Acts 18). For a year and half, Paul stayed there laying a foundation for the church, and then returned to Antioch. Following up the Corinthian ministry, Paul wrote them a letter, the so-called "previous letter" (1 Cor 5:9), which has been lost. While staying in Ephesus during the third missionary journey (Acts 19), upon receiving a report from the Corinthian church (1 Cor 16:17), the apostle sent a reply letter, which is 1 Corinthians. Probably after a short "painful visit" to Corinth (2 Cor 2:1), Paul subsequently wrote them out of anguish a "tearful letter" (2 Cor 2:3–4), which did not survive either. The last letter to the church, 2 Corinthians, was written after his companion Titus came back to Paul with positive news from Corinth. Paul wrote at least four or more letters to the Corinthian church. Also, it is reasonable to assume that during that period the Corinthians sent letters or messages to Paul at least four times.[74]

First Thessalonians is one of the earliest letters of Paul.[75] However, although not mentioned in the letter or in any other documents, "it is quite possible that Paul had written to them when he first sent Timothy to them and it is highly probable that they in return wrote him for

73. Eusebius, *Hist. eccl.* 6.20.

74. Paul received a report of church factions from Chloe's household (1 Cor 1:11), a report of sexual immorality (1 Cor 5:1), and another report of division at the Lord's Supper (1 Cor 11:18). Stephanas, Fortunatus, and Achaicus visited Paul possibly with a letter from Corinth, where the Corinthians raised a wide range of questions (cf. περὶ δέ phrases at 7:25; 8:1; 12:1; 16:1, 12).

75. Bruce, *1 and 2 Thessalonians*, iiiiv–iiiv.

advice."[76] When Timothy returned with the information about the Thessalonians and possibly with their letter, Paul responded to them with 1 Thessalonians. Therefore, the possibility cannot be ruled out that there had been a letter prior to 1 Thessalonians. In Col 4:16, Paul gives an instruction to the readers: "Now when this epistle is read among you, see that it is read also in the church of the Laodiceans, and that you likewise read the epistle from Laodicea." What was this "letter from Laodicea"? Most scholars agree that the phrase does not literally mean "letter *from* Laodicea," written by the Laodicean church to Paul or to the Colossians.[77] Given that verse 4:16 is a reminder of the circulation of letters, it is most probable that Paul here refers to a letter, which had been written by Paul himself to the Laodiceans, and now to be passed on to the Colossians. In short, Paul wrote quite a few letters to meet the various needs of Christian communities.

Funk introduces the concept of "apostolic *parousia*" in Paul's ministry, which signifies the presence of apostolic authority and power to his congregations. According to him, the apostolic *parousia* takes "three different but related aspects," i.e., "the aspect of the letter, the apostolic emissary, and his own personal presence."[78] Further, he presents an order of importance among the three aspects: "Since Paul gives precedence to the oral word, the written word will not function as a primary medium of his apostleship."[79] However, as Llewelyn and Kearsley question, why did Paul write such long letters if the function of emissaries and oral words was superior to that of written letters?[80] Mitchell thus doubts about the hierarchy of presence assumed by Funk: "The evidence indicates that there may have been no fixed hierarchy of presence, but that in each situation Paul chose which of the three—a letter, an envoy, a personal visit (or some combination)—would be most effective."[81]

It is unlikely that Paul conceived of his letter-writing as a substitute for his personal visit or sending an envoy. The primary reason for Paul's letter-writing was that he regarded it to be most pertinent and effective in the situation. In this light, Paul's "tearful letter" (2 Cor 2:3–4) may have

76. Malherbe, "Did the Thessalonians Write to Paul?," 255.

77. See Moo, *Colossians and Philemon*, 350–51 and Wright, *Colossians and Philemon*, 164–65.

78. Funk, "Apostolic *Parousia*, 249.

79. Funk, "Apostolic *Parousia*, 260.

80. Llewelyn and Kearlsey, *New Documents Illustrating Early Christianity*, 52–53.

81. Mitchell, "New Testament Envoys," 642–43.

served what other methods were inept to do. After the "painful visit" (2 Cor 2:1), Paul did not visit Corinth for some time, not because of any outward circumstances, but because of his concerns for the Corinthians. Paul made it clear: "I call God as witness to my soul, that to spare you I came no more to Corinth" (2 Cor 1:23). Instead, he wrote the "tearful letter" to the Corinthians, and it turned out to be very effective, prompting repentance and reconciliation (2 Cor 7:8–9). Paul's letters played a substantial role.

Hezser rightly says that "mobility in and of itself . . . would have had a significant impact on social, economic, cultural, religious, and literary developments in ancient Jewish society."[82] In the same way, the frequent exchange of letters and couriers in Paul's ministry, in and of itself, brought about the close network of Paul's churches, the circle of instruction and fellowship, and decades later, the development of biblical canon. In understanding letters, according to Stowers, "it is more helpful to think of letters in terms of the actions that people performed by means of them."[83] Viewed at this angle, Paul's frequent letter-writing itself seems to tell what the apostle emphasizes the most, that is, relationship, fellowship, and unity among the Christians and Christian communities. Evidence for such emphasis is plentiful also in the lines of his letters, which is to be examined in the following sections.

Co-Senders/Co-Authors

One of the most notable features in Paul's letters is the inclusion of co-senders in his letter-writing. For examples, Paul starts 1 and 2 Thessalonians with the conventional salutation, "Paul, Silvanus, and Timothy, to the church of the Thessalonians" (1 Thess 1:1). Out of the thirteen letters attributed to Paul, eight letters bear one or two names as co-senders.[84] For the proper understanding of this feature, a question needs to be addressed: was the inclusion of co-senders in letters an ordinary custom

82. Hezser, *Jewish Travel in Antiquity*, 3.

83. Stowers, *Letter Writing*, 15.

84. Letters without co-senders are Romans, Ephesians, and three pastoral letters. Those with co-senders are 1 Corinthians (Sosthenes), 2 Corinthians (Timothy), 1 and 2 Thessalonians (Silvanus and Timothy), Philippians (Timothy), Colossians (Timothy), and Philemon (Timothy). Unlike others, Galatians has unspecified co-senders, "all the brothers with me" (Gal 1:2). See Appendix 4 "Paul's Letters: Senders, Receivers, and Persons in Greeting."

in Hellenistic and Roman letter-writing? According to Thiselton, it was "extremely rare in Greek letters apart from Paul's."[85] Byrskog claims that "Greco-Roman letters mention several senders very rarely."[86] However, a more thorough research by Fulton shows that "the inclusion of co-senders in the prescripts of the Pauline letters was not an innovation in letter writing but rather a development of an already existing practice."[87] Although proposing a literary resemblance, Fulton still acknowledges significant differences between Paul's letters and extra-biblical letters.[88] At least, the prevalence of co-senders in Paul's letters cannot be matched by Greco-Roman letters, of which only one fifth has co-senders.[89] It can be reasonably said that the practice of multiple senders was quite characteristic of Paul's letter-writing.

Another question to be answered is whether a co-sender is equivalent to a co-author? Pertaining to 1 and 2 Thessalonians, Byrskog suggests that "the consistent use of the first person plural together with the presentation of the three senders as on the same level lend some probability to the view that the co-senders are also co-authors."[90] Ehrensperger is more assertive: "I cannot see how the first person plural could not refer to all of the three, Paul, Silvanus and Timothy as authors as well as senders of the letter."[91] On the other hand, Donfried takes the first person plurals in 1 Thessalonians as "rhetorical plurals" and argues that Paul wrote the letter "in the presence of Silvanus and Timothy."[92] Fulton again resorts to the

85. Thiselton, *First Epistle to the Corinthians*, 69.

86. Byrskog, "Co-senders, Co-authors," 233.

87. Fulton, "Phenomenon of Co-Senders," 149. She examines many letters contained in Jewish literature, extra-biblical Christian writings, Oxyrhynchus Papyri, and ancient inscriptions from around the Roman Empire. Her research discloses that approximately one fifth of ancient letters had co-senders.

88. Fulton, "Phenomenon of Co-Senders," 151–52. The differences are: (1) extra-biblical letters are considerably shorter than the Pauline letters; (2) extra-biblical letters with co-senders are proportionately very few whereas Paul's letters with co-senders are predominant; and (3) extra-biblical letters with co-senders occur mostly in routine administrative matters whereas Paul's letters intend to build relationships and encourage Christian living.

89. Fulton, "Phenomenon of Co-Senders," 56, 102, 149.

90. Byrskog, "Co-senders, Co-authors," 238.

91. Ehrensperger, *Paul and the Dynamics*, 39.

92. Donfried, *Paul, Thessalonica, and Early Christianity*, 211–12. For the grammatical discussion of "epistolary/rhetorical plural," See Wallace, *Greek Grammar Beyond the Basics*, 394–97.

Greco-Roman letter-writing and argues that Paul's co-senders, "joined him [Paul] in taking responsibility for the letter and would be perceived by the recipients as being in agreement with its contents."[93]

It is hard to determine "to what extent Silvanus and Timothy actively participated in the composition of the letter."[94] Although scholars are equivocal about the extent, the main point here is very clear that Paul intended to include fellow workers in his letter-writing, and the inclusion of co-senders was not a mere epistolary style but rather a straightforward expression of his partnership ministry. Obviously, Paul shared certain issues of the Thessalonian church with Silvanus and Timothy, who were themselves founders of the church. They may also have discussed the needs of the church, which were later reflected into the letters. In letter-writing, like all other missionary works, Paul did not think of himself "as commissioned to lead or to minister as an isolated individual, without collaboration with co-workers."[95]

Co-senders in Paul's letters were not confined to a few of inner circle members. Gal 1:1–2 makes it clear: "Paul . . . and all the brothers who are with me, to the churches of Galatia." "All the brothers" may refer to Paul's traveling companions or church leaders at Antioch, where Paul is writing the letter. However, by using the emphatic πάντες, "all," Paul seems to envisage a larger group of believers, even the whole Christian community at Antioch. The church at Antioch had sent out Paul and Barnabas (Acts 13:2–3), who went to Galatia and evangelized the region. After missionary works there, they returned to Antioch and reported on their Galatian missions. Then, the Antiochenes came to know about the new congregations in Galatia, and surely prayed for them. At this juncture, while writing a letter to the Galatians, Paul included "all the brothers with me" as the letter's co-senders. At any rate, the writing of letters for Paul was not a personal job but a group or community project. This means that "the church at Antioch" sent a letter to "the churches of Galatia." In sum, Paul's practice of including co-senders—few or many in number, significant or less significant in contribution—does indicate the element of relationship and partnership in Paul's ministry.

93. Fulton, "Phenomenon of Co-Senders," 229.

94. Wanamaker, *Epistles to the Thessalonians*, 67.

95. Thiselton, *First Epistle to the Corinthians*, 69.

Greetings for Multiple People

Another notable feature of Paul's letter-writing is that he frequently conveys greetings from believers to believers other than himself and the recipients. Nine letters of the Pauline corpus contain various types of greeting. According to Mustakallio, there are three types of greeting in the Greco-Roman and New Testament letters, corresponding to the three persons of the verb ἀσπάζομαι ("to greet").[96] In the first-person type of greeting, the letter-writer sends greeting to someone, usually the addressee. In the second-person type, the writer requests the addressee to greet someone else for him/her. In the third-person type, the writer relays a third party's greeting to the addressee. For example, Titus 3:15 has both the second-person and the third-person type of greetings: "All who are with me greet you (third-person type). Greet those who love us in the faith (second-person type)."[97]

The first-person type of greeting occurs only once in Rom 16:22, in which Tertius, Paul's scribe for Romans, adds his own greeting: "I, Tertius, who write the letter, greet (ἀσπάζομαι) you in the Lord." The scarcity of the first-person type of greeting may reflect an "innate humility on the part of the writers" or some "cordiality between the writer and the reader," which may negate the necessity of greeting.[98] However, it seems more plausible that the first-person type of greeting was substituted by the normal form of salutation ("from . . . to . . .") in the prescripts of the letter. Extra greeting may be unnecessary for the letter writer.

The second-person type of greeting is most common in the New Testament. In particular, it occurs as many as sixteen times in Rom 16:3–15.[99] Paul does not simply list the names of his acquaintances; his greetings convey genuine concern and intimacy for each of those greeted. The third-person type of greeting is also found in Romans 16. Four times, Paul relays the greetings of his fellow workers and believers to the believers at Rome. Those who greet through Paul to the Romans are: "all the

96. Mustakallio, "Very First Audiences of Paul's Letters," 228. Mustakallio here draws on Mullins's analysis of greeting as a literary form. See Mullins, "Greeting as a New Testament Form," 418–26.

97. Another verse that has both type of greetings is Phil 4:21: "Greet every saint in Christ Jesus (second-person type). The brothers who are with me greet you (third-person type)."

98. Mullins, "Greeting as a New Testament Form," 424.

99. It is unparalleled that Paul in the passage greets twenty-six individuals by name and a number of unspecified people.

churches of Christ" (Rom 16:16); Timothy, Lucius, Jason, and Sosipater (16:21); and Gaius, Erastus, and Quartus (16:23). According to Paul's description, most of them are church leaders representing the whole community of believers and house churches in Corinth. It would be fair to say that the church at Corinth comes into contact with the church at Rome through Paul's letter.

The inclusion of multiple people in greetings can be observed in almost all the Pauline letters. In Phil 4:21–22, Paul delivers greetings to "every saint in Christ" at Philippi, from (1) "the brothers who are with me" (probably in prison), (2) "all the saints" at Rome, and (3) "those of Caesar's household." Paul's letter links the believers at Rome to the believers at Philippi. In similar words, Paul sends to the Corinthians the greetings from (1) "the churches in the province of Asia," (2) "Aquila and Priscilla, and their house church members," and (3) "all the brothers here" (1 Cor 16:19–20). Paul plays a role of connector between the churches in Asia and the churches in Corinth.

Philemon, one of the most personal and occasional letters, is addressed not only to Philemon but also to Apphia, Archippus, and the church at Philemon's house (Phlm 1:1–2). More than that, Paul probably had in mind other churches as well, since the incident of Onesimus could affect the entire Christian community at Colossae and the Lycus valley. In this sense, even the letter to Philemon is not simply "the private correspondence of one friend to another."[100] The communal aspect is also true for the pastoral letters. Paul communicates people's greetings to Timothy, "Eubulus greets you, also Pudens and Linus and Claudia and all the brothers" (2 Tim 4:21). The letter to Titus, as mentioned above, ends with a community greeting, "All who are with me greet you. Greet those who love us in faith" (Titus 3:15), and a congregational benediction, "Grace be with you all."

In the second-person type of greeting, explains Mullins, "the writer of the letter becomes the principal and the addressee becomes his agent in establishing a communication with a third party" (e.g., Rom 16:3–15), and in the third-person type of greeting, "the writer of the letter becomes the agent through whom a third party greets the addressee or greets some fourth party through the addressee" (e.g., Rom 16:16, 21, 23).[101] The crux of the matter is that the epistolary greetings signify and entail the

100. Gehring, *House Church and Mission*, 152.

101. Mullins, "Greeting as a New Testament Form," 420–21.

"relationships which exist beyond the writer-reader dialogue and beyond the specific occasion of the letter."[102] Paul's words in his greetings—i.e., multiple names, "the church in his/her house," "all those with me," "all the saints," etc.—reveal his extensive relationship with many others, locally and trans-locally. Further, encompassing a wide range of people and communities, Paul's letters seem more public than private, and more communal than personal. Paul's letter-writing needs to be examined with more emphasis on its public and communal dimension.

References to Other Churches

In addition to the wide scope of the salutation and greeting, Paul frequently refers to other believers and churches in the course of writing the letter. Stenschke's question is to the point: "in what way do the references to Christians other than the addressees of a letter function in Paul's argumentation?"[103] It concerns the implication of the references to other churches in Paul's letters.

Paul in 1 Thess 1:7–8 speaks highly of the Thessalonians: "you became an example to all the believers . . . not only in Macedonia and Achaia, but also in every place your faith toward God has gone forth." Although it is hard to determine who were "all the believers" and the geographical extent of "every place," no one will dispute that Paul heard about the Thessalonians from other believers, and now reports it back to the Thessalonians. It is noteworthy that: (1) vital networks existed among Paul's churches, through which the news of various Christian communities spread over the Mediterranean world; (2) Paul was at the hub of the networks, for he heard of news from "people everywhere" (1 Thess 1:9); and to be more relevant, (3) Paul commended the Thessalonians for their exemplary faith, relaying compliments from other believers and churches. Similar statements occur when Paul praises the Romans: "your faith is being reported all over the world" (Rom 1:8) and "the report of your obedience has reached to all" (Rom 16:19). Again, in the letter to the Ephesians, Paul gives thanks to God, "having heard of your faith . . . and love" (Eph 1:15–16).

Paul's commendation is more active and straightforward in 2 Thess 1:4, "therefore, we ourselves boast of you among the churches of God

102. Mullins, "Greeting as a New Testament Form," 422.

103. Stenschke, "Significance and Function," 189.

for your perseverance and faith." Still, other "churches of God" are mentioned here. To speak highly of the faithfulness of the Thessalonians to other churches would bring about three positive results: (1) it challenges and stimulates the faith of others who hear the commendation; (2) it encourages the Thessalonians to continue in the faith; (3) it produces a psychological connection between them, who become aware of each other's status. Paul's characteristic way of complimenting the addressees must be effective to enhance the relation and cohesion of Paul's churches.

Another example of referring to other churches is found in the "collection" discourse (2 Cor 8–9). Beginning the exhortation, Paul gives a lengthy account of the Macedonians: "we make known to you . . . beyond their ability, they gave willingly . . . for the favor of partnership in the support of the saints" (2 Cor 8:1–5). Paul reminds the Corinthians of the sacrificial deeds of the Macedonians. At the end of the chapter, Paul again mentions the Macedonian churches: "Therefore show to them, *before the churches*, the proof of your love and of our boasting on your behalf" (2 Cor 8:24; italics mine). Interestingly enough, Paul earlier boasted about the Corinthians to the Macedonians, "Achaia [Corinth] has been prepared since last year," and in fact the Corinthians' zeal "has stirred up the majority of the Macedonians" (2 Cor 9:2). Now, in turn, Paul stirs up the Corinthians by referring to the zeal of the Macedonians. According to Ascough, Paul appeals to the Corinthians by calling forth "the rivalry for honour, often found among members of religious associations."[104] The churches may be prompted by a competitive spirit. More properly saying, however, Paul appeals to the mutual relationship of example and stimulus, which is compatible with an active community of faith, the churches of God. The interaction between the churches at Corinth and at Macedonia reflects a genuine form of relationship and collaboration, which is indebted primarily to Paul's ministry including his letter-writing.

A reference to other churches reflects a larger body of Christian communities beyond the immediate community of the letter-writer and the recipients. Further, it implies certain commonality and unity of the larger body because of Paul's teachings in the letter. In 1 Cor 4:17, Paul notifies the Corinthians: "I have sent to you Timothy . . . he will remind you of my ways which are in Christ, just as I teach everywhere in every church." The repetition of "everywhere, in every church" is not redundant but emphatic in Paul's mind. Thus, the teaching of Paul to the Corinthians

104. Ascough, "Completion of a Religious Duty," 598.

is "not narrow or idiosyncratic but general and universal," as it is taught in all other churches scattered around the Mediterranean world.[105]

This ecumenical dimension of Paul's teaching appears repeatedly throughout the letter.[106] In 1 Cor 7:17, after giving instructions on marriage relationships, Paul concludes the pericope by saying "and thus I direct in all the churches." Concerning the form of worship style, Paul affirms that "but if anyone is contentious, we have no such custom, nor do the churches of God" (1 Cor 11:16). Even in the matter of fundraising, Paul offers a guideline that applies to other churches as well. He advises, "Now concerning the collection for the saints, as I directed the churches of Galatia, so do you also" (1 Cor 16:1). What he taught to the Galatians, he now teaches to the Corinthians. Paul's churches had a common ground, namely, Paul's teachings and instructions, which must have held together various churches in various places. In this sense, Hartman claims that "Paul wrote his letters to be more than occasional correspondence. He intended them to be read more widely."[107]

The reference to other churches is also related to the circulation of letters and their wide readership. Paul says to the Colossians: "Now when this epistle is read among you, see that it is read also in the church of the Laodiceans, and that you likewise read the epistle from Laodicea" (Col 4:16). Churches in the Lycus valley—Colossae, Laodicea, and Hierapolis (Col 2:1; 4:13)—had close communications since they resided less than ten miles apart from one another along the Lycus river. Paul's letters exerted a unifying effect on the community as they called forth the gathering of believers for public reading. The circulation of letters surely connected the churches in the area and undergirded them with the same Christian thoughts and traditions.

As for the Thessalonian letter, Paul orders more seriously: "I charge you by the Lord that this epistle be read to all the brothers" (1 Thess 5:27). The phrase "all the brothers" seems to indicate the whole community of Christians in the vicinity beyond the group of the first readers of the letter. Circulation of Paul's letters was established by Paul himself. Although

105. Ciampa and Rosner, *First Letter to the Corinthians*, 189.

106. The frequent reference to other churches particularly in 1 Corinthians seems to reflect the Corinthians' attitude of self-importance and self-sufficiency. Paul may be admonishing the Corinthians that they are not "*a self-contained autonomous entity: they are not a self-sufficient community; they are not the only pebble on the beach*" (italics in original). Thiselton, *First Epistle to the Corinthians*, 74.

107. Hartman, "On Reading Others' Letters," 145.

not mentioned explicitly, the letter to the Ephesians may also have been written for all the churches in Asia. Arnold thus argues that the letter "was intended in the first instance to circulate among the various local churches in the city of Ephesus, then to other churches in nearby villages, and possibly to churches in cities as far away as Smyrna, Miletus, and the Maeander and Lycus valleys."[108] The Corinthian letters, addressed "to the church of God which is at Corinth, with all the saints who are in all Achaia" (2 Cor 1:1), must have been read at Corinth, Cenchrea, and other cities in the province. The letter to the Romans, addressed "to all who are beloved of God in Rome" (Rom 1:7), had to be passed around from house church to house church in Rome. Beyond doubt, Paul's letters caused more communication and contact, and reinforced closer relationship among the churches.

Collaboration through Visitations

Luke presents the missionary works of Paul "in the form of successive tours."[109] The successive tours made Paul travel approximately 15,500 miles throughout the Mediterranean world.[110] Accordingly, Luke refers to about seventy names of the cities and provinces that Paul visited during his missionary journeys. Considering the places omitted or unnamed by Luke and the fact that Paul visited most of the places twice or more times, it can be said that Paul made a huge number of visits to places and persons for evangelistic and pastoral purposes. This section looks into those visitations and examines their implications in the context of New Testament church relationships. First, travels and visitations are explained along with the related topics of sending envoys and rendering hospitality. Second, biblical accounts are explored to examine the nature of Paul's visits to local churches. Third, Paul's visits to Jerusalem are explored to determine the dynamics of relationship between Paul and the Jerusalem church.

108. Arnold, *Ephesians*, 29.

109. Marshall, "Luke's Portrait," 102.

110. For more information, see the first section, "Greco-Roman and Jewish Contexts," the first subsection, "Travel and Letters in the Greco-Roman World."

Visitation, Envoy, and Hospitality

It was noted in the first section that early Christians relied on the travel structures and communicational mediums which had been constructed by the Roman Empire. Whereas the Roman Empire provided infrastructures for mobility, the widespread Jewish communities provided the base and the model for the socio-religious network of early Christians. Whenever arriving at a mission field, for instance, Paul went to the local Jewish synagogue and announced the gospel, starting missionary works in the area.[111] The first Christians, who were mostly Jews, utilized their Jewish connections in spreading the new faith in Christ. It is, therefore, natural that the earliest churches started and developed where the Jewish communities were present.

Travels and visitations were frequent in the earliest churches, reflecting the mobile trend of the ancient Jewish society. Numerous stories of travels and visitations are handed down in the Jewish traditions. For example, rabbinic documents often provide the account of travels made by rabbis and rabbinic students. It is interesting that many tannaitic stories are introduced by a typical phrase, "he was/they were walking on the way."[112] By means of such travels and visitations, Jewish communities in Palestine as well as in the Diaspora were able to maintain their communal relationships and common identity. The same was true of the first-century Christian communities.

A striking example of the earliest Christians' travels can be observed in Paul's letter to the Romans. Paul greets twenty-six named individuals and an unspecified number of unnamed people in the letter's closing chapter. It clearly suggests that there had been intensive mobility among the believers across the Mediterranean basin. Priscilla and Aquilla, for example, were so mobile as to be found in many places at various times.[113] Epaenetus, "the first fruits of Asia for Christ" (Rom 16:5b), moved from

111. Such strategy was consistently executed in Paul's missionary journeys. See Acts 13:5, 14; 14:1; 17:1–2, 10, 17; 18:4–5, 19; 19:8.

112. Hezser, *Jewish Travel in Antiquity*, 215.

113. Priscilla and Aquilla lived in Rome prior to the edict of Claudius, which expelled all the Jews from the city (Acts 18:2). The couple came to Corinth and made friends with Paul, working together (Acts 18:3). When Paul left Corinth back to Syria, they accompanied Paul as far as Ephesus and remained there (Acts 18:19). In Rom 16:3, Paul asks the recipients to greet Priscilla and Aquilla, who were sponsoring a house church in Rome. In 2 Tim 4:19, Paul urges Timothy to greet the couple. They resided in Ephesus.

Ephesus to Rome, probably along with Priscilla and Aquilla.[114] Andronicus and Junia (Rm 16:7) originally belonged to the Hellenistic Jewish community in Jerusalem, became "fellow-prisoners" with Paul probably in Ephesus, and later stayed at Rome.[115] These people, for various reasons, moved from the Eastern Mediterranean to Rome. Malherbe writes that "it was this mobility of the early church that was responsible for the spread of the faith."[116] In addition to Paul and his coworkers, there were many other traveling Christians, and "in this way they would have contributed to the unity of the church and to whatever continuities characterized early Christianity."[117]

In Phil 2:25–26, Paul writes, "I thought it necessary to send to you Epaphroditus . . . because he was longing for you all and was distressed because you had heard that he was sick." Paul's word implies that several messengers have been exchanged between Rome and Philippi: (1) the news of Paul's imprisonment was delivered to the Philippians; (2) the Philippians responded by sending Epaphroditus to Paul along with a financial gift (4:18); (3) the news of Epaphroditus's illness reached Philippi (2:26); and (4) the Philippians' anxiety over Epaphroditus was reported back to those in Rome (2:26). Furthermore, Paul expects three more travels in the near future: (1) Paul was about to send Epaphroditus to Philippi with his letter (2:25, 28); (2) Paul hoped to send Timothy as soon as he could (2:19–23); and (3) Paul himself planned to visit Philippi (2:24).

Philippi was a long way from Rome, approximately one thousand miles.[118] So the occurrence of the first four travels in a short span of time, according to Hansen, "seems to conflict with the sense given by Philippians of messages being sent quickly back and forth."[119] On this ground, some scholars challenge the Roman provenance of Philippians and choose Ephesus as a likely alternative on account of its proximity

114. Jewett argues that "Epainetos was probably associated with Prisca and Aquila's house church on the basis of his conversion during the period of their Ephesian residence" (*Romans*, 959–60).

115. Most commentators are in favor of the feminine name "Junia" (NKJV, NIV, NET, NRSV) over the masculine name "Junias" (NASB, RSV), and regard "Andronicus and Junia" as husband and wife. See Jewett, *Romans*, 961; Dunn, *Romans 9–16*, 894–95; and Moo, *Romans*, 921–23.

116. Malherbe, *Social Aspects of Early Christianity*, 65.

117. Malherbe, *Social Aspects of Early Christianity*, 65.

118. Carson and Moo, *Introduction to the New Testament*, 504.

119. Hansen, *Philippians*, 21.

to Philippi.[120] However, put differently, if Rome was the place of letter-writing, a reasonable inference is that the travelers and news in antiquity moved much faster than the scholars have generally assumed and that the exchange of letter-carriers or envoys between Rome and Philippi was quite frequent and swift. This is likely what happened to Paul in Rome and the Philippian church.

Paul wrote many letters. That means that he had to send out envoys or letter-carriers, frequently. Paul's envoys, usually his coworkers, communicated news and instructions by delivering a letter (written communication) and/or by conveying Paul's message (verbal communication) to the local churches. It should be noted that Paul's envoys functioned not only as the letter-carriers but, more importantly, as Paul's representatives, playing a significant role in the communication. Comparing Paul's letters with Greco-Roman letters, Mitchell observes two similarities between them: "proper reception of the envoy necessarily entails proper reception of the one who sent him"[121] and "they [envoys] have the significant power and authority to speak for those who sent them in accordance with their instructions."[122] Most pertinent in this regard is the text of Col 4:7–9, where Paul says, "Tychicus will tell you all the news about me . . . I am sending him to you for this purpose that you may know about our circumstances and that he may encourage your hearts . . . He is coming with Onesimus . . . They will tell you everything that is happening here."[123] In fact, in the letter itself, nothing is told about Paul's trial process or his gospel ministry in prison. Such news is to be told in person by his emissaries, Tychicus and Onesimus. Also, they were supposed to encourage the believers in Colossae along with the letter. Head thus rightly argues that Paul's envoys functioned as "the earliest interpreters of the individual letters."[124]

120. See Koester, "Paul and Philippi," 52–53. For a more extensive discussion on this subject, see Hawthorne, *Philippians*, xxxix–l.

121. Mitchell, "New Testament Envoys," 645.

122. Mitchell, "New Testament Envoys," 649. Emphasizing the importance of envoys, she argues that "Paul sent envoys not as mere substitutes for himself but also with the understanding that they could perform special functions that he himself could not perform *even if present*" (643).

123. Paul similarly writes to the Ephesians: "You also may know about my circumstances, how I am doing, Tychicus . . . will make everything known to you. And I have sent him to you for this very purpose, so that you may know about us, and that he may comfort your hearts" (Eph 6:21–22).

124. Head "Named Letter-Carriers," 298.

When envoys were sent out with or without letters, they were expected to bring the news of the recipients back to the sender.[125] In this way, news and instructions were shared together by the two separated communities, enhancing mutual understanding and relationship. This bilateral function of envoys is well demonstrated in two similar, impressive passages, 1 Thess 3:6–8 and 2 Cor 7:6–7, in which Paul expresses his own feeling of relief and comfort at the return of Timothy and Titus, respectively, and at the news of the churches brought by them.[126] In Phil 2:19, Paul explicitly discloses his purpose for sending Timothy: "I . . . send Timothy to you shortly, so that I also may be encouraged when I learn of your condition." The word κἀγώ ("I also") is emphatic "because of its presence as well as its position in the sentence," and signifies "a twofold purpose in view, namely that (1) Paul himself might be encouraged by good news about the Philippians and that (2) they might be cheered by good news concerning him."[127] Paul's saying clearly shows that he received from the Philippians not only financial support but psychological support as well. Paul's relationship with his churches was not one-sided but two-sided enough to be reciprocal and collaborative with each other.

The prevalence of travels and visitations by Paul, envoys, and other believers, implicated the prevalence of hospitality among the first-century Christian communities. Hospitality was essential, since the early Christians, like the Jews, mostly avoided public inns "because of their bad reputation" and then "usually sought out lodging in the private homes of their fellow believers."[128] Paul thus stayed at the house of Lydia in Philippi (Acts 16:15), the house of Jason in Thessalonica (Acts 17:7), and the house of Gaius in Corinth (Rom 16:23). Also, Paul in his letters requests or orders the addressees to offer hospitality for him (1 Cor 16:6; Phlm 22) as well as for his coworkers, Timothy (1 Cor 16:10), Epaphroditus

125. Apparent examples are many in Paul's letters. Paul sent Timothy to Thessalonica to "strengthen and encourage" the new believers there (1 Thess 3:1–3), and Timothy returned to Paul with news about the church (1 Thess 3:6–8). Stephanas, Fortunatus, and Achaicus came to Ephesus with the news (written or verbal) of the Corinthian church (1 Cor 16:17), and probably carried home Paul's letter to the Corinthians (1 Corinthians). Titus worked as a messenger from Paul to the Corinthians, and from the Corinthians to Paul (2 Cor 2:13; 7:6, 13).

126. Concerning Timothy and Titus as the envoys to Thessalonica and Corinth, respectively, see chapter 2, section "Paul's Coworkers in the Trans-local Ministry," subsection "Paul's Travel Companions and Messengers."

127. O'Brien, *Philippians*, 317.

128. Gehring, *House Church and Mission*, 183.

(Phil 2:29), Phoebe (Rom 16:2), and Zenas the lawyer and Apollos (Titus 3:13). It is noticeable that Paul writes these passages in quite a casual and cursory manner. In the New Testament, practicing hospitality was common and further encouraged among the believers (Rom 12:3).

When Paul received Stephanas, Fortunatus, and Achaicus coming from Corinth (1 Cor 16:17), he likely "had to rely on the hospitality of other people in the church in Ephesus. Thus the delegates from Corinth were put in contact with fellow believers in Ephesus."[129] As the guests and hosts had fellowship together, "Christian families received news of other churches, their horizons were broadened . . . and formed a sense of community larger than their urban area."[130] In Rom 16:1–2, Paul commends Phoebe to the Roman Christians and requests "that you receive her . . . and that you assist her in whatever matter she may have need of you." As Paul's envoy, Phoebe might have read and explained the letter in the whole assembly of the Roman Christians or, more plausibly, in various house churches in Rome. Phoebe was a leader of the house church at Cenchrea and "a helper/benefactor" for Paul and many other Christians in Achaia. Considering her local and trans-local activities, it is not too much to say that "Paul's old house church network from the Aegean was now providing entry into the new house church networks in Rome, through the exercise of letter-writing and hospitality."[131] Through visitations and hospitality, Paul and his coworkers expanded their missionary field and strengthened inter-community relationships.

Paul's Visitation to Local Churches

Communication between people is most effective face to face. When physically present with each other, people can directly exchange thoughts, emotions, and opinions with a clearer understanding of each other. In this sense, the Apostle John says, "Having many things to write to you, I do not want to do so with paper and ink; but I hope to come to you and speak face to face, that our joy may be full" (2 John 12). Likewise, Paul writes to the Romans, "I long to *see* you that I may impart to you some spiritual gift, so that you may be established" (Rom 1:11; italics mine). Paul earnestly wanted to share with the Romans the grace of God and nurture them in faith, and "his visit with them would provide the

129. Hvalvik, "All Those," 141.

130. Osiek and Balch, *Families*, 207.

131. White, *Building God's House*, 106.

opportunity to accomplish that purpose."[132] Paul's desire for all to be saved and strengthened in faith drove him constantly on the road to visit and meet people everywhere face to face.

Visitation was Paul's basic and primary way of carrying out his missions. Writing on Paul's first missionary journey, Luke refers to many cities, Seleucia, Cyprus, Salamis, Paphos, Perga, Pamphylia, Pisidian Antioch, Iconium, Lystra, Lycaonia, Derbe, and so on (Acts 13:4—14:21). The travel route is noteworthy in that Paul and Barnabas returned at Derbe back to Antioch, taking exactly the same route in reverse order (Acts 14:21–26). The selection of the route seems to be intentional: that is, Paul and Barnabas wanted to revisit the people who had been converted through their recent ministry, "encouraging them to continue in the faith" (Acts 14:22) and "appointing elders for them in every church" (Acts 14:23). The purpose of visitation is reiterated when they are planning the second missionary journey: "Let us now go back and visit (ἐπισκεψώμεθα) our brethren in every city . . . and see how they are doing" (Acts 15:36).[133] Again, the third missionary journey was made for the same purpose: "Paul set out from there and traveled from place to place throughout the region of Galatia and Phrygia, strengthening all the disciples" (Acts 18:23). Paul's letters and the book of Acts describe Paul as always revisiting or desiring to revisit his churches in order to encourage the local believers. Portraying Paul's missionary journeys in broad strokes, Marshall thus says, "the picture of a warm, loving relationship emerges."[134]

In his farewell speech to the Ephesian elders, Paul adumbrates his preaching ministry at Ephesus: "I did not hesitate to preach anything that would be helpful but taught you publicly [possibly in the school of Tyrannus (Acts 19:9)] and from house to house" (Acts 20:20). Stowers comments that "the house appears as the characteristic place for Paul's teaching activity during his long stays in Ephesus and Corinth aside from the peculiar situation of the *scholē* of Tyrannus."[135] Further, examining the circumstances of Paul's preaching activity, he concludes that first, "Paul used the synagogue on numerous occasions, although this often led to conflict and could not be a permanent locus for his preaching,"

132. Mounce, *Romans*, 67.

133. The term ἐπισκέπτομαι denotes "to go to see a person(s) with helpful intent, visit" or "to make a careful inspection, look at, examine, inspect," or even "look for with interest in selection, select" (Acts 6:3). See BDAG, s.v. "ἐπισκέπτομαι."

134. Marshall, "Luke's Portrait," 105.

135. Stowers, "Social Status," 70.

and second, "the private house provided the most important place for his work."[136] In short, Paul's preaching and teaching ministry was done by visitations "from house to house" in the setting of house churches.

House churches in a given area were bound together by the visitation of Paul or his envoys. When Paul sent Timothy to Corinth, the Corinthian house churches must have assembled to receive him, Paul's envoy. The delivery of Paul's message, "what I teach everywhere in every church" (1 Cor 4:17), must have enhanced a sense of oneness in the church. Most of all, Paul's presence and ministry rallied the churches over the Mediterranean basin for the gospel of Christ. By their common recognition of Paul as the apostle of Christ and common link with him, the churches naturally formed a communal network with Paul at its center. In addition, since Paul had the "opportunity to observe the practice of the churches of his mission firsthand,"[137] Paul's visitations from place to place may also have a unifying effect on the general form of church worship and polity. Paul thus says, "There is one body and one Spirit . . . one Lord, one faith, one baptism" (Eph 4:4–5).

The literary block of Acts 20:1 to 21:17 relates to the process of Paul's final journey to Jerusalem. While giving an eyewitness account of the itinerary,[138] Luke presents, in particular, four occasions—Paul's visits to the four Christian communities at Troas, Miletus (Ephesus), Tyre, and Caesarea.[139] Paul's visits to these cities on the way to Jerusa-

136. Stowers, "Social Status," 81. He also says, "Paul followed the pattern of Hellenistic teachers, a pattern which was continued by Christian teachers in the second century and later."

137. Willis, "Networking of the Pauline Churches," 76.

138. This portion, along with Acts 16:10–17 and Acts 27–28, contains "we" passages.

139. Luke's travel note is quite systematic: stay (narrative) and move (travelogue) are recorded in turn.

20:1–6	After missions in Macedonia and Achaia, Paul and his companions went to Troas.
20:7–12	(1) In Troas, the local believers assembled to break bread and to hear Paul's preaching.
20:13–16	Travelogue from Troas to Miletus, the port city of Ephesus.
20:17–38	(2) In Miletus, Paul gives a farewell instruction to the elders from Ephesus.
21:1–3	Travelogue from Miletus to Tyre, Syria.
21:4–6	(3) In Tyre, the believers told Paul not to go up to Jerusalem.
21:7–8	Travelogue from Tyre to Caesarea.
21:9–14	(4) In Caesarea, Agabus and the believers urged Paul not to go up to Jerusalem.
21:15–17	Travelogue from Caesarea to Jerusalem

lem probably brought the sense of a larger body of Christ to the local believers. First, since Paul arrived from a place and would soon move on to another place, the local believers may have become more aware and heedful of other Christian communities across the Aegean or Mediterranean Sea. Second, there was imminent danger worrying all the churches, namely, the "chains and afflictions" looming over Paul (Acts 20:23). The churches would have been of one mind in praying for him (Acts 20:36; 21:5). Third, Paul was carrying the charity funds for the Jerusalem church which had been collected from the churches in Galatia, Asia, Macedonia, and Achaia. Paul and his traveling companions representing the donor churches unmistakably reminded the local believers of the financial collaboration of many trans-local churches for the Jerusalem church.

Examining the narrative structure of the literary block, Acts 20:1—21:17, Gaventa highlights "three scenes of community life (the gatherings in Troas, Miletus, and Caesarea, respectively) alternating with four accounts of travel."[140] The believers of each community gathered "for worship (20:7–12), instruction (20:18–35), or prophecy (21:7–14)."[141] Paul's visitations called forth community life and reinforced cohesion of the local community. More importantly, Paul's visitations brought about trans-local effects, too. Gaventa rightly argues that "these scenes of community life do not stand as isolated vignettes about ἐκκλησίαι in particular and unrelated places, but are connected by Paul's journey."[142] She finds that Luke, by alternately narrating the travel reports and community gatherings, presents "the connectedness of groups of believers scattered around the Aegean and back to Caesarea."[143] Paul's regular visits to so many local churches demonstrate the presence of close church networks in the first-century world. In other words, Paul's travels and visitations helped develop such close networks among the earliest churches, local and trans-local.

140. Gaventa, "Theology and Ecclesiology," 38. In her analysis, the occasion in Tyre is not included. Gaventa may consider that Paul's meeting with the Christians in Tyre was not significant enough to be noted. However, their fellowship was apparently meaningful and sincere. Paul and his travel companions stayed there for seven days, and the disciples kept telling Paul through the Spirit not to go to Jerusalem (Acts 21:4). When Paul's company was departing, Luke writes, "They all accompanied us, with wives and children, till we were out of the city. And we knelt down on the shore and prayed" (Acts 21:5).

141. Gaventa, "Theology and Ecclesiology," 40.

142. Gaventa, "Theology and Ecclesiology," 42.

143. Gaventa, "Theology and Ecclesiology," 43.

Paul's Visitation to Jerusalem

The issue of Paul's visits to Jerusalem has been controversial in terms of their numbers and interpretation. Varying views are embedded in the issue that while Galatians mentions only two visits to Jerusalem (Gal 1:18; 2:1), the book of Acts records five visits (Acts 9:26; 11:30; 15:2; 18:22; 21:15).[144] The main debate is about the Jerusalem visit in Gal 2:1–10 in relation to the Jerusalem Council in Acts 15.[145] Some scholars equate the Jerusalem visit in Galatians 2 with the Jerusalem Council and dismiss the relief visit of Acts 11:27–30 as Luke's misrepresentation of his sources or misplacement of the final visit to a much earlier period.[146] On the contrary, accepting the book of Acts to be historically correct and devoid of serious errors, other scholars equate the relief visit in Acts 11 with the one in Gal 2:1–10.[147] The present volume follows the latter view.[148]

144. Paul's five visits in Acts were made: (1) following his escape from Damascus (Acts 9:26); (2) to deliver relief gifts from Antioch church to Jerusalem (Acts 11:30); (3) to participate in the Jerusalem Council and settle the circumcision issue for gentile converts (Acts 15:1–4); (4) as a passing visit on the way to Antioch at the end of the second missionary journey (Acts 18:22); and (5) as the final visit followed by his arrest, imprisonment, and transport to Rome (Acts 21:15).

145. On the other hand, it is a consensus view that both Gal 1:18 and Acts 9:26 indicate Paul's first visit to Jerusalem after his conversion.

146. According to them, Luke, misunderstanding his sources, turned one Jerusalem event into two incidents by making up another visitation story of Acts 11:27–30 in addition to Acts 15. Some others claim that the famine visit (Acts 11:30) is, in fact, a misplaced report of the final visit (Acts 21:15) that was made along with a relief fund. See Knox, *Chapters in a Life of Paul*, 49–50.

147. See Marshall, *Acts of the Apostles*, 216–17; Bruce, *Acts*, 229–31; and Peterson, *Acts*, 358. Also, they generally espouse that Galatians was written shortly before the Jerusalem Council (Acts 15).

148. The basis of the first view is the similarity between the two passages, respectively, in Acts 15 and Gal 2:1–10. Both deal with the same issue of observing the Mosaic Law by gentile Christians. In both, the decision was made in favor of law-free gentile missions. However, the two accounts also show a considerable difference. Was the Jerusalem visit made in response to a revelation (Gal 2:2) or by the commission of the Antioch church (Acts 15:2)? Did Paul have a private meeting with a few leaders (Gal 2:2) or a public conference with a number of people (Acts 15:4)? Besides the differences in description, if the meeting of Gal 2:1–10 represents the Jerusalem Council, Paul makes two serious omissions in his letter: he leaves out the famine relief visit and the decision of the Jerusalem Council. It is unreasonable that Paul fails to mention the famine visit while he is trying to explain the nature of his contact and relationship with the Jerusalem leaders. Much more inconceivable is the omission of the Jerusalem Council because its decision would have been decisive for the Galatian situation.

Paul's visits to Jerusalem exhibit some distinctive aspects compared to the visits to other cities. First, Paul visited many places to preach the gospel or to strengthen local churches. In relation to the Jerusalem church, however, Paul never mentioned, explicitly or implicitly, such intentions or concerns. Visits to Jerusalem could not be for evangelistic work, since Paul "aspired to preach the gospel, not where Christ was already named" (Rom 15:20). They could not be for instruction or pastoral care since the Jerusalem church were being led by the apostles and elders. Second, according to biblical evidence, Paul made more visitations to the Jerusalem church than to any other churches. He visited his own churches—even the major Christian communities at Corinth, Philippi, and Ephesus—no more than three times, whereas he visited Jerusalem five times.

Third, Paul's trips to Jerusalem were made mostly in difficulty and adversity. Luke describes Paul's first visit to Jerusalem with the word πειράζω, which means "to make an effort to do something . . . at times in a context indicating futility."[149] At first, Paul probably failed to meet the Jerusalem apostles because "they were all afraid of him, not believing that he was a disciple" (Acts 9:26). Only through the mediation of Barnabas, did Paul meet with Peter and James (Acts 9:27; Gal 1:18–19). During the second visit, Paul and his companions, Barnabas and Titus, had to deal with the "false brothers" who had crept in to bring them into bondage (Gal 2:4). In the third visit for the Jerusalem Council, Paul encountered hostile opposition from "certain ones of the sect of the Pharisees," who insisted that the gentile Christians be circumcised and obliged to observe the Law of Moses (Acts 15:5). Paul's fifth and final visit to Jerusalem met the most hateful and violent counteraction and resulted in arrest and imprisonment. Paul himself knew that "chains and afflictions" were awaiting him (Acts 20:23) but determined "not only to be bound, but also to die at Jerusalem for the name of the Lord Jesus" (Acts 21:13).

Paul visited the Jerusalem church the most times and despite difficulties and dangers. If the visits were neither evangelistic nor pastoral, what then was his purpose for the visits? Paul's first visit to Jerusalem is described in Acts 9:26–30. After escaping from Damascus, Paul made his way to Jerusalem, introduced himself through Barnabas to the apostles, and stayed with them for fifteen days (Gal 1:18), preaching the gospel together (Acts 9:28–29). Luke in Acts 9:26 uses the term κολλάω, which means "to join closely together, bind closely, unite someone with or to

149. BDAG, s.v. "πειράζω."

someone."[150] That is, Paul purposed and endeavored to join with the Jerusalem apostles. This account of Luke corroborates Paul's own words: "I went up to Jerusalem to become acquainted (ἱστορῆσαι) with Cephas" (Gal 1:18). Here, ἱστορῆσαι is used in the sense of "making someone's acquaintance" and "*visit* for the purpose of coming to know someone or something."[151] Paul went to Jerusalem to see Cephas. He probably thought it important to acquaint himself with "the leader of the original apostles, who was also at this time the unchallenged leader of the Jerusalem church."[152] To be more relevant, however, the verb ἱστορέω better be rendered as "to visit, with the purpose of obtaining information—'to visit and get information.'"[153] Paul most wanted to hear about Jesus' life and teaching directly from the eyewitnesses, the original apostles. Paul's visit to Jerusalem signified his acknowledgement of one faith and one church founded by Jesus Christ and proclaimed by the Twelve.

Paul's second trip to Jerusalem was a relief visit as recorded in Acts 11:29–30. Paul and Barnabas were sent to Jerusalem with the contribution collected by the Antiochene Christians. The visitation was to give assistance to the poor in the Jerusalem church. The third visit to Jerusalem took place sometime after the first missionary journey and just before the second missionary journey. Paul and Barnabas were again sent out by the Antiochene church to attend the Jerusalem Council (Acts 15), which showed early church collaboration for the cause of the gospel ministry. Paul visited Jerusalem to resolve the law-free versus law-observant or the Jewish versus gentile conflict in the New Testament churches. Paul's fourth trip to Jerusalem was a passing visit. On the way to Antioch, finishing the second missionary journey, Paul visited the Jerusalem church again (Acts 18:22).[154] In a sense, this visit may best represent the connection between Paul and Jerusalem, since it was not made for a particular cause but for a customary greeting. The trip may have been "to assert his

150. BDAG, s.v. "κολλάω."

151. BDAG, s.v. "ἱστορέω."

152. Bruce, *Galatians*, 98.

153. L&N, s.v. "34.52 ἱστορέω." In this sense, NET renders the infinitive verb ἱστορῆσαι as "to get information from him."

154. Luke does not explicitly say Paul visited Jerusalem: "And when he had landed at Caesarea, he went up and greeted the church, and went down to Antioch." However, from the use of "went up," "went down," and "the church," it can be inferred that Paul visited Jerusalem en route to Antioch.

continuing fidelity to the original apostolic community"[155] and also "to maintain good links between the Gentile churches and the centre from which the gospel first came."[156]

Paul's final trip to Jerusalem is recorded in several places (Acts 21:15–18; Rom 15:25–28; 1 Cor 16:3–4). Arriving at the city, Paul immediately went to see James and all the Jerusalem elders (Acts 21:18). When the Jerusalem leaders heard of Paul's report on what God had done among the gentiles through his ministry, they praised God (Acts 21:19–20). Furthermore, they kindly advised Paul to perform certain Judaic rites to stay clear from the threat of ill-willed Jewish believers in Jerusalem (Acts 21:20–25). According to these accounts, Paul and the Jerusalem church leaders were in the harmonious relationship with each other. Besides, Paul and his companions were presenting financial gifts from various churches to the Jerusalem church. As Luke portrays, Paul and his churches identified with the Jerusalem church, cooperating and collaborating together for the gospel of Christ. In sum, Paul's five visits to Jerusalem embodied his close relationship with the Jerusalem apostles and enhanced the networking of the churches, Pauline and non-Pauline, as one body of Christ.

Collaboration through Conferences

Whereas letter-writing or visitation indicates, relatively, a simple mutual relationship, a conference often implicates multilateral relations with more parties and more issues involved. Conferences bear more communal features than other forms of communication. In this sense, the reality of New Testament church relationship and collaboration can be observed, most apparently, in church conferences. That is why Meeks, referring to early church relationships, argues that "the primary means for resolving conflicts seems to have been meeting and talking."[157] This section discusses, in particular, three church conferences that occurred in connection with Paul's ministry—Paul's conference with the Jerusalem apostles (Gal 2:1–10), the Antioch incident (Gal 2:11–14), and the Jerusalem Council (Acts 15).[158] In each subsection, a brief exegetical study

155. Johnson, *Acts of the Apostles*, 335.

156. Peterson, *Acts*, 522.

157. Meeks, *First Urban Christians*, 113.

158. In this volume, the "Jerusalem Council" refers to the general assembly of Acts

will be done on key texts in order to reconstruct and understand the situation of the three conferences.

Paul's Conference with the Jerusalem Apostles (Gal 2:1–10)

The narrative of Gal 2:1–10 reveals the nature of ministry relationship between two parties, Paul and Barnabas from Antioch on the one hand, and the apostles at Jerusalem on the other. It starts with ἔπειτα ("then" or "next"), which implies that "Paul is omitting nothing material to his argument—in particular, that he is omitting no visit to Jerusalem or other contact with the church there or its leaders."[159] That is, there has been no interactions between Paul and the Jerusalem church since his first visit to the city (Gal 1:18). "After fourteen years" could be understood as "fourteen years after his conversion" or "fourteen years after the first visit to Jerusalem."[160] Either way, at the time of the Jerusalem conference, Paul had been preaching the gospel to the Gentiles for many years and "there is no question about the gospel that he preaches being fully developed by now."[161]

Because of the prepositional phrase "by revelation" (κατὰ ἀποκάλυψιν) (Gal 2:2), many scholars relate the Jerusalem conference to the famine visit in Acts 11:28–30, where a prophet named Agabus announced by the Spirit a great famine approaching, and the Antiochene church sent a relief fund to Jerusalem by the hands of Barnabas and Paul. The point is that Paul claims he went up to Jerusalem due to the Spirit's leading, not to any order or instruction from the Jerusalem leaders. Ἀνατίθημι (ἀνεθέμην) means "to lay something before someone for consideration . . . with connotation of request for a person's opinion."[162] At the beginning of his ministry, Paul did not consult with anyone or go up to Jerusalem to see the apostles there (Gal 1:16–17); fourteen years later, he went up to Jerusalem and submitted (ἀνεθέμην) to them the gospel that he preached among the gentiles (Gal 2:2). The phrase, "for fear that I might be running, or had run, in vain,"

15, and the "Jerusalem conference" denotes the meeting of Paul and Barnabas with the Jerusalem apostles as narrated in Gal 2:1–10.

159. Bruce, *Galatians*, 106.

160. Those who espouse the South Galatian hypothesis normally take the former view "fourteen years after his conversion," dating the incident earlier than the scholars of the latter view do. The South Galatian hypothesis contends that Galatians was written to the churches in southern Galatia rather than the cities in the north.

161. Cole, *Galatians*, 100.

162. BDAG, s.v. "ἀνατίθημι."

suggests that Paul was cautious about a potential problem: disagreement with the Jerusalem church might damage the effectiveness of his ministry and hurt the truthfulness of his gospel that claimed, "neither Jews nor Gentiles in Christ Jesus" (Gal 3:28).

The passage of Gal 2:3–5 functions "as an extended parenthesis within Paul's account of his second Jerusalem visit."[163] It starts with the strong adversative ἀλλά, indicating that the subsequent passage conveys what is contrasting to the previous statement in verse 2. In the passage, Paul affirms "the truth of the gospel" (Gal 2:5) by refusing to circumcise Titus. Semantically, the clause "being a Greek" (Ἕλλην ὤν) is opposite to the phrase "Titus who was with me" (Τίτος ὁ σὺν ἐμοί) since Jews were not supposed to make company with gentiles. Most English Bibles therefore interpret the clause as concessive: Titus, although a Greek, was not compelled to be circumcised (Gal 2:3). The "false brethren" who sneaked in to spy out Paul and his colleagues (Gal 2:4) were probably connected with the Judaizers of Acts 15:1, who came down from Judea and taught the Antiochene Christians, "Unless you are circumcised according to the custom of Moses, you cannot be saved." The fact that Paul and his colleagues did not surrender to them "even for a moment" (Gal 2:5 NET) emphasizes "the absoluteness of their unyielding attitude in face of the Judaizers' demands."[164]

In describing the Jerusalem leaders, Paul repeatedly uses the word "esteem" (δοκέω).[165] In what sense does he use the word? In the present context, Paul does not seem to compliment those esteemed in Jerusalem; rather, the nuance is that "they may be highly regarded, but I am not concerned with human reputation or recognition, I live and work before the Lord." The participle "knowing" (γνόντες) (v. 9) is in apposition to "seeing" (ἰδόντες) (v. 7), and both are causal in syntax, related to the principal verb "gave" (ἔδωκαν) (v. 9). The Jerusalem authorities recognized the work of God in Paul's missions and offered a ministry fellowship (Gal 2:7–9). Although Paul did not ask for endorsement, the Jerusalem apostles acknowledged Paul's ministry. The implied verb of the ἵνα clause is most likely

163. Longenecker, *Galatians*, 49. It is clear from the context: the preceding verse 2 refers to οἱ δοκοῦντες ("those esteemed"), which reappears in verse 6, ἀπὸ δὲ τῶν δοκούντων ("from those esteemed").

164. Fung, *Galatians*, 94.

165. Paul writes "to those esteemed" (τοῖς δοκοῦσιν) (v. 2); "from those esteemed" (Ἀπὸ δὲ τῶν δοκούντων) (v. 6); "those esteemed" (οἱ δοκοῦντες) (v. 6); and "who were esteemed to be pillars" (οἱ δοκοῦντες στῦλοι εἶναι (v. 9).

"to go" (πορεύομαι) or "to evangelize" (εὐαγγελίζω). That is, both parties agreed on the demarcation of two evangelistic missions, one "to the Jews" (εἰς τὴν περιτομήν) and the other "to the Gentiles" (εἰς τὰ ἔθνη).

From this brief exegetical study of Gal 2:1–10, it can be perceived that Paul had quite contrasting attitudes toward the Jerusalem apostles. He was somehow dependent on them and, at the same time, clearly independent of them. The dependent side is that: (1) Paul occasionally went up to Jerusalem to visit the church; (2) Paul "submitted" (ἀνατίθημι) to the apostles the gospel that he preached among the gentiles; and (3) he was concerned about how the apostles would appraise his gentile ministry. The independent side is more divergent: (1) there had been no contact between Paul and the Jerusalem church for fourteen years; (2) the Jerusalem conference occurred "because of revelation," not at the request of the Jerusalem authorities; (3) Paul did not succumb to the pressure of some Jewish leaders that Titus should be circumcised; and (4) the Jerusalem apostles of high reputation contributed nothing to Paul. Certainly, Paul's attitude toward the Jerusalem church and its leaders seems ambivalent. Making a comment on this ambivalence, Bruce says that "*dissociation* from Jerusalem would imply in practice severance from the birthplace of Christianity; yet *dependence* on Jerusalem would be a denial of his receiving his apostolic call direct from Christ."[166] Holmberg's remark is more succinct: "the dialectic between being independent of and being acknowledged by Jerusalem is the keynote of this important text and must not be forgotten."[167]

The inner tension in Paul reflects the delicate relationship between Paul and the Jerusalem leaders, which in turn represents the incipient inter-church relationship, for the "private council [Gal 2:1–10] was a meeting between two churches, Antioch and Jerusalem, and their respective leaders Paul and Barnabas for Antioch, and James, Peter, and John, whom Paul calls pillars in the Jerusalem church."[168] Between the two groups, when they first encountered, there might have been "confrontation in the air."[169] Tension might have been felt as "Paul took Titus along, and made it clear that he would not yield to pressure from those

166. Bruce, "Paul and Jerusalem," 5.

167. Holmberg, *Paul and Power*, 16.

168. Just, "Apostolic Councils," 266–67.

169. Grothe, "Missionary in Fellowship," 9.

who insisted on circumcision."[170] Hidden opponents were trying to find fault with Paul's gentile missions. More importantly, both sides had yet little understanding of each other's theology and ministry, and Paul was anxious about the acceptance of his gospel by the Jerusalem apostles. To be sure, there were certain issues to be clarified in the meeting.

Despite the "confrontation in the air," the Jerusalem conference turned out to be successful. The pillars of the Jerusalem church offered Paul "the right hand of fellowship" (Gal 2:9) denoting "the mutual fellowship and partnership existing between himself and the leaders at Jerusalem."[171] How did such a positive outcome come about? First, the apostles saw that the ministry of Paul to the gentiles was equivalent to that of Peter to the Jews (Gal 2:7–8). This acknowledgment suggests a prior understanding that the gospel proclaimed by Paul was not different from the gospel proclaimed by the Jerusalem apostles.[172] Second, the Jerusalem authorities, considering the context (Gal 2:3–5), seemed to affirm the circumcision-free mission with regard to the gentiles. Third, they divided the gospel ministry into Jewish missions and gentile missions, laying down a strategy of teamwork, not a framework of opposing or competing missions. Finally, they agreed to work together not only for evangelistic missions but also for the charitable act, "remembering the poor" in Jerusalem (Gal 2:10). They confirmed the partnership of the churches even in financial matters.

It goes without saying that the conference must have proceeded with genuine concerns and sincere discussions about the gospel of Christ, its meaning and ministry. In the course of the meeting, though undocumented, some adjustments might have been made to their theological thoughts and ecclesial practices. After all, even in the midst of ill-willed "false brothers," the leaders of both communities were united for the gospel ministry. David Sim says that "after much disputation he [Paul] convinced the three pillar apostles . . . This led in turn to an agreed demarcation of the Christian mission."[173] Rather, it would be more reasonable to say that after much *discussion*, Paul, Barnabas, and the three pillar apostles reached an amicable agreement of ministry and specialization. In

170. Grothe, "Missionary in Fellowship," 9.

171. Longenecker, *Galatians*, 58.

172. Put in Bruce's words, "There is no hint of any difference with regard to the *substance* of the gospel. . . . Still less was there any essential difference between the two groups with regard to the person of Christ" ("Paul and Jerusalem," 9).

173. Sim, "Matthew, Paul and the Origin," 381.

the spirit of cooperation, the attendants produced positive results beyond the initial tension in their relationship. The Jerusalem conference was an example of inter-group open talk and solution. Through the conference, Paul and the Jerusalem apostles were able to confirm their commonality in the gospel and establish a collaborative ministry for the gospel.

The Antioch Incident (Gal 2:11–14)

If there was "a confrontation in the air" at the Jerusalem conference, an open and blunt confrontation took place during the so-called Antioch incident (Gal 2:11–14). When Peter came to Antioch, he ate together with the gentile Christians.[174] Then, when some people came from James, Peter feared them and withdrew from the table-fellowship with the gentile Christians (Gal 2:12). Paul then openly condemned Peter for not acting on "the truth of the gospel" (Gal 2:14). This short passage has long been the focal text for most scholars to explain and determine the nature of the first-century church relationship. Particularly, since the latter half of the nineteenth century, New Testament scholarship has largely been influenced by Baur's interpretation of the incident: "In drawing this distinction between the Jewish and the Gentile Christians, he [Peter] practically declared that he no longer recognized the latter to be on the same level with the former."[175] For example, Dunn claims that the Antioch incident brought forth: (1) a breach between Paul and the Antioch church; (2) a breach between Paul and Barnabas; (3) a breach between Paul and the churches of Syria and Cilicia with which Paul had worked; and (4) an effective breach with the Jerusalem church.[176] Did the Antioch incident really bring such disunity to early Christianity?

It started with Peter's visitation to Antioch, "but when Cephas came to Antioch" (Gal 2:11). We are not told about when Cephas came to the city. It is most natural to reckon that the Antioch incident (Gal 2:11–14) occurred after the Jerusalem conference (Gal 2:1–10) as in the order of Paul's narrative of those events.[177] Since Paul does not refer or allude

174. The imperfect form of "eat with" (συνήσθιεν) indicates that Peter repeatedly or habitually ate with the gentile Christians in Antioch. Therefore, NASB and NIV render the passage as "he used to eat with the Gentiles."

175. Baur, *Church History*, 54.

176. See Dunn, *Beginning from Jerusalem*, 489–94; "Relationship between Paul and Jerusalem," 473–74.

177. Bruce, *Galatians*, 128.

to the Jerusalem Council (Acts 15), it must have happened before the Council.[178] Bauckham thus says, "the Antioch incident (Gal 2:11–14) belongs to the events which led immediately to the Jerusalem council" and "Galatians would have been written in the heat of this debate at Antioch, shortly before the Jerusalem council."[179] The phrase κατεγνωσμένος ἦν constitutes a periphrastic participle, meaning "he was to be blamed" (NKJV) or "he stood condemned" (NASB). The imperfect ἦν here "reads like a pluperfect and heightens the idea of a past existing state."[180] Paul's language conveys the certitude of his judgment on Peter.

After the general description of the incident (Gal 2:11), Paul gives a more detailed account, explaining the reason for his confrontation with Peter. The word ἐλθεῖν is an adverbial (temporal) infinitive. With the proposition πρό and the subject τινας ἀπὸ Ἰακώβου, the clause reads "before the coming of certain men from James" (Gal 2:12). Yet, who were the "certain men from James" and why did they come to Antioch? Many scholars have attempted to sort out the situation and proposed many views of their identity. Betz believes that "James himself was behind the 'men from James.' It is only because of Acts 15 that scholars have doubted this."[181] In contrast, Bockmuehl contends that the "men from James" may not have been commissioned by James himself and that they should be "carefully distinguished from Jewish and Judaizing opponents to Paul."[182] George's argument sounds more plausible: they were "zealous members of the ultra-right-wing party" and "were shocked when they saw how freely Peter was sharing table fellowship with uncircumcised believers in evident disregard for the usual practice of Jewish Christians at home."[183] Whatever the case, the majority of scholars agree that the "men from

178. The chronology taken in this book is as follows: (1) the Jerusalem conference and the strategic division of the gospel ministry (Gal 2:1–10, cf. Acts 11:30); (2) the first missionary journey to the Southern Galatia (Acts 13:2—14:28); (3) the Antioch incident (Gal 2:11–14); and (4) the Jerusalem Council (Acts 15). See the subsection "Paul's Visitations to Jerusalem" of the above section "Collaboration through Visitations."

179. Bauckham, "James and the Jerusalem Church," 469–70.

180. Longenecker, *Galatians*, 72.

181. Betz, *Galatians*, 108. In Acts 15:24, Jerusalem leaders say, "Since we have heard that some of our number to whom we gave no instruction have disturbed you with their words, unsettling your souls."

182. Bockmuehl, *Jewish Law in Gentile Churches*, 71–72.

183. George, *Galatians*, 175–76.

James" were related, one way or another, to James, the principal leader of the Jerusalem church.

Another question of identity needs to be raised: who were "those of the circumcision" (οἱ ἐκ περιτομῆς) at the end of the verse? Is this an appositive phrase indicating the people from James? If not, who were they? Bruce posits that "those of the circumcision" may have various meanings according to the context: (1) "circumcision party," i.e., the Judaizers within the church who held a particular partisan view of circumcision (Acts 11:2; 15:1; Gal 2:4; Titus 1:10); (2) circumcised members of the church, i.e., Jewish Christians in a non-partisan sense (Acts 10:45; Col 4:11); (3) circumcised people, i.e., non-Christian Jews (Rom 4:12).[184] For a more precise representation of the Jewish Christians, it is advisable to divide the second group further into two sub-groups—i.e., more conservative, law-abiding Jewish Christians and less conservative, tolerant Jewish Christians. If the former held strictly to the Mosaic laws and traditions, the latter accepted them in a more flexible way. If the former was represented by James, the latter, probably, by Peter.

Longenecker takes οἱ ἐκ περιτομῆς simply as Jews on the grounds that in the immediately preceding episode (Gal 2:7–9) ἡ περιτομή is used three times, all referring "to Jews and not to Jewish Christians or to Gentiles who had assumed Jewish ideas and ways."[185] Yet, were there any reasons for Peter to fear (φοβέομαι) the Jews in general? On the other hand, Esler opts for the literal meaning of οἱ ἐκ περιτομῆς. He speculates that "in Antioch, following the secession by Peter and the other Jews (Gal 2:12–13), circumcision had been demanded of the Gentile Christians."[186] If that was what really happened, that means the agreement of the Jerusalem conference (Gal 2:1–10) was breached by Peter and James. In fact, Esler claims, "there were strong pressures on James and Peter to abrogate the agreement, pressures to which they eventually succumbed in Antioch."[187] However, it is hardly conceivable that "James would have gone so quickly against the decision he had made with Paul and Barnabas in the private council with Peter and John."[188] Besides, according to the account of Paul, the main issue of the Antioch incident was not about circumcision but

184. Bruce, *Galatians*, 131.

185. Longenecker, *Galatians*, 73.

186. Esler, "Making and Breaking an Agreement," 262.

187. Esler, "Making and Breaking an Agreement," 264.

188. Just, "Apostolic Councils," 269.

about the table-fellowship with the gentiles. Therefore, the most natural reading of the passage will take οἱ ἐκ περιτομῆς as appositional to τινας ἀπὸ Ἰακώβου. "Those of the circumcision" indicates the aforementioned "men from James." It is to be further noted that they were not equivalent to "false brothers" (Gal 2:4) or the "circumcision party" (Acts 15:1, 24), who insisted on circumcision regarding the gentile believers.[189] Most probably, "certain men from James" ("those of the circumcision") were, as above mentioned, those who belonged to the "more conservative, law-abiding Jewish Christians" within the Jerusalem church.

Most New Testament scholars propose that Peter did not acquiesce to Paul's rebuke and that the confrontation became "a primary cause for the split between Paul and Barnabas as well as the reason that Antioch is never mentioned by Paul in any of his subsequent letters."[190] However, Luke clearly records that Paul and Barnabas split because of "a sharp disagreement" over the companionship of Mark, leaving no hint of the Antioch incident (Acts 15:36–40). At the Council of Jerusalem, "Barnabas stood four square with Paul" (Acts 15:12)[191] and they went out together as the emissaries of the Council (Acts 15:25–26). Years later, Paul still "associated himself with Barnabas in a positive manner" (1 Cor 9:5–6).[192] After the second missionary journey to Macedonia and Achaia, Paul returned to Antioch via Jerusalem (Acts 18:22–23) as he had normally done in the past. These biblical accounts are not congruent with the claim that the Antioch incident severed the relationship between Paul and Barnabas or the Antioch church. Concerning Paul's relationship with Peter, the alleged estrangement between the two finds no biblical or extra-biblical support. Instead, standing up for the law-free gospel of Christ at the Jerusalem Council (Acts 15:7–11), Peter supported the position of Paul and Barnabas.

It should be noted that the Antioch church, like any other New Testament churches, was in the volatile stage of identity formation as a new community of faith. Although the "Christians" at Antioch (Acts 11:26) held some typical beliefs about Jesus, "the earliest Christianity was not yet seen as something separate and distinct from Judaism."[193] As such, the

189. See Longenecker, *Galatians*, 73; Bruce, *Galatians*, 130.

190. Gibson, *Peter Between Jerusalem and Antioch*, 14.

191. Cole, *Galatians*, 118.

192. George, *Galatians*, 176. Paul says, "Or do only I and Barnabas not have the right not to work?" (1 Cor 9:6). Although they were not working together at this time, Paul still regarded Barnabas as his close coworker.

193. Dunn, "Incident at Antioch," 5.

Judaic laws and customs were still operative among the Christian Jews in the city. Within the Christian Jews, in addition, there must have been a range of different opinions and factions concerning the observance of Jewish traditions. It is very tenable that even the decision made by Paul and the "pillar" apostles (Gal 2:1–10) did not completely settle the controversy over circumcision and purity laws in the church. In this context, it is not surprising that "certain men from James" stirred up confusion and conflict in the Antioch church, which was made up of both Jews and gentiles.

It is inappropriate to view the Antioch incident, like Baur or Dunn, as a culmination of schism whereby two different camps of Christianity arose. First, as the passage clearly shows, the confrontation was not about heresy or apostasy, but about inconsistency of behavior. Serious as it was, a matter of table-fellowship with gentiles would not alienate Paul from Peter or vice versa.[194] Second, considering the "diversity and complexity of early Christianity," a dialectic analysis is "inadequate for understanding early Christianity, which cannot be simplified into a struggle between two parties."[195] Third, the determination of the New Testament church relationship should not be contingent on the interpretation of an incident, which might have been brief and transitory. It should be based on more substantial evidences, namely, more biblical references and allusions that corroborate the nature of the early church relationship.

To be sure, the Antioch incident was not characteristic of the church conference intended for collaboration and decision-making. Nevertheless, the meeting involved several factions of the earliest church and occasioned frank interactions, which led even to the point of stern confrontation. The confrontation may have brought about a temporary uneasiness in their relationship, but it did not cause a substantial opposition or separation. As Alexander rightly affirms, "real unity, real communion in Christ . . . is the kind we are able to maintain with people with whom

194. In this connection, think of Paul's fundamental ministry principle stated in 1 Cor 9:20–22: "And to the Jews I became as a Jew that I might win Jews; to those who are under the Law, as under the Law . . . I have become all things to all men that I may by all means save some." Paul would have accepted all things for the cause of the gospel of Christ. Also, even though Peter drew back from the table-fellowship with the gentiles in certain situation, he probably used to eat with the gentiles since his vision in Acts 10:9–16. Related to the table-fellowship with the gentiles, the Antioch incident could hardly be a turning point for Peter's life-ling gospel ministry.

195. Taylor, *Paul, Antioch and Jerusalem*, 23. He rightly points out that the diversity and complexity of early Christianity "are more fully appreciated today than was the case with Baur."

we disagree."[196] In this sense, the incident at Antioch rather intimated a genuine relationship of early church leaders. Bruce argues that the Jerusalem Council was convened in large measure to solve the social issues which had arisen to the surface during the Antioch incident.[197] George observes that the Antioch incident (Gal 2:11–14) rendered "an important link" between the Jerusalem conference (Gal 2:1–10; Acts 11:30) and the Jerusalem Council (Acts 15).[198] The incident of confrontation may have served as a momentum to straighten up the truth of the gospel among the New Testament churches.

The Jerusalem Council (Acts 15)

Controversy at Antioch became more acute when some men arrived from Judea and insisted "unless you are circumcised according to the custom of Moses, you cannot be saved" (Acts 15:1). "A fierce argument" (GNT) broke out between the men form Judea, and Paul and Barnabas.[199] So the Antioch church sent Paul and Barnabas to Jerusalem to consult with the apostles and the elders about the dispute (Acts 15:2). It is worth observing a textual variant in this verse. The Western text (Codex Bezae) reads, "those who came from Jerusalem ordered them—Paul, Barnabas, and some others—to go up [to Jerusalem]."[200] The men from Judea, instead of the Antioch church, are said to have arranged the expedition. In other words, the men associated with the Jerusalem church were directly involved in the activity of the Antioch believers. Epp comments on this that "the early church is one of unity, and Paul can be portrayed as willing

196. Alexander, "Community and Canon," 47. Referring to a letter written by Irenaeus, Bishop of Lyons, to Victor, Bishop of Rome, around 190 AD, Alexander affirms the ecclesiastical cooperation and unity in the midst of conflict and disagreement.

197. Bruce, *Galatians*, 128.

198. George, *Galatians*, 170.

199. "A fierce argument" is originally "no small dissention and debate" (στάσεως καὶ ζητήσεως οὐκ ὀλίγης). "No small" is here used as an expression of emphasis. The noun στάσις also means "riot" or "insurrection" (Luke 23:19, 25; Acts 19:40). So the men from Judea and their teaching gave rise to "great" (NASB), "sharp" (NIV), and "vehement" (NLT) disturbance and debate in the church. It should be noticed that Paul and Barnabas were on the same side debating in opposition to the circumcision party.

200. Rius-Camps and Read-Heimerdinger, *Message of Acts*, 174–75. The Western text reads, οἱ δὲ ἐληλυθότες ἀπὸ Ἰερουσαλὴμ παρήγγειλαν αὐτοῖς τῷ Παύλῳ καὶ τῷ Βαρναβᾷ καί τισιν ἄλλοις ἀναβαίνειν.

to be examined at Jerusalem rather than risk a breach of that unity."[201] Although the following verse 3 confirms that the sending was arranged by the Antioch church (Acts 15:3), the emphasis of the Western text is worthy of note: Antioch and Jerusalem were willing to forge a common ground of faith as one body of Christ.

When the Antiochene delegates arrived at Jerusalem, they were "received" (παρεδέχθησαν) by the whole church including "the apostles and the elders." The Greek verb παραδέχομαι is not a word of neutral meaning: it signifies "to acknowledge something to be correct" or "to accept the presence of someone in a hospitable manner, receive, accept."[202] The reception of the Jerusalem church was warm and positive (Acts 15:4). However, when Paul and Barnabas reported their gentile missions, some of the believers who belonged to "the sect of the Pharisees" stood up and demanded that the gentiles should be circumcised and required to obey the law of Moses (Acts 15:5). So the Jerusalem Council (Acts 15:6) was convened. Luke's account of the event gives the impression that the opposing group of Pharisaic Christians was small in number compared to the majority of the Jerusalem congregation who heartily welcomed the brothers from Antioch. Myllykoski thus argues that "those who demanded circumcision of the Gentiles were but a tiny and independent minority in the church of Jerusalem."[203]

The apostles and the elders had "much debate" (πολλή ζήτησις) on the issue of gentiles and Jewish laws (Acts 15:7). Afterwards, Peter stood up and said: "God bore witness to the Gentiles, giving them the Holy Spirit, just as He also did to us . . . we are saved through the grace of the Lord Jesus, in the same way as they also are" (Acts 15:8–11).[204] Peter's words are reminiscent of Paul's in Acts 13:38–39.[205] Both emphasiz the sole competency of the grace of God in Christ for the salvation of all men, Jews and gentiles alike. All the attendants might have embraced Peter's words, since, as Barrett describes the scene, "Peter's speech silenced the ζήτησις of verse 7."[206] It is noteworthy that Peter, though rebuked by

201. Epp, *Theological Tendency of Codex Beaze*, 96–97.

202. BDAG, s.v. "παραδέχομαι."

203. Myllykoski, "James the Just," 92.

204. Peter's testimony is related to his own experience at the house of Cornelius in Caesarea. Peter and all the other Jews with him "were amazed, because the gift of the Holy Spirit had been poured out upon the Gentiles also" (Acts 10:45).

205. Conzelmann, *Acts*, 117.

206. Barrett, *Acts*, 721.

Paul recently, spoke out for Paul's stance and gentile missions. Just argues that Peter served "as spokesman for Paul/Barnabas and for the Antioch church," which was "an act of great kindness to Paul by Peter."[207] If the Jerusalem apostles and the elders took Peter's speech seriously, which is most probable, they must also have listened to the subsequent testimony of Paul and Barnabas in a positive manner (Acts 15:12). Finally, after the debate, the words of Peter, and the testimony of Paul and Barnabas, James gave a concluding statement (ἐγὼ κρίνω) based on Amos 9:11–12, confirming Peter's remark (Acts 15:13–18).

James proposed that the gentile believers should not be inflicted with the burden of circumcision and the Mosaic laws except the abstinence from food polluted by idols, sexual immorality, what is strangled, and blood. The decree enacted two principles, that is, "a formal rejection of the demand of the Judaizers" (Acts 15:19) and "a fourfold challenge to Gentiles not to offend Jews" (Acts 15:20–21).[208] The former upheld the claim of Paul and the Antioch church and reinforced the mission to the gentiles. The latter preserved the basic tenet of the Law, keeping "the lines of fellowship open with Jewish believers."[209] As Alexander lucidly presents, the decree of the Jerusalem Council represented "a minimalist formula for maintaining communion between Jewish and Gentile believers, not a compromise but a common platform for engaging difference, allowing both sides to maintain *communitas* while continuing to respect the irreducible diversity of each other's experience of Gospel and Spirit."[210]

Since the conflict and confusion arose from the instigation of the "men from Judea" (Acts 15:1), it may have been necessary to send to Antioch not just a letter of notice but also certain official delegates fully authorized and accredited by the Jerusalem church. The apostles and the elders, with the whole church, chose Judas and Silas, the leading men of their own, and sent them to Antioch with Paul and Barnabas, along with the letter conveying the decision of the Council (Acts 15:22). While the letter starts with the common style of greeting, it characterizes both the senders and the receivers as "brothers": "the apostles and the elders, [your]

207. Just, "Apostolic Councils," 280–81.

208. Peterson, *Acts*, 423.

209. Peterson, *Acts*, 440.

210. Alexander, "Community and Canon," 77.

brothers, to the brothers in Antioch, Syria, and Cilicia" (Acts 15:23).[211] The language seems to be "intended to stress the close brotherly feeling that existed between churches."[212] Immediately after the greeting, the letter acknowledges that "the men from Judea" were not those authorized by the Jerusalem church, thereby officially denouncing the claim of the circumcision party (Acts 15:24). On the other hand, it commends Paul and Barnabas for their faithful ministry, describing them as "our beloved brothers" (Acts 15:25) and "men who have risked their lives for the name of our Lord Jesus Christ" (Acts 15:26). Reading between the lines, one can perceive that the Jerusalem church was seeking to resolve the Law-related issues and keep a good relationship with the gentile churches.

When the Antioch believers read the decree of the Jerusalem Council, they "rejoiced at the encouragement" (παράκλησις) (Acts 15:30–31). Judas and Silas, the emissaries of the Jerusalem church, also encouraged the Antioch brothers (Acts 15:32), and after some time, were sent off in peace from the brothers back to Jerusalem (Acts 15:33). Luke uses the words παράκλησις and παρακαλέω, indicating that the Jerusalem Council brought comfort and encouragement to the gentile believers. In other words, Luke is claiming that "Gentile Christianity is free from the Law and that the unity of the church had been preserved."[213] Later on, commissioned by the Antioch church, Paul and Silas set out for the second missionary journey (Acts 15:40–41). Yet, what they did, traveling from town to town, was to deliver the decrees of the Jerusalem Council for the believers to observe (Acts 16:4). That is, Paul and Silas served as the emissaries of the Jerusalem church as well as the missionaries of the Antioch church. Not only the Antioch church but also the churches in Syria, Cilicia, and Galatia must have been renewed and reinforced in their relationship with the mother church at Jerusalem. Luke concludes the long narrative related to the Jerusalem Council: "So the churches were being strengthened in the faith and were increasing in number daily" (Acts 16:5).

211. Various translations may be possible for the phrase, οἱ ἀπόστολοι καὶ οἱ πρεσβύτεροι ἀδελφοὶ: "the apostles and the brethren who are elders" (NASB); "the apostles, the elders, and the brethren" (NKJV); "the apostles and elders, your brothers" (NIV); and "the brothers, both the apostles and the elders" (NRSV). Given the repeated occurrence of "the apostles and the elders" in the context (Acts 15:2, 4, 6, 22), the phrase is best translated as "the apostles and the elders, who are your brothers."

212. Marshall, *Acts*, 269.

213. Barrett, *Acts*, 748–49.

The Jerusalem Council has been described as "watershed event in the early Christian church, the most significant decision in the church's history up to that point."[214] After the Council, the claim of the Judaizers or Pharisaic Christians lost ground to the law-free gospel of Christ. Gentile Christians secured the freedom from the Jewish laws in communion with Jewish Christians. The axis of missions shifted from the Jews to the gentiles, with the twelve apostles fading out and Paul taking center stage in the story of the church, i.e., in the book of Acts. Besides the epoch-making change, another significance of the Council was the fact that it exhibited intensive inter-church communication and cooperation for the unity of the church. Kloha perceptively says, "there was the assumption, indeed the necessity, of sharing the same confession and practice, even though the congregations themselves were located in very different cultural contexts."[215] Therefore, the Antioch church was "determined not to dodge the issue, but to send delegates to Jerusalem to lay the dispute before the apostles and the elders," and the Jerusalem church also showed "a commitment to κοινωνία," by welcoming the delegates and holding the conference open to the whole church.[216] Concluding the discussion of the Jerusalem Council, Peterson presents the crux of the conference:

> Here we find an important manifestation of the church as an entity involving local congregations in partnership, working together to maintain the truth of God's word and promote the work of the gospel. The Jerusalem Council makes the gospel of salvation by faith alone the key to defining the true nature of this church, which involves Jewish and Gentile believers together.[217]

Conclusion

New Testament churches, in relation with Paul's ministry, had many occasions for communication, which included writing letters, sending and receiving envoys, visitations, local or trans-local conferences, etc. The numerous accounts of these communicative activities in the book of Acts

214. Just, "Apostolic Councils," 276. He adds, "in the book of Acts, the council appears at the midpoint: the first fourteen chapters contain 12,385 words, and the final fourteen chapters contain 12,502 words."

215. Kloha, "Trans-Congregational Church," 176.

216. Alexander, "Community and Canon," 75.

217. Peterson, *Acts*, 443.

and Paul's letters strongly suggest that the ministry of partnership was prominent and prevalent among Paul, his churches, and other churches. This chapter explored various communicative activities in light of the networking and collaboration of New Testament churches. It showed how the churches, beyond Pauline and non-Pauline distinction, were related to one another and worked together for the common cause of the gospel ministry.

In the first section, since the church arose in the Greco-Roman world, the Jewish and Hellenistic contexts of communication were briefly surveyed—ancient travels and letter-writing, the interrelationship of voluntary associations, and the social network of Jewish communities in the Diaspora. It is undeniable that New Testament churches took shape, being influenced by the Greco-Roman society. The second section discussed one of the most important means of communication, lettering-writing. Paul wrote many letters, which turned out to be crucial not only to the shaping of Christian theology but also to the construction of the church as one body of Christ. His letters connected many Christian communities together, reinforcing the sense of unity and the ministry of partnership. The third section concerned Paul's travels and visitations to local churches and Jerusalem. Paul's visits to local churches not only strengthened the congregations individually but also strengthened the relationships between the congregations. His continuous visits to Jerusalem speak for his compliant and cooperative attitude toward the apostles and the elders of the Jerusalem church. The final section reviewed the three conferences—the Jerusalem conference (Gal 2:1–10), the Antioch incident (Gal 2:11–14), and the Jerusalem Council (Acts 15). These conferences brought about challenge, reconciliation, and cooperation among the first-century churches beyond the Pauline and non-Pauline demarcation.

Concerning the communicative activities of the churches, Stewart rightly points out that "the extant evidence represents only a fraction of the communication that took place. Paul made trips and visited individuals for whom no records exist. He sent messengers with oral presentations for which there is no evidence. He wrote letters which are no longer extant."[218] The New Testament churches were in active communication and cooperation with one another, presumably, more than has generally been recognized.

218. Stewart, "Communication Networks and Social Cohesion," 84.

5

Conclusion

Summary of Findings

The present study began with the belief that a careful look at Paul's partnership ministry would offer a much richer understanding of the interrelationship of Paul's churches, which would further reflect the first-century church relations involving both Pauline and non-Pauline churches. Based on this understanding, this study investigated the partnership ministry of Paul, his coworkers, and local churches in the context of the first-century Greco-Roman world. What is the result of this investigation? That is, what does the New Testament say about the relationship of the earliest churches? Put concisely, the present study demonstrated that Paul's partnership ministry significantly contributed to the establishment of networking and collaboration among the New Testament churches.

The first chapter, as an introduction, laid out a blueprint for the present work. It examined three areas of Paul's partnership ministry—coworkers, financial assistance, and communicative activities—paying attention to their implications in local and trans-local church relationships. These three ministry areas formed three major chapters of this book. In addition, the study was done, as much as possible, with the scope of ministry in view—local, translocal, and beyond the Pauline churches. Therefore, Paul's partnership ministry and church relationships were observed, first, among the house churches in a local area, second, among the major churches in trans-local areas, and finally, among Pauline and non-Pauline churches.

Arguments in this study rested on the concrete activities and events that happened in the life and work of Paul, his coworkers, and the local churches. Therefore, for a better understanding of those historical occurrences, a brief review of their socio-religious backgrounds was presented in each chapter. Particularly, since "the long-established Jewish networks of contact and communication were the best conduits through which the messianic movement could travel,"[1] the social networks and activities of the Jewish Diaspora were given more attention in light of Paul's partnership ministry and church relations.

Most church and inter-church activities in the New Testament were related to the ministry of Paul and his coworkers. Consequently, New Testament church relationships can be traced by examining the ministry of Paul and his coworkers. Chapter 2 therefore explored the missionary activities of Paul's coworkers. In the first section, some relevant concepts were laid down for discussion. Various definitions and functions of Paul's coworkers were explained based on the Greek vocabulary of "coworkers" in the book of Acts and Paul's letters. Paul's coworkers were categorized roughly into three groups according to their primary field of missions: local, trans-local, and beyond the Pauline boundary. For contextual understanding, the section surveyed the Greco-Roman customs of household and patronage, which were assimilated into the structure of Paul's ministry and his churches. More importantly, this section also discussed the position of Paul's coworkers in relation with the local churches. It provided an important premise for the present study, that is, the inseparable relationship between the ministry of Paul and his coworkers on the one hand, and the ministry of the local churches on the other.

The second section focused on the local ministry of Paul's coworkers. Paul's missionary works mostly resulted in the development of house churches in the area. When Paul departed, Paul's coworkers continued the missionary works and also maintained the new community of believers. The community sometimes went through internal dispute and disunity. Nevertheless, they jointly sent out missionaries, collected for financial assistance, and shared Paul's letters with one another. Despite occasions of tension and conflict, the house churches continued to assemble for

1. Barclay, "Jews of the Diaspora," 27.

worship and ministry as one body of Christ. At the center of this networking and collaboration were Paul's coworkers.

The third section investigated trans-local coworkers in the order of (1) Paul's travel companions and emissaries, (2) Paul's ministry associates from the local churches, and (3) messengers of the local churches. As messengers either from Paul to local churches or from local churches to Paul, they played a crucial role in facilitating communication between Paul and the local churches. Local churches also participated in Paul's missions by sending their own members to Paul to assist his ministry. Partnership ministry through Paul's coworkers naturally led to inter-church collaborations since the ministry of Paul and his coworkers was closely interwoven with the ministry of local churches.

In the final section, independent coworkers were examined. They were "independent" because they were engaged in non-Pauline missions as well. For example, although Apollos and Barnabas were Paul's important coworkers, they also conducted missionary campaigns on their own. Aquila and Priscilla moved around the metropolitan areas, continuing missionary works and hosting the local believers in their house church. Though independent, they were in communication with Paul. Barnabas was also a bridge builder relating people to people and church to church. He made a significant contribution to the establishment of the Antioch church and her relationship with the Jerusalem church. Silas's mission was unique. As a prophet from Jerusalem, he accompanied Paul in the Aegean mission and, afterwards, worked for Peter as a messenger. Mark was a connecting link between Paul and Peter. The most important fact found in this section was that these independent coworkers turned out to be effective connectors for trans-local church relationships, particularly, correlating Pauline and non-Pauline churches, gentile and Jewish missions. Their activities revealed the overall spirit of unity and cooperation among the New Testament churches.

Chapter 3 discussed financial assistance in Paul's partnership ministry. First, widespread poverty in antiquity, particularly in the area of Jerusalem, was surveyed for the background understanding of financial needs and actions among the earliest churches. This section dealt with two social equivalents of Paul's churches, i.e., Greco-Roman voluntary associations and Jewish communities in the Diaspora. The practice of financial assistance among voluntary associations was common and well-known to the first-century world. Given the prevalence of voluntary associations in the society, it is unlikely that "early Christian followers in

Corinth or Macedonia did not know how to collect money or that Paul was somehow innovative in organizing a collection."[2] More importantly, with their ethnic and religious link, the custom of Jewish communities in the Diaspora had a substantial effect on the financial ministry of the Christian communities around the Mediterranean world.

The second section discussed financial activities of the local churches under the titles of "Community of Goods" in Jerusalem, "Brotherly Love" in Macedonian, and "Ministry to the Saints" in Achaia. It is to be noted that each title did not represent an exclusive character confined to the titled community. Rather, New Testament churches, though differing in specifics, all shared similar characters in ministering fellow Christians. To provide financial assistance, house churches had to develop a communal network and collaborate with one another. Although biblical data for financial assistance at the local level was limited, a careful reading of some biblical texts was able to intimate the practice of financial assistance among the house churches in the local area.

In the third section, the financial assistance for Paul was examined. It noticed the importance of self-support in Paul's ministry and argued that Paul's self-supporting policy was for the sake of the gospel ministry as well as for the benefit of fellow believers. An impressive finding was that the ministry of self-support was for Paul based on the mutual support and cooperation rather than the independence itself. The financial gifts from the Philippians enabled Paul to carry out his missions effectively in Corinth and later in Rome. It means that the Philippians participated in Paul's ministry in Corinth and in Rome, and the partnership means that "the new churches were indebted to the older ones."[3] New Testament churches, directly or indirectly, advertently or inadvertently, networked and collaborated with one another in supporting Paul's missions.

The fourth section examined the financial contributions for the Jerusalem church made by the Antioch church and then by Paul's churches. First, the temple tax system in the Diaspora was discussed to understand the Jewish context of the financial assistance for the Jerusalem church. The collection of the half-shekel tax certainly contributed to the maintenance of cultic system in the Jerusalem temple. A more significant role of the collection was to spiritually muster all the diasporan Jewish communities toward Jerusalem, the capital of the Jews. Second, with regard

2. Kloppenborg and Ascough, *Greco-Roman Associations*, 12.

3. Hvalvik, "All Those," 128. Here, the new churches represent those at Corinth and Rome, the older ones, the churches at Philippi.

to the contribution of the Antioch church, it was noted that each member of the church contributed "in the proportion that any of the disciples had means" (Acts 11:29). It means that all the house churches in Antioch joined together in the financial ministry. Third, this section examined Paul's "collection" for the Jerusalem church. While most scholars tended to present theological explanations, the present study was devoted primarily to the facts and events of church relations in the process of collecting funds. Concerning the collection, it is to be noted, "*all* the members of the churches were contributors as, indeed, were *all* the communities."[4] Unmistakably, Paul's collection ministry was a concerted act of cooperation among the New Testament churches, local or trans-local, Pauline or non-Pauline.

Chapter 4 examined Paul's partnership ministry through various communicative activities, such as letter-writing, visitations, and conferences. The first section surveyed three topics of the Greco-Roman social networking and communication: travels and letters in the first-century world, social networks of the voluntary association, and social networks of the Jewish community. Even a brief survey was enough to reveal that the first-century world was considerably mobile and communicative much more than usually thought. Such social traffic reinforced inter-personal and inter-community relations around the Mediterranean basin, including the widespread Pauline communities.

Paul's ministry greatly impacted the shape of early Christianity. The most lasting impact would be his letters. Besides the critical role of the main repository of Christian doctrines, Paul's letters served as important mediums for building up the network of communication and cooperation, which was indispensable for the development of early Christianity. So, the second section discussed several styles characteristic of Paul's letter-writing. It explained Paul's customary practice of including co-senders. Certainly, Paul teamed up with his coworkers in letter-writing. In addition, two more epistolary styles were examined, that is, greetings for multiple people and frequent references to other churches in his letters. These letter-writing styles must have reminded the readers that they belonged to one and the same community with Paul, his coworkers, the community where Paul stays, and any other churches cited by Paul. Paul's letters helped advance mutual awareness and relationship among the local house churches as well as among the trans-local churches over the

4. Meggitt, *Paul, Poverty, and Survival*, 159.

Empire. Paul's letters need to be studied with more emphasis on their public and communal nature.

It is comprehensible to say that "Paul should be seen as a 'professional traveler.'"[5] As such, Paul visited numerous cities and villages, and met with numerous individuals and groups in preaching the gospel of Christ and in nurturing the new believers. In the third section, it was shown that Paul's visitation to local churches prompted the local believers to perceive a larger body of Christ beyond their boundaries and to develop relationships with other believers in distant lands as well as in the neighborhood. In addition, Paul's frequent visits to Jerusalem demonstrated that there was a shared understanding of one church and one gospel between Paul and the Jerusalem apostles. Paul's churches and the Jerusalem church belonged to the same body of Christ and were committed to the same missions for the gospel of Christ.

The last section of chapter 4 examined the three conferences that took place during the earliest days of church development—Paul's conference with the Jerusalem apostles (Gal 2:1–10), the Antioch incident (Gal 2:11–14), and the Jerusalem Council (Acts 15). Meeting face to face in a conference, people usually communicate and interact more effectively. In that sense, the examination of the three conferences displayed the intensity of communication, interaction, and cooperation existent among the Christian communities. The conferences also exhibited some conflict and confusion in the church. However, they proceeded with a genuine concern for the whole church and resulted in a united solution, overcoming the conflict and confusion. Holding a conference itself was a clear sign of communal effort to preserve the common faith in Christ and the unity of the church.

Biblical and Ecclesial Implications

In the middle of the nineteenth century, F. C. Baur advocated a hypothesis that the first-century church was divided into two opposing groups, Petrine/Judean Christianity versus Pauline/gentile Christianity. Although his theory has not been fully accepted by the majority of modern New Testament scholars, the concept of conflict and opposition in early Christianity has continued to influence much of the agenda and methodology of the contemporary New Testament scholarship. Particularly,

5. Rapske, "Acts, Travel and Shipwreck," 1.

Baur's analysis of the Antioch incident (Gal 2:11–14) has provided for subsequent generations a frame of reference to the relationship between Paul and the Jerusalem apostles. That is, with difference in degree, most scholars tended to think that the Antioch incident led to a split between Paul and Jerusalem.

In a similar vein, the term "Paul's opponent" has become almost proverbial in Pauline study, bringing forth numerous books and articles on that subject.[6] On the contrary, however, Paul's friends or coworkers, though specifically named and more frequently referred to, have not been paid as much attention as they should have been, with only a few scholarly works published on the topic. Even allowing for that "Paul's epistolary responses are often in rebuttal of opposition,"[7] the apparent imbalance in the treatment of "Paul's opponents" and "Paul's friends/coworkers" cannot be adequately explained without recourse to the effect of Baur's hypothesis. Likewise, it may well be that the nature of cooperative relationships among New Testament churches has been unfairly shadowed by the Bauerian concept of opposition for more than a century. Baur's legacy still remains in contemporary New Testament scholarship.

Based on this understanding, the present study endeavored to shed light on the cooperative nature of New Testament churches. It demonstrated that a great number of Paul's coworkers were actively involved in Paul's ministry. Their local and trans-local activities enabled Paul's churches to relate to one another and also to other non-Pauline churches. Most Pauline churches provided financial assistance not only for their own communities or Paul's ministry, but also for the Jerusalem church. No one can refute the mutual care and cooperation between Pauline and non-Pauline churches embodied through the sharing of financial resources. In addition, the vigor of communicative activities—letters, visitations, and conferences—evidenced in the book of Acts and Paul's letters is more than enough to confirm the vitality of networking and collaboration among the New Testament churches. Particularly, Paul's consistent visits to Jerusalem and meetings with the Jerusalem leaders represent the presence of partnership between Paul and his churches on the one hand, and the apostles and the Jerusalem church on the other. In

6. There has been much study on "Paul's opponents." Some of influential works are: Ellis, "Paul and his Opponents," 264–98; Georgi, *Opponents of Paul in Second Corinthians*; Lüdemann, *Opposition to Paul in Jewish Christianity*; Sumney, *Identifying Paul's Opponents*; Sumney, *'Servants of Satan'*; and Porter, *Paul and His Opponents*.

7. Barnett, "Opponents of Paul," 644.

short, contrary to Baur's hypothesis, the earliest church was, overall, in unity and cooperation rather than in conflict and opposition.

A paradigm is important in the development of one's perception and judgment. It will thus make a considerable difference whether one has the paradigm of the church in unity or the paradigm of the church in conflict. For example, according to the church relationship discussed so far, it is quite probable that the Jerusalem church accepted the collection money contributed by their fellow Christian communities. On the contrary, however, those with the paradigm of the church in conflict would argue that "the collection may have failed in its basic purpose and that the Jerusalem church refused to accept any of it for itself."[8] The paradigm of conflict is also obvious in Sim's interpretation of a biblical text. Discussing the Great Commission in Matt 28:16–20, he argues that "the mission to which they were called was fully Law-observant for both Jew and Gentile," which was "directly contrary to the claims of Paul."[9] Further, Sim even contends that the Matthean pericope was "specifically designed by the evangelist to counter the person, the theology and the mission of Paul."[10] Behind Sim's view of the biblical text is Baur's concept of two opposing Christian missions.

However, given the findings of the present study, most biblical accounts of church occasion and incident in the New Testament need to be approached in the light of unity and cooperation. Even the confrontation at Antioch (Gal 2:11–14) is to be understood in a larger context of early church development and relationship-building. Otherwise, one may attach too much importance to the confrontation itself, which may have been not-so-unusual to the fledgling stage of early Christianity.[11] When viewed from the perspective of the church in unity, all the conferences discussed in chapter 4, in one way or another, have certain aspects of correlating and consolidating the churches together. George, probably in

8. Wedderburn, "Paul's Collection," 110.

9. Sim, "Matthew, Paul and the Origin," 390.

10. Sim, "Matthew, Paul and the Origin," 390.

11. For example, Dunn emphasizes that Paul's attitude towards the Jerusalem apostles dramatically changed from dependence to independence and separation ("Relationship between Paul and Jerusalem," 471–74). Chilton maintains that since the incident Paul "was isolated from every other Christian Jew" and the isolation quickly led him to develop a distinctive approach to the Scripture, "the dialectic between grace and law" ("James, Peter, Paul," 7). Similarly, many scholars regard the Antioch incident as a culmination of great schism or a watershed point that diverted the stream of first-century Christian movement.

this sense, argues that "the incident at Antioch was an important link between Paul's earlier agreement with the Jerusalem leaders on missionary strategy and the later settlement of the Jerusalem Council regarding the inclusion of Gentiles into the Christian fellowship."[12]

In Phil 4:2, Paul writes, "I plead with Euodia and I plead with Syntyche to agree with each other in the Lord." Paul's exhortation for agreement reveals that there was a conflict in the church between the church leaders. However, it is quite probable that the Philippians listened to Paul's exhortation, met together, and recovered rapprochement. Even the Corinthians, infamous for internal division (1 Cor 1:12), may have accepted Paul's admonition against disunity. According to *1 Clement*, one of the earliest extra-biblical documents, the Corinthians may have responded to Paul's letter written "in the Spirit concerning himself and Cephas and Apollos" in sorrow and repentance (cf. 2 Cor 7:9).[13] Regarding the church conflict in the book of Acts, Johnson makes a perceptive statement: "Luke clearly sees conflict and debate as legitimate and perhaps even necessary elements in the process of discernment . . . Luke is unembarrassed by it, for such disagreement serves to reveal the true bases for fellowship and elicit the fundamental principles of community identity."[14] Even in the midst of church conflict, a positive construction of relationship is possible and reasonable. Observed from the viewpoint of the church in unity, conflict is also a part of the process bound for oneness in Christ.

It is worth recalling the questions posed at the very beginning of this study. What type of relationship did the New Testament churches have with one another? Was it, as Baur and his followers have claimed, a relationship of conflict and opposition? Or was it like a loose aggregation of individual churches scattered over the Greco-Roman world? Or can it be rather described as a cohesive partnership for the common cause of the gospel of Christ? The present study affirms the last question: New Testament churches, Pauline and non-Pauline, were basically in cooperative relationship with one another, far from being in conflict or competition. It is also true that the paradigm of the earliest churches in unity will

12. George, *Galatians*, 170.

13. 1 Clem. 47.3. Later, the Corinthians fell again into conflict and disunity among themselves. However, the conflict among the Corinthians should not be taken as the Bauerian conflict of the earliest churches divided into Pauline/gentile vs. Petrine/Jewish churches.

14. Johnson, *Acts of the Apostles*, 271.

have an important bearing on the understanding of some biblical texts and on the view of early church development.

Without the partnership ministry of Paul, would it have been possible that the wide-spread early churches remained joined and held together? Without the spirit of oneness and collaboration, would it have been possible that the churches overcame internal and external obstacles and moved on through the subsequent centuries? The answers seem to be both negative. That is, Paul's partnership ministry played an indispensable role in the formation and development of early churches as the body of Christ. It laid a groundwork for the coming age of Christianity. At this juncture, twenty-first century churches may find the importance of Paul's partnership ministry to themselves as they reach out to the new field of post-modern world. They may find useful strategies from Paul's missionary works and New Testament church relations. As the community of one faith and one hope (Eph 4:4–5), what can the Christian church glean from the partnership ministry of Paul, his coworkers, and the local churches?

First, concerning the ideal of the churches in unity, Thomassen notes that "it was an ideal that had practical implications insofar as it inspired individual communities to actively seek and maintain contact with one another, through traveling, correspondence, counseling, and exchanges of gifts."[15] That is, the church in unity is accordant, more than anything else, with actual contacts and collaborations among individual Christian communities. The networking and cooperation of Pauline and non-Pauline churches had to do with the miles that Paul and other Christians traveled, the number of times they conferred, and the amount of money they contributed for financial assistance. This is true of the church today. The first step to the ideal of the church(es) in unity will be to communicate and confer with one another, work together for the gospel ministry, and support fellow members in need as much as possible.

Second, the church in unity is not equivalent to the church in uniformity. Paul declares to the Galatians: "There is neither Jew nor Greek, there is neither slave nor free man, there is neither male nor female; for you are all one in Christ Jesus" (Gal 3:28). However, he also exhorts to the Corinthians: "Let each one remain in that, in the calling which he was called" (1 Cor 7:20). To be sure, Paul did not abrogate the social structure of the ancient world. While each of the Corinthians was an equal and essential part that made up the Corinthian church, everyone remained

15. Thomassen, "Orthodoxy and Heresy," 248–49.

the same in his/her old status. The Jerusalem conference (Gal 2:1–10) acknowledged two different paths of mission, Pauline/gentile and Petrine/Judean, which were not of division but of diversity for the effectiveness of the gospel ministry. The Jerusalem Council (Acts 15) did not issue a decree of uniform actions required for all churches. Rather, it recognized and affirmed the respective position of gentile and Jewish Christians. The concept of the church(es) in unity presupposes differences and disagreements existing in the church.

Third, the call for unity needs to appropriate certain dynamics of church relationship. In Paul's missionary journeys, two directions of movement were noticeable, one toward Jerusalem and the other toward the local churches in the Diaspora. That is, Paul continually visited the local churches around the Mediterranean, but always returned to Jerusalem.[16] Paul's churches sent their representatives and contributions to the Jerusalem church. The Jerusalem church, on the other hand, sent out its emissaries to the Christian communities abroad. This two-way movement may signify the coexistence of two discrete concepts—the sense of oneness and the sense of independence—in early church relationships. This conception is also meaningful to present-day churches and denominations. For example, according to McBeth, two basic ideas have stood out in the Baptist tradition: first, each church is complete within itself, a distinct body under Christ's lordship, and second, each church should relate to other churches in their life and work.[17] He succinctly states that "the Baptists established two anchors of their ecclesiology: each church is independent, and all the churches are interdependent."[18] As discussed in the previous chapters, Paul maintained bold independence from the Jerusalem church, but at the same time, displayed genuine reliance on the church. The application of these two concepts to the contemporary Christian communities will guard against indiscriminate ecumenism on the one hand, and unbiblical denominationalism on the other. The concept of independence and interdependence in balance is crucial for the growth of the church as one body of Christ.

Based on Paul's partnership ministry, some principles were laid down for the advancement of the church(es) in unity and cooperation. Practical and specific methods of application will need to be developed

16. Porter, "How Do We Define," 7.

17. McBeth, "Cooperation and Crisis," 36.

18. McBeth, "Cooperation and Crisis," 36.

according to the distinct circumstance of different churches and different denominations. Yet, fundamental truth is that Christian communities—regardless of their localities or ecclesial forms or nonessential theologies—exist as the body of Christ, i.e., the church(es) in unity and cooperation. "So we, the many, are one body in Christ, and individually members of one another" (Rom 12:5).

Appendix 1

Paul's Coworkers in the Local Ministry

Community	Coworkers	Biblical Sources
Philippi	Lydia	Acts 16:13–15, 40
	Euodia, Syntyche	Phil 4:2–3
Thessalonica	Jason	Acts 17:7; Rom 16:21 (?)
Corinth	Titus Justus	Acts 18:7
	Crispus (synagogue ruler)	Acts 18:8; 1 Cor 1:14
	Gaius	1 Cor 1:14; Rom 16:23
	Quartus	Rom 16:23
	Stephanas	1 Cor 1:16; 16:15–18
	Fortunatus, Achaicus	1 Cor 16:17–18
Cenchrea	Phoebe	Rom 16:1–2
Ephesus	Onesiphorus	2 Tim 1:16–18; 4:19
Colossae	Philemon (& Apphia?)	Phlm 1:1–2
	Archippus	Col 4:17; Phlm 1:2

Laodicea	Nympha	Col 4:15
Troas	Carpus	2 Tim 4:13
Rome	Epenetus, Mary, Andronichus, Junias, Ampliatus, Urbanus, Stachys, Apelles, Aristobulus, Herodion, Narcissus, Tryphena, Tryphosa, Persis, Rufus, et al.	Rom 16

- Some coworkers also worked trans-locally, e.g., Stephanas along with Fortunatus and Achaicus (1 Cor 16:17), Phoebe (Rom 16:1), Onesiphorus (2 Tim 1:17), etc.

Appendix 2

Paul's Coworkers in the Trans-Local Ministry

Category	Coworkers (Community)	Biblical Sources
Travel Companions & Messengers	Aristarchus (Thessalonica)	Acts 19:29; 20:4; 27:2; Col 4:10; Phlm 24
	Artemas	Titus 3:12
	Erastus (Corinth)	Acts 19:22; Rom 16:23 (?); 2 Tim 4:20
	Gaius (Macedonia)	Acts 19:29
	Gaius (Derbe)	Acts 20:4
	Luke	Col 4:14; 2 Tim 4:11; Phlm 1:24
	Secundus (Thessalonica)	Acts 20:4
	Sospater (Berea)	Acts 20:4; Rom 16:21 (?)
	Sosthenes (Corinth)	Acts 18:17; possibly 1 Cor 1:1
	Timothy	Acts 16:1; 17:14–15; 18:5; 19:22; 20:4; 1 Cor 4:17; 16:10; 2 Cor 1:1, 19; 1 Thess 1:1; 3:1–3, 6–7; 2 Thess 1:1; Phil 1:1; 2:19–23; Col 1:1; Phlm 1:1; 1Tim 1:2, 18; 2 Tim 1:2; Heb 13:23
	Titus	Gal 2:1; 2 Cor 2:12–13; 7:5–7; 8:6, 16–17, 23; 12:18; Titus 1:4; 2 Tim 4:10
	Trophimus (Ephesus)	Acts 20:4; 21:29; 2 Tim 4:20
	Tychicus (Asia)	Acts 20:4; Eph 6:21–22; Col 4:7; Titus 3:12; 2 Tim 4:12
	Zenas, Apollos	Titus 3:13

Ministry Associates from Local Churches	Epaphras (Colossae)	Col 1:7–8; 4:12; Phlm 1:23
	Epaphroditus (Philippi)	Phil 2:25–29; 4:18
	Onesiphorus (Ephesus)	2 Tim 1:16–17; 4:19
	Onesimus (Colossae)	Col 4:9; Phlm 1:10
Coworkers beyond Pauline Missions	Apollos	Acts 18:24, 27–28; 1 Cor 16:12; Titus 3:13 (?)
	Aquila and Priscilla	Acts 18:1–3, 18–19, 26; 1 Cor 16:19; Rom 16:3–4; 2 Tim 4:19
	Barnabas	Acts 4:36; 9:27; 11:22–26, 30; 13:2–3; 14:26–28; 15:1–2, 39; Gal 2:1, 13; 1 Cor 9:6; Col 4:10
	Mark	Acts 12:12, 25; 13:5, 13; 15:39; Col 4:10; Phlm 1:24; 2 Tim 4:11; 1 Pet 5:13
	Silas	Acts 15:22, 27, 40; 16:19, 25; 17:10, 14–15; 18:5; 1 Thess 1:1; 2 Thess 1:1; 2 Cor 1:19; 1 Pet 5:12

- Paul's trans-local coworkers comprise travel companions, messengers, and ministry associates. Many of them were sent by local churches on behalf of Paul's missionary works. Biblical sources in this chart describe significant events and developments in each coworker's ministry.
- Some coworkers are difficult to categorize into any categories of the present classification. Tertius (Rom 16:22) was Paul's amanuensis for the letter to the Romans. Demas (Col 4:14; Phlm 1:24; 2 Tim 4:10) assisted Paul in Rome, but later deserted him. Others, known only by name, were with Paul in Rome, e.g., Jesus called Justus (Col 4:11), Crescens (2 Tim 4:10), Eubulus, Pudens, Linus, and Claudia (2 Tim 4:21). They are not included in the above lists, local or trans-local.

Appendix 3

Biblical Accounts in Relation to Financial Assistance

Category	Biblical Sources	Comments
Assistances for the Local Community	Acts 2:44–45/4:32–35	Jerusalem community
	Acts 6:1	Jerusalem community
	Gal 6:9–10	"doing good" to "households of faith"
	1 Thess 4:9–10	"brotherly love" in Macedonia
Assistances for Paul's Missions	Acts 16:15, 40	Lydia's service
	Acts 20:34	Paul's support for his companions.
	1 Cor 9:4–15	Paul's self-support
	1 Cor 16:6	Corinthians' support
	2 Cor 11:8–9	local supports for Paul's mission
	Rom 16:1	hospitality
	Phil 1:5; 4:10, 15–16	Philippians' mission support
Assistances for the Jerusalem Church	Acts 11:29–30	Antiochian Church's financial aid for Jerusalem
	Acts 20:4	church representatives for collection
	Acts 20:17–24	delivery of the collection
	Gal 2:10	"remember the poor"
	1 Cor 16:1–4, 17	Corinthian participation in collection
	2 Cor 8 & 9	Paul's instructions on collection
	Rom 15:25–27, 31	Paul's remark on collection

- In addition, the practice of financial support and hospitality in the early church can be inferred from following texts: Rom 12:13; Eph 4:28; 1 Thess 1:7–8; 4:10; 1 Tim 3:2; 5:16; Heb 6:10; 13:1–2; 1 Pet 4:9, et al.

Appendix 4

Paul's Letters: Senders, Receivers, and Persons in Greeting

Letters	Sender(s)/Persons Greeting	Receiver(s)/Persons Greeted
Galatians	"Paul . . . and all the brothers with me" (1:1–2)	"the churches in Galatia" (1:2)
1 Thessalonians	Paul, Silvanus, and Timothy (1:1)	"the church of the Thessalonians" (1:1)
		"Greet all the brothers with a holy kiss" (5:26)
2 Thessalonians	Paul, Silvanus, and Timothy (1:1)	"the church of the Thessalonians" (1:1)
1 Corinthians	Paul and Sosthenes (1:1)	"the church of God in Corinth . . . with all those everywhere who call . . ." (1:2)
	"the churches of Asia, Aquila and Priscilla, the church in their house, and all the brothers" (16:19–20)	"Greet one another with a holy kiss." (16:20)
2 Corinthians	Paul and Timothy (1:1)	"the church of God in Corinth, together with all the saints throughout Achaia" (1:1)
	"All the saints greet you." (13:12)	"Greet one another with a holy kiss." (13:11)

Romans	Paul (1:1)	"all who are in Rome, beloved of God, called saints" (1:7)
	People greet Romans. (16:16, 21–23)	Paul greets many individuals at Rome. (16:3–16)
Ephesians	Paul (1:1)	"the saints who are in Ephesus" (1:1)
Colossians	Paul and Timothy (1:1)	"the saints in Colossae" (1:2)
	Aristarchus, Mark, Jesus (Justus), Epaphras, Luke, Demas (4:10–14)	"Greet the brothers in Laodicea, and Nymphas, and the church in his house" (4:15) Archippus (4:17)
Philemon	Paul and Timothy (1:1)	"to Philemon . . . to Apphia, to Archippus . . . and to the church in your house" (1:1–2)
	"Epaphras, my fellow prisoner . . . Mark, Aristarchus, Demas, and Luke, my fellow workers." (1:23–24)	
Philippians	Paul and Timothy (1:1)	"all the saints . . . in Philippi together with the overseers and deacons" (1:1)
	"The brothers with me greet you. All the saints greet you, especially those of Caesar's household" (4:21–22)	"Greet every saint in Christ Jesus" (4:21)
1 Timothy	Paul (1:1)	Timothy (1:2)
Titus	Paul (1:1)	Titus (1:4)
	"All those with me greet you" (3:15)	"Greet those who love us" (3:15)
2 Timothy	Paul (1:1)	Timothy (1:2)
	Erastus, Trophimus (4:20) "Eubulus greets you, also Pudens, Linus, Claudia, and all the brothers." (4:21)	"Greet Priscilla and Aquila and the household of Onesiphorus." (4:19)

Bibliography

Aasgaard, Reidar. *My Beloved Brothers and Sisters: Christian Siblingship in the Apostle Paul*. Studies of the New Testament and Its World. London: T. & T. Clark, 2004.

Adamopoulo, Themistocles A. "Elements of the Earliest Evangelisation of Gentiles in the Roman Empire: Caesarea Maritima, Antioch, and Rome." *Phronema* 13 (1998) 65–87.

Adams, Edward. "First-Century Models for Paul's Churches: Selected Scholarly Developments since Meeks." In *After the First Urban Christians: The Social-Scientific Study of Pauline Christianity Twenty-Five Years Later*, edited by Todd D. Still and David G. Horrell, 60–78. London: T. & T. Clark, 2009.

Adams, Edward, and David G. Horrell, eds. *Christianity at Corinth: The Quest for the Pauline Church*. Louisville: Westminster John Knox, 2004.

Ådna, Jostein. "James' Position at the Summit Meeting of the Apostles and the Elders in Jerusalem (Acts 15)." In *The Mission of the Early Church to Jews and Gentiles*, edited by Jostein Ådna and Hans Kvalbein, 125–61. WUNT 127. Tübingen: Mohr Siebeck, 2000.

Agosto, Efrain. "Paul's Use of Greco-Roman Conventions of Commendation." PhD diss., Boston University, 1996.

Aland, Barbara, et al., eds. *Novum Testamentum Graece*. 28th ed. Stuttgart: Deutsche Bibelgesellschaft, 2012.

Alexander, Loveday. "Chronology of Paul." In *DPL*, 115–23. 1993.

———. "Community and Canon: Reflections on the Ecclesiology of Acts." In *Einheit der Kirche im Neuen Testament: Dritte europäische orthodox-westliche Exegetenkonferenz in Sankt Petersburg, 24.–31. August 2005*, edited by Anatoly A. Alexeev et al., 45–78. WUNT 218. Tübingen: Mohr Siebeck, 2008.

———. "'In Journeyings Often': Voyaging in the Acts of the Apostles and in Greek Romance." In *Luke's Literary Achievement: Collected Essays*, edited by C. M. Tuckett, 17–49. JSNTSup 116. Sheffield: Sheffield Academic, 1995.

———. "Mapping Early Christianity: Acts and the Shape of Early Church History." *Interpretation* 57 (2003) 163–73.

———. "Paul and the Hellenistic Schools: The Evidence of Galen." In *Paul in His Hellenistic Context*, edited by Troels Engberg-Pedersen, 60–83. Minneapolis: Fortress, 1995.

Anderson, Graham. *Sage, Saint and Sophist: Holy Men and Their Associates in the Early Roman Empire*. London: Routledge, 1994.

Aneziri, Sophia. "World Travelers: The Associations of Artists of Dionysus." In *Wandering Poets in Ancient Greek Culture: Travel, Locality and Pan-Hellenism*, edited by Richard Hunter and Ian Rutherford, 217–36. Cambridge: Cambridge University Press, 2009.

Applebaum, Shimon. *Jews and Greeks in Ancient Cyrene*. Leiden: Brill, 1979.

———. "The Organization of the Jewish Communities in the Diaspora." In *The Jewish People in the First Century: Historical Geography, Political History, Social, Cultural and Religious Life and Institutions*, edited by Shemuel Safrai and Menahem Stern, 464–503. CRINT 1.1. Philadelphia: Fortress, 1974.

Arnold, Clinton E. *Ephesians*. ZECNT. Grand Rapids: Zondervan, 2010.

Arterbury, Andrew E. *Entertaining Angels: Early Christian Hospitality in Its Mediterranean Setting*. Sheffield: Sheffield Phoenix, 2005.

Ascough, Richard S. "The Completion of a Religious Duty: The Background of 2 Cor 8:1–15." *NTS* 42 (1996) 584–99.

———. "Greco-Roman Philosophic, Religious, and Voluntary Associations." In *Community Formation in the Early Church and the Church Today*, edited by Richard N. Longenecker, 3–19. Peabody, MA: Hendrickson, 2002.

———. *Lydia: Paul's Cosmopolitan Hostess*. Paul's Social Network: Brothers and Sisters in Faith. Collegeville, MN: Liturgical, 2009.

———. *Paul's Macedonian Associations: The Social Context of Philippians and 1 Thessalonians*. WUNT 2/161. Tübingen: Mohr Siebeck, 2003.

———. "The Thessalonian Christian Community as a Professional Voluntary Association." *JBL* 119 (2000) 311–28.

———. "Translocal Relationships among Voluntary Associations and Early Christianity." *JECS* 5 (1997) 223–41.

———. "Voluntary Associations and Community Formation: Paul's Macedonian Christian Communities in Context." PhD diss., University of St. Michael's College, Toronto School of Theology, 1997.

———. *What Are They Saying about the Formation of the Pauline Churches?* New York: Paulist, 1998.

Ascough, Richard S., et al., eds. *Associations in the Greco-Roman World: A Sourcebook*. Waco, TX: Baylor University Press, 2012.

Associations in the Greco-Roman World: An Expanding Collection of Inscriptions, Papyri, and Other Sources in Translation. "Puteoli." http:// philipharland.com/ greco-roman-associations/317–letter-of-the-tyrian-settlers-at-puteoli-to-the-city-of-tyre/.

Aune, David E. The *New Testament and Early Christian Literature in Greco-Roman Context: Studies in Honor of David E. Aune*. NovTSup 122. Leiden: Brill, 2006.

———. *The New Testament in Its Literary Environment*. Library of Early Christianity 8. Philadelphia: Westminster, 1987.

Baird, William Robb, Jr. "Letters of Recommendation: A Study of 2 Cor 3:1–3." *JBL* 80 (1961) 166–72.

Bakke, Odd Magne. *Concord and Peace: An Analysis of the First Letter of Clement with an Emphasis on the Language of Unity and Sedition*. WUNT 2/143. Tübingen: Mohr Siebeck, 2001.

Balz, Horst, and Gerhard Schneider, eds. *Exegetical Dictionary of the New Testament*. 3 vols. Translated by James W. Thompson and John W. Medendorp. Grand Rapids: Eerdmans, 1990–1993

Banks, Robert. *Paul's Idea of Community*. Rev. ed. Peabody, MA: Hendrickson, 1994.

Barclay, John M. G. *Jews in the Mediterranean Diaspora from Alexander to Trajan (323 BCE–117 CE)*. Edinburgh: T. & T. Clark, 1996.

———. "The Jews of the Diaspora." In *Early Christian Thought in Its Jewish Context*, edited by John Barclay and John Sweet, 27–40. Cambridge: Cambridge University Press, 1996.

———. "Money and Meetings: Group Formation among Diaspora Jews and Early Christians." In *Vereine, Synagoge und Gemeinden im kaiserzeitlichen Kleinasien*, edited by Andreas Gutsfeld and Dietrich-Alex Koch, 113–27. Studien und Texte zu Antike und Christentum 25. Tübingen: Mohr Siebeck, 2006.

———. "Paul Among Diaspora Jews: Anomaly or Apostate?" *JSNT* 60 (1995) 89–120.

———. *Pauline Churches and Diaspora Jews*. WUNT 275. Tübingen: Mohr Siebeck, 2011.

———. "Pauline Churches, Jewish Communities and the Roman Empire: Introducing the Issues." In *Pauline Churches and Diaspora Jews*, 3–33. WUNT 275. Tübingen: Mohr Siebeck, 2011.

———. "Poverty in Pauline Studies: A Response to Steven Friesen." *JSNT* 26 (2004) 363–66.

———. "Thessalonica and Corinth: Social Contrasts in Pauline Christianity." In *Christianity at Corinth: The Quest for the Pauline Church*, edited by Edward Adams and David G. Horrell, 183–96. Louisville: Westminster John Knox, 2004.

Barentsen, Jack. *Emerging Leadership in the Pauline Mission: A Social Identity Perspective on Local Leadership Development in Corinth and Ephesus*. Princeton Theological Monograph Series 168. Eugene, OR: Pickwick Publications, 2011.

Barnett, Paul. "Opponents of Paul." In *DPL*, 644–53. 1993.

———. *The Second Epistle to the Corinthians*. NICNT. Grand Rapids: Eerdmans, 1997.

Barnikol, Ernst. "The Non-Pauline Origin of the Parallelism of Peter and Paul in Galatians 2:7–8." *Journal of Higher Criticism* 5 (1998) 285–300.

Barrett, C. K. *A Commentary on the First Epistle to the Corinthians*. HNTC. New York: Harper & Row, 1968.

———. *A Critical and Exegetical Commentary on the Acts of the Apostles*. ICC. Edinburgh: T. & T. Clark, 1998.

———. *On Paul: Aspects of His Life, Work and Influence in the Early Church*. London: T. & T. Clark, 2003.

Bartchy, S. Scott. "Community of Goods in Acts: Idealization or Social Reality?" In *The Future of Early Christianity: Essays in Honor of Helmut Koester*, edited by Birger A. Pearson, 309–18. Minneapolis: Fortress, 1991.

———. "Divine Power, Community Formation, and Leadership in the Acts of the Apostles." In *Community Formation in the Early Church and the Church Today*, edited by Richard N. Longenecker, 89–104. Peabody, MA: Hendrickson, 2002.

Barton, S. C., and G. H. R. Horsley. "A Hellenistic Cult Group and the New Testament Churches." *Jahrbuch für Antike und Christentum* 24 (1981) 7–41.

Bauckham, Richard. "Barnabas in Galatians." *JSNT* 2 (1979) 61–70.

———. "For Whom Were Gospels Written?" In *The Gospels for All Christians: Rethinking the Gospel Audiences*, edited by Richard Bauckham, 9–48. Grand Rapids: Eerdmans, 1998.

———, ed. *The Gospels for All Christians: Rethinking the Gospel Audiences*. Grand Rapids: Eerdmans, 1998.

———. "James and the Gentiles (Acts 15.13–21)." In *History, Literature, and Society in the Book of Acts*, edited by Ben Witherington III, 154–84. Cambridge: Cambridge University Press, 1996.

———. "James and the Jerusalem Church." In *The Book of Acts in Its Palestinian Setting*, edited by Richard Bauckham, 415–80. The Book of Acts in Its First Century Setting 4. Grand Rapids: Eerdmans, 1995.

———. "James, Peter, and the Gentiles." In *The Missions of James, Peter, and Paul: Tensions in Early Christianity*, edited by Bruce Chilton and Craig A. Evans, 91–142. NovTSup 115. Leiden: Brill, 2005.

———. *Jude, 2 Peter*. WBC 50. Waco, TX: Word, 1983.

Baur, F. C. *Church History of the First Three Centuries*. 2 vols. 3rd ed. Translated and edited by Allan Menzies. London: Williams & Norgate, 1878.

Ben Zeev, Miriam Pucci. *Jewish Rights in the Roman World: The Greek and Roman Documents Quoted by Josephus Flavius*. Texts and Studies in Ancient Judaism 74. Tübingen: Mohr Siebeck, 1998.

Berding, Kenneth. "John or Paul? Who Was Polycarp's Mentor?" *TynBul* 58 (2007) 135–43.

Best, Ernest. "Paul's Apostolic Authority?" *JSNT* 27 (1986) 3–25.

Betz, Hans Dieter. *Galatians: A Commentary on Paul's Letter to the Churches in Galatia*. Hermeneia. Philadelphia: Fortress, 1989.

Beyer, Hermann W. "διακονέω, διακονία, διάκονος." In *TDNT* 2:81–93.

Billings, Bradly S. "From House Church to Tenement Church: Domestic Space and the Development of Early Urban Christianity—the Example of Ephesus." *JTS* 62 (2011) 541–69.

Bird, Michael F. "Mark: Interpreter of Peter and Disciple of Paul." In *Paul and the Gospels: Christologies, Conflicts and Convergences*, edited by Michael F. Bird and Joel Willitts, 30–61. LNTS 411. London: T. & T. Clark, 2011.

Blue, Bradley B. "Acts and the House Church." In *The Book of Acts in Its Graeco-Roman Setting*, edited by David W. J. Gill and Conrad H. Gempf, 119–222. The Book of Acts in Its First Century Setting 2. Grand Rapids: Eerdmans, 1994.

———. "The Influence of Jewish Worship on Luke's Presentation of the Early Church." In *Witness to the Gospel: The Theology of Acts*, edited by I. Howard Marshall and David Peterson, 473–97. Grand Rapids: Eerdmans, 1998.

Blumell, Lincoln H. "Travel and Communication in the NT." In *NIDB* 5:652–58.

Bock, Darrell L. *Acts*. BECNT. Grand Rapids: Baker, 2007.

Böckh, August, ed. *Corpus Inscriptionum Graecarum*. Berlin: Reimer, 1825–77.

Bockmuehl, Markus. "1 Thessalonians 2:14–16 and the Church in Jerusalem." *TynBul* 52 (2001) 1–31.

———. "Antioch and James the Just." In *James the Just and Christian Origins*, edited by Bruce Chilton and Craig A. Evans, 155–98. NovTSup 98. Leiden: Brill, 1999.

———. *Jewish Law in Gentile Churches: Halakhah and the Beginning of Christian Public Ethics*. Edinburgh: T. & T. Clark, 2000.

———. *Simon Peter in Scripture and Memory: The New Testament Apostle in the Early Church*. Grand Rapids: Baker Academic, 2012.

———. "Why not Let Acts Be Acts?: In Conversation with C. Kavin Rowe." *JSNT* 28 (2005) 163–66.

Bonz, Marianne P. "Differing Approaches to Religious Benefaction: The Late Third-Century Acquisition of the Sardis Synagogue." *HTR* 86 (1993) 139–54.

Böttger, Paul C. "Paulus und Petrus in Antiochien: zum Verständnis von Galater 2:11–21." *NTS* 37 (1991) 77–100.

Brown, Raymond E., and John P. Meier. *Antioch and Rome: New Testament Cradles of Catholic Christianity*. 1983. Reprint. New York: Paulist, 2004.

Bruce, F. F. *1 and 2 Thessalonians*. WBC 45. Grand Rapids: Zondervan, 1982.

———. *The Book of Acts*. NICNT. Grand Rapids: Eerdmans, 1988.

———. "Conference in Jerusalem—Galatians 2:1–10." In *God Who Is Rich in Mercy: Essays Presented to Dr. D. B. Knox*, edited by Peter T. O'Brien and David G. Peterson, 195–212. Homebush West, NSW, Australia: Lancer, 1986.

———. *The Epistle of Paul to the Galatians: A Commentary on the Greek Text*. NIGTC. Grand Rapids: Eerdmans, 1982.

———. "Galatian Problems: 5. Galatians and Christian Origins." *Bulletin of the John Rylands Library* 55 (1973) 264–84.

———. "Jews and Christians in the Lycus Valley." *BSac* 141 (1984) 3–15.

———. *Men and Movements in the Primitive Church: Studies in Early Non-Pauline Christianity*. Exeter: Paternoster, 1979.

———. "Paul and Jerusalem." *TynBul* 19 (1968) 3–25.

———. "Paul in Acts and Letters." In *DPL*, 679–92. 1993.

———. *The Pauline Circle*. Grand Rapids: Eerdmans, 1985.

———. *Peter, Stephen, James, and John: Studies in Early Non-Pauline Christianity*. Grand Rapids: Eerdmans, 1980.

———. "The Roman Debate—Continued." In *The Romans Debate*, edited by Karl P. Donfried, 175–94. Peabody, MA: Hendrickson, 1991.

Bultmann, Rudolf. *Theology of the New Testament*. 2 vols. Translated by Kendrick Grobel. London: SCM, 1951–1955.

Byrskog, Samuel. "Co-senders, Co-authors, and Paul's Use of the First Person Plural." *ZNW* 87 (1996) 230–50.

Campbell, Joan Cecelia. *Phoebe: Patron and Emissary*. Paul's Social Network: Brothers and Sisters in Faith. Collegeville, MN: Liturgical, 2009.

Campbell, R. Alastair. *The Elders: Seniority within Earliest Christianity*. Edinburgh: T. & T. Clark, 1994.

Campbell, William S. *Paul and the Creation of Christian Identity*. LNTS 322. New York: T. & T. Clark, 2006.

Campenhausen, Hans von. *Ecclesiastical Authority and Spiritual Power in the Church of the First Three Centuries*. Translated by J. A. Baker. Stanford, CA: Stanford University Press, 1969.

Capes, David B., et al. *Rediscovering Paul: An Introduction to His World, Letters, and Theology*. Downers Grove, IL: IVP Academic, 2007.

Capper, Brian J. "The Palestinian Cultural Context of Earliest Christian Community of Goods." In *The Book of Acts in Its Palestinian Setting*, edited by Richard Bauckham, 323–56. The Book of Acts in Its First Century Setting 4. Grand Rapids: Eerdmans, 1995.

———. "Reciprocity and the Ethic of Acts." In *Witness to the Gospel: The Theology of Acts*, edited by I. Howard Marshall and David Peterson, 499–518. Grand Rapids: Eerdmans, 1998.

Carson, D. A. *Showing the Spirit: A Theological Exposition of 1 Corinthians 12–14*. Grand Rapids: Baker, 1996.

Carson, D. A., and Douglas J. Moo. *An Introduction to the New Testament*. 2nd ed. Grand Rapids: Zondervan, 2005.

Cassidy, Richard J. *Paul in Chains: Roman Imprisonment and the Letters of St. Paul*. New York: Crossroad, 2001.

Casson, Lionel. *Travel in the Ancient World*. Baltimore: Johns Hopkins University Press, 1994.

Catchpole, David R. "Paul, James and the Apostolic Decree." *NTS* 23 (1977) 428–44.

Catto, Stephen K. *Reconstructing the First-Century Synagogue: A Critical Analysis of Current Research*. LNTS 363. New York: T. & T. Clark, 2007.

Chadwick, Henry. *The Early Church*. Rev. ed. New York: Penguin, 1993.

Chilton, Bruce. "James, Peter, Paul, and the Formation of the Gospels." In *The Missions of James, Peter, and Paul: Tensions in Early Christianity*, edited by Bruce Chilton and Craig A. Evans, 3–28. NovTSup 115. Leiden: Brill, 2005.

Ciampa, Roy E., and Brian S. Rosner. *The First Letter to the Corinthians*. PNTC. Grand Rapids: Eerdmans, 2010.

Clarke, Andrew D. "'Refresh the Hearts of the Saints': A Unique Pauline Context?" *TynBul* 47 (1996) 277–300.

———. *Serve the Community of the Church: Christians as Leaders and Ministers*. Grand Rapids: Eerdmans, 2000.

Claussen, Carsten. "Meeting, Community, Synagogue—Different Frameworks of Ancient Jewish Congregations in the Diaspora." In *The Ancient Synagogue from Its Origins until 200 C.E.: Papers Presented at an International Conference at Lund University, October 14–17, 2001*, edited by Birger Olsson and Magnus Zetterholm, 144–67. ConBNT 39. Stockholm: Almqvist & Wiksell, 2003.

Cohen, Shaye J. D. "Did Ancient Jews Missionize?" *BRev* 19 (2003) 40–47.

———. *From the Maccabees to the Mishnah*. 2nd ed. Louisville: Westminster John Knox, 2006.

Cole, R. Alan. *The Epistle of Paul to the Galatians*. TNTC 9. Downers Grove, IL: InterVarsity, 1989.

Collins, Raymond F. *The Birth of the New Testament: The Origin and Development of the First Christian Generation*. New York: Crossroad, 1993.

Colson, F. H., et al., eds. *Philo with an English Translation*. 10 vols. and 2 supplementary vols. LCL. Cambridge, MA: Harvard University Press, 1929–1941.

Conzelmann, Hans. *1 Corinthians: A Commentary on the First Epistle to the Corinthians*. Translated by James W. Leitch. Philadelphia: Fortress, 1975.

———. *Acts of the Apostles*. Hermeneia. Philadelphia: Fortress, 1987.

Court, John M. "Rivals in the Mission Field." *ExpTim* 113 (2002) 399–403.

Craffert, Pieter F. "The Pauline Household Communities: Their Nature as Social Entities." *Neotestamentica* 32 (1998) 309–41.

Cranfield, C. E. B. *A Critical and Exegetical Commentary on the Epistle to the Romans*. 2 vols. ICC. Edinburgh: T. & T. Clark, 2001.

Dahl, Nils A. "Euodia and Syntyche and Paul's Letter to the Philippians." In *The Social World of the First Christians: Essays in Honor of Wayne A. Meeks*, edited by L. Michael White and O. Larry Yarbrough, 3–15. Minneapolis: Fortress, 1995.

Dauer, Anton. *Paulus und die Christliche Gemeinde im Syrischen Antiochi: Kritische Bestandsaufnhme der Modernen Orschung mit Einigen Weiterfhrenden Überlegungen*. Bonner Biblische Beiträge 106. Weinheim: Beltz Athenäum, 1996.

Davids, Peter H. *The First Epistle of Peter*. NICNT. Grand Rapids: Eerdmans, 1990.

———. "James and Peter: The Literary Evidence." In *The Missions of James, Peter, and Paul: Tensions in Early Christianity*, edited by Bruce Chilton and Craig A. Evans, 29–52. NovTSup 115. Leiden: Brill, 2005.

Davies, W. D. *Paul and Rabbinic Judaism: Some Rabbinic Elements in Pauline Theology*. 4th ed. Philadelphia: Fortress, 1980.

Davis, Thomas W. "The Business Secrets of Paul of Tarsus." *SWJT* 59 (2017) 219–34.

De Vos, Craig S. *Church and Community Conflicts: The Relationships of the Thessalonian, Corinthian and Philippian Churches*. Society of Biblical Literature Dissertation Series 168. Atlanta: Scholars, 1999.

DeWitt, Norman W. *Epicurus and His Philosophy*. Minneapolis: University of Minnesota Press, 1954.

Di Berardino, Angelo. "Patterns of *Koinonia* in the first Christian Centuries." *Concilium* 3 (2001) 45–58.

Dickson, John P. *Mission-Commitment in Ancient Judaism and in the Pauline Communities: The Shape, Extent and Background of Early Christian Mission*. WUNT 2/159. Tübingen: Mohr Siebeck, 2003.

Donfried, Karl P. *Paul, Thessalonica, and Early Christianity*. Grand Rapids: Eerdmans, 2002.

Downing, Francis Gerald. *Cynics, Paul, and the Pauline Churches: Cynics and Christian Origins II*. New York: Routledge, 1998.

Downs, David J. *The Offering of the Gentiles: Paul's Collection for Jerusalem in Its Chronological, Cultural, and Cultic Contexts*. WUNT 2/248. Tübingen: Mohr Siebeck, 2008.

———. "Paul's Collection and the Book of Acts Revisited." *NTS* 52 (2006) 50–70.

Du Toit, Andreas B. "'God's Beloved in Rome' (Rm 1:7): The Genesis and Socio-Economic Situation of the First Generation Christian Community in Rome." *Neotestamentica* 32 (1998) 367–88.

Dunn, James D. G. *Beginning from Jerusalem: Christianity in the Making*. Grand Rapids: Eerdmans, 2009.

———. *The Epistle to the Galatians*. BNTC. Peabody, MA: Hendrickson, 1993.

———. "The Incident at Antioch (Gal. 2:11–18)." *JSNT* 18 (1983) 3–57.

———. "One Church—Many Churches." In *Einheit der Kirche im Neuen Testament: Dritte europäische orthodox-westliche Exegetenkonferenz in Sankt Petersburg, 24.–31. August 2005*, edited by Anatoly A. Alexeev et al., 3–22. WUNT 218. Tübingen: Mohr Siebeck, 2008.

———. *Paul's Letter to the Philippians*. NICNT. Grand Rapids: Eerdmans, 1995.

———. "The Relationship between Paul and Jerusalem according to Galatians 1 and 2." *NTS* 28 (1982) 461–78.

———. *The Romans 9–16*. WBC 38B. Waco, TX: Word, 1988.

———. *The Theology of Paul the Apostle*. Grand Rapids: Eerdmans, 1998.

———. "Who Did Paul Think He Was? A Study of Jewish-Christian Identity." *NTS* 45 (1999) 174–93.

Ehrensperger, Kathy. *Paul and the Dynamics of Power: Communication and Interaction in the Early Christ-Movement*. LNTS 325. New York: T. & T. Clark, 2007.

Elliott, John H. *1 Peter*. AB 37B. New York: Doubleday, 2000.
———. *A Home for the Homeless: A Social-Scientific Criticism of 1 Peter, Its Situation and Strategy*. 1990. Reprint, Eugene, OR: Wipf and Stock, 2005.
———. "Jesus the Israelite Was Neither a 'Jew' nor a 'Christian': On Correcting Misleading Nomenclature." *JSHJ* 5 (2007) 119–54.
———. "Peter, Silvanus and Mark in 1 Peter and Acts: Sociological-Exegetical Perspectives on a Petrine Group in Rome." In *Wort in der Zeit: Neutestamentliche Studien: Festgabe Für Karl Heinrich Rengstorf zum 75. Geburtstag*, edited by Wilfrid Haubeck and Michael Bachmann, 250–67. Leiden: Brill, 1980.
Ellis, E. Earle. "Coworkers, Paul and His." In *DPL*, 183–89. 1993.
———. "Paul and His Co-Workers." *NTS* 17 (1971) 437–52.
———. "Paul and His Opponents." In *Christianity, Judaism and Other Greco-Roman Cults*, edited by Jacob Neusner, 264–98. Studies in Judaism in Late Antiquity 12. Leiden: Brill, 1975.
Ellis, Jeffrey S. "Stephanas: A New Testament Example of Frontier Member Care." *International Journal of Frontier Missions* 12 (1995) 171–75.
Elmer, Ian J. *Paul, Jerusalem and the Judaisers: The Galatian Crisis in Its Broadest Historical Context*. WUNT 2/258. Tübingen: Mohr Siebeck, 2009.
Elsner, Jaś, and Ian Rutherford, eds. *Pilgrimage in Graeco-Roman and Early Christian Antiquity: Seeing the Gods*. Oxford: Oxford University Press, 2006.
Engberg-Pedersen, Troels. "The Material Spirit: Cosmology and Ethics in Paul." *NTS* 55 (2009) 179–97.
———. *Paul and the Stoics*. Louisville: Westminster John Knox, 2000.
———, ed. *Paul in His Hellenistic Context*. Minneapolis: Fortress, 1995.
———. "The Relationship with Others: Similarities and Differences between Paul and Stoicism." *ZNW* 96 (2005) 35–60.
The Epistles of St. Clement of Rome and St. Ignatius of Antioch. Translated by James A. Kleist. Westminster: Newman, 1961.
Epp, Eldon Jay. "New Testament Papyrus Manuscripts and Letter Carrying in Greco-Roman Times." In *The Future of Early Christianity: Essays in Honor of Helmut Koester*, edited by Birger A. Pearson, 35–56. Minneapolis: Fortress, 1991.
———. *The Theological Tendency of Codex Beaze Cantabrigiensis in Acts*. Eugene: Wipf & Stock, 2001.
Esler, Philip F. "Community and Gospel in Early Christianity: A Response to Richard Bauckham's Gospels for All Christians." *SJT* 51 (1998) 235–48.
———. *Conflict and Identity in Romans: The Social Setting of Paul's Letter*. Minneapolis: Fortress, 2003.
———. "Making and Breaking an Agreement Mediterranean Style: A New Reading of Galatians 2:1–14." In *The Galatians Debate*, edited by Mark D. Nanos, 261–81. Peabody, MA: Hendrickson, 2002.
Eusebius. *Eusebius: The Church History: A New Translation with Commentary*. Translated and Commentary by Paul L. Maier. Grand Rapids: Kregel, 1999.
Evans, Craig A. *Ancient Texts for New Testament Studies: A Guide to the Background Literature*. Grand Rapids: Baker Academic, 2005.
Everts, Janet Meyer. "Financial Supports." In *DPL*, 295–300. 1993.
Farmer, William R. "James the Lord's Brother, according to Paul." In *James the Just and Christian Origins*, edited by Bruce Chilton and Craig A. Evans, 133–53. NovTSup 98. Leiden: Brill, 1999.

Feddes, David J. "Caring for God's Household: A Leadership Paradigm among New Testament Christians and Its Relevance for Church and Mission Today." *CTJ* 43 (2008) 274–99.

Fee, Gordon D. *The First Epistle to the Corinthians*. NICNT. Grand Rapids: Eerdmans, 1987.

Feldman, Louis H. "Diaspora Synagogues: New Light from Inscriptions and Papyri." In *Sacred Realm: The Emergence of the Synagogue in the Ancient World*, edited by Steven Fine, 48–66. New York: Oxford University Press/Yeshiva University Museum, 1996.

Feldman, Louis H., and Meyer Reinhold, eds. *Jewish Life and Thought among Greeks and Romans: Primary Readings*. Minneapolis: Fortress, 1996.

Ferguson, Everett. *Backgrounds of Early Christianity*. 3rd ed. Grand Rapids: Eerdmans, 2003.

———. "The Church at Corinth outside the New Testament." *ResQ* 3 (1959) 169–72.

Fiensy, David. "The Composition of the Jerusalem Church." In *The Book of Acts in Its Palestinian Setting*, edited by Richard Bauckham, 213–36. The Book of Acts in Its First Century Setting 4. Grand Rapids: Eerdmans, 1995.

Fiorenza, Elizabeth Schüssler. "Missionaries, Apostles, Coworkers: Romans 16 and the Reconstruction of Women's Early Christian History." *Word and World* 6 (1986) 420–33.

Fisk, Bruce N. "Paul: Life and Letters." In *The Face of New Testament Studies: A Survey of Recent Research*, edited by Scot McKnight and Grant R. Osborne, 283–325. Grand Rapids: Baker Academic, 2004.

Fitzmyer, Joseph A. *The Acts of the Apostles: A New Translation with Introduction and Commentary*. AB 31. New York: Doubleday, 1998.

Foster, Paul, ed. *The Writings of the Apostolic Fathers*. London: T. & T. Clark, 2007.

Freedman, David Noel, ed. *Anchor Bible Dictionary*. 6 vols. New York: Doubleday, 1992

Frey, Jean Baptiste. *Corpus of Jewish Inscriptions: Jewish Inscriptions from the Third Century B.C. to the Seventh Century A.D.* 1936. Reprint, Library of Biblical Studies. New York: Ktav, 1975.

Friberg, Timothy, Barbara Friberg, and Neva F. Miller. *Analytical Lexicon of the Greek New Testament*. Grand Rapids: Baker, 2000.

Friesen, Steven J. "Paul and Economics: The Jerusalem Collection as an Alternative to Patronage." In *Paul Unbound: Other Perspectives on the Apostle*, edited by Mark D. Given, 27–54. Peabody, MA: Hendrickson, 2010.

———. "Poverty in Pauline Studies: Beyond the So-called New Consensus." *JSNT* 26 (2004) 323–61.

Fulton, Karen E. "The Phenomenon of Co-Senders in Ancient Greek Letters and the Pauline Epistles." PhD diss., University of Aberdeen, 2011.

Fung, Ronald Y. K. *The Epistle to the Galatians*. NICNT. Grand Rapids: Eerdmans, 1988.

Funk, Robert W. "The Apostolic Parousia: Form and Significance." In *Christian History and Interpretation: Studies Presented to John Knox*, edited by W. R. Farmer, C. F. D. Moule, and R. R. Niebuhr, 249–68. Cambridge: Cambridge University Press, 1967.

Furnish, Victor Paul. *2 Corinthians*. AB 32A. New York: Doubleday, 1984.

Garland, David E. *1 Corinthians*. BECNT. Grand Rapids: Baker Academic, 2003.

Gaventa, Beverly R. "Theology and Ecclesiology in the Miletus Speech: Reflections on Content and Context." *NTS* 50 (2004) 36–52.

Gehring, Roger W. *House Church and Mission: The Importance of Household Structures in Early Christianity*. Peabody, MA: Hendrickson, 2004.

Gempf, Conrad. "Before Paul Arrived in Corinth: The Mission Strategies in 1 Corinthians 2:2 and Acts 17." In *The New Testament in Its First Century Setting: Essays on Context and Background in Honour of B. W. Winter on His 65th Birthday*, edited by P. J. Williams et al., 126–42. Grand Rapids: Eerdmans, 2004.

George, Timothy. *Galatians: An Exegetical and Theological Exposition of Holy Scripture*. NAC 30. Nashville: Broadman & Holman, 1994.

Georgi, Dieter. *The Opponents of Paul in Second Corinthians*. Philadelphia: Fortress, 1986.

———. *Remembering the Poor: The History of Paul's Collection for Jerusalem*. Nashville: Abingdon, 1991.

Gerberding, Kieth A. "Women Who Toil in Ministry, Even as Paul." *Currents in Theology and Mission* 18 (1991) 285–91.

Gibson, Jack J. *Peter between Jerusalem and Antioch: Peter, James, and the Gentiles*. WUNT 2/345.Tübingen: Mohr Siebeck, 2013.

Gibson, Richard J. "Paul and the Evangelization of the Stoics." In *The Gospel to the Nations: Perspectives on Paul's Mission: In Honour of Peter T. O'Brien*, edited by Peter Bolt and Mark Thompson, 309–26. Downers Grove, IL: InterVarsity, 2000.

Glad, Clarence E. *Paul and Philodemus: Adaptability in Epicurean and Early Christian Psychagogy*. NovTSup 81. Leiden: Brill, 1995.

Glaze, R. E., Jr. "Onesimus: Runaway or Emissary?" *The Theological Educator: A Journal of Theology and Ministry* 54 (1996) 3–11.

Goodman, Martin. "The Pilgrimage Economy of Jerusalem in the Second Temple Period." In *Judaism in the Roman World: Collected Essays*, 60–68. Ancient Judaism and Early Christianity Series 66. Leiden: Brill, 2007.

Gottheil, Richard. "Adiabene." http://jewishencyclopedia.com/articles /7525-helena.

Goulder, Michael D. *Paul and the Competing Mission in Corinth*. Peabody, MA: Hendrickson, 2001.

———. *St. Paul versus St. Peter: A Tale of Two Missions*. Louisville: Westminster John Knox, 1995.

Grant, Robert M. *Paul in the Roman World: The Conflict at Corinth*. Louisville: Westminster John Knox, 2001.

Green, Gene L. *Jude and 2 Peter*. BECNT. Grand Rapids: Baker Academic, 2008.

———. *The Letters to the Thessalonians*. PNTC. Grand Rapids: Eerdmans, 2002.

Green, Joel B. "The Book of Acts as History/Writing." *LTQ* 37 (2002) 119–27.

Grothe, Jonathan F. "A Missionary in Fellowship with the Church." *Lutheran Theological Review* 2 (1990) 7–14.

Hansen, G. Walter. *The Letter to the Philippians*. PNTC. Grand Rapids: Eerdmans, 2009.

Hanson, K. C., and Douglas E. Oakman. *Palestine in the Time of Jesus: Social Structures and Social Conflicts*. Minneapolis: Fortress, 1998.

Harland, Philip A. "Associations and the Economics of Group Life: A Preliminary Case Study of Asia Minor and the Aegean Islands." *Svensk Exegetisk Årsbok* 80 (2015) 1–37.

———. *Associations, Synagogues, and Congregations: Claiming a Place in Ancient Mediterranean Society*. Minneapolis: Fortress, 2003.

———. "Honouring the Emperor or Assailing the Beast: Participation in Civic Life among Associations (Jewish, Christian and Other) in Asia Minor and the Apocalypse of John." *JSNT* 77 (2000) 99–121.

Harrill, J. Albert. "Ignatius, Ad Polycarp. 4.3 and the Corporate Manumission of Christian Slaves." In *Christianity and Society: The Social World of Early Christianity*, edited by Everett Ferguson, 279–314. New York: Garland, 1999.

Harris, Murray J. *The Second Epistle to the Corinthians: A Commentary on the Greek Text*. The NIGTC. Grand Rapids: Eerdmans, 2005.

Harris, William V. "Poverty and Destitution in the Roman Empire." In *Rome's Imperial Economy: Twelve essays*, edited by William V. Harris, 27–54. Oxford: Oxford University Press, 2011.

Harrison, James R., and L. L. Welborn, eds. *The First Urban Churches 2: Roman Corinth*. Atlanta: SBL Press, 2016.

———. *The First Urban Churches 3: Ephesus*. Atlanta: SBL, 2018.

Hartin, Patrick J. *Apollos: Paul's Partner or Rival?*. Paul's Social Network: Brothers and Sisters in Faith. Collegeville, MN: Liturgical, 2009.

Hartman, Lars. "On Reading Others' Letters." *HTR* 79 (1986) 137–46.

Hauck, Friedrich. "κοινός." In *TDNT* 3:789–809.

Hawthorne, Gerald F. *Philippians*. Rev. ed. WBC 43. Grand Rapids: Zondervan, 2004.

Head, Peter M. "Named Letter-Carriers among the Oxyrhynchus Papyri Source." *JSNT* 31 (2009) 279–99.

Hegermann, Harald. "The Diaspora in the Hellenistic Age." In *The Hellenistic Age*, edited by W. D. Davies and Louis Finkelstein, 115–66. Cambridge: Cambridge University Press, 1989.

Hemer, Colin J. "Address of 1 Peter." *ExpTim* 89 (1978) 239–43.

———. *The Book of Acts in the Setting of Hellenistic History*. Winona Lake, IN: Eisenbrauns, 1990.

———. *The Letters to the Seven Churches of Asia in Their Local Setting*. JSNTSup 11. Sheffield: JSOT, 1986.

Hengel, Martin. *Acts and the History of Earliest Christianity*. Translated by John Bowden. Philadelphia: Fortress, 1980.

———. *Between Jesus and Paul: Studies in the Earliest History of Christianity*. Translated by John Bowden. 1983. Reprint, Eugene, OR: Wipf & Stock, 2003.

———. *Judaism and Hellenism: Studies in Their Encounter in Palestine during the Early Hellenistic Period*. Translated by John Bowden. 1981. Reprint, Eugene, OR: Wipf & Stock, 2003.

———. *Saint Peter: The Underestimated Apostle*. Translated by Thomas H. Trapp. Grand Rapids: Eerdmans, 2010.

Hengel, Martin, and Anna Maria Schwemer. *Paul between Damascus and Antioch: The Unknown Years*. Translated by John Bowden. Louisville: Westminster John Knox, 1997.

Hertig, Young L. "Cross-cultural Mediation: From Exclusion to Inclusion." In *Mission in Acts: Ancient Narrative in Contemporary Context*, edited by Robert L. Gallagher and Paul Hertig, 59–72. Maryknoll, NY: Orbis, 2004.

Hezser, Catherine. *Jewish Travel in Antiquity*. Texts and Studies in Ancient Judaism 144. Tübingen: Mohr Siebeck, 2011.

Hiigel, John L. *Leadership in 1 Corinthians: A Case Study in Paul's Ecclesiology*. Studies in the Bible and Early Christianity 57. Lewiston, NY: Mellen, 2003.

Hock, Ronald F. "'By the Gods, It's My One Desire to See an Actual Stoic': Epictetus' Relations with Students and Visitors in His Personal Network." *Semeia* 56 (1991) 121–42.

———. *The Social Context of Paul's Ministry: Tentmaking and Apostleship*. Philadelphia: Fortress, 1980.

Hodge, Caroline Johnson. "Apostle to the Gentiles: Constructions of Paul's Identity." *Biblical Interpretation* 13 (2005) 270–88.

Holmberg, Bengt. *Paul and Power: The Structure of Authority in the Primitive Church as Reflected in the Pauline Epistles*. Lund: Gleerup, 1978.

Horbury, William, and David Noy. *Jewish Inscriptions of Graeco-Roman Egypt: With an Index of the Jewish Inscriptions of Egypt and Cyrenaica*. Cambridge: Cambridge University Press, 1992.

Horden, Peregrine, and Nicholas Purcell. *The Corrupting Sea: A Study of Mediterranean History*. Oxford: Blackwell, 2000.

Horrell, David G. "Domestic Space and Christian Meetings at Corinth: Imagining New Contexts and the Buildings East of the Theatre." *NTS* 50 (2004) 349–69.

———. "From ἀδελφοί to οἶκος θεοῦ: Social Transformation in Pauline Christianity." *JBL* 120 (2001) 293–311.

———. "Pauline Churches or Early Christian Churches?: Unity, Disagreement, and the Eucharist." In *Einheit der Kirche im Neuen Testament: Dritte europäische orthodox-westliche Exegetenkonferenz in Sankt Petersburg, 24.–31. August 2005*, edited by Anatoly A. Alexeev et al., 185–203. WUNT 218. Tübingen: Mohr Siebeck, 2008.

———. "Paul's Collection: Resources for a Materialist Theology." *Epworth Review* 22 (1995) 74–83.

———. "The Product of a Petrine Circle? A Reassessment of the Origin and Character of 1 Peter." *JSNT* 24 (2002) 29–60.

———. *The Social Ethos of the Corinthian Correspondence: Interests and Ideology from 1 Corinthians to 1 Clement*. Edinburgh: T. & T. Clark, 1996.

Horsley, Richard A. *Paul and Politics: Ekklesia, Israel, Imperium, Interpretation: Essays in Honor of Krister Stendahl*. Harrisburg, PA: Trinity, 2000.

Houwelingen, P. H. R. (Rob) van. "Jerusalem, the Mother Church: The Development of the Apostolic Church from the Perspective of Jerusalem." *Sárospataki Füzetek* 16 (2012) 11–22.

Hunter, A. M. "Apollos the Alexandrian." In *Biblical Studies: Essays in Honor of William Barclay*, edited by Johnston R. McKay and James F. Miller, 147–56. Philadelphia: Westminster, 1976.

Hurd, John Coolidge. *The Origin of 1 Corinthians*. London: SPCK, 1965.

Huttner, Ulrich. *Early Christianity in the Lycus Valley*. Ancient Judaism and Early Christianity 85. Leiden–Boston: Brill, 2013.

Hvalvik, Reidar. "All Those Who in Every Place Call on the Name of Our Lord Jesus Christ." In *The Formation of the Early Church*, edited by Jostein Ådna, 123–43. WUNT 183. Tübingen: Mohr Siebeck, 2005.

———. "Paul as a Jewish Believer—according to the Book of Acts." In *Jewish Believers in Jesus: The Early Centuries*, edited by Oskar Skarsaune and Reidar Hvalvik, 121–53. Peabody, MA: Hendrickson, 2007.

Instone-Brewer, David. *Traditions of the Rabbis from the Era of the New Testament*, Vol. 1: *Prayer and Agriculture*. Grand Rapids: Eerdmans, 2004.

———. *Traditions of the Rabbis from the Era of the New Testament*, Vol. 2A: *Feasts and Sabbaths: Passover and Atonement*. Grand Rapids: Eerdmans, 2011.

Instone-Brewer, David, and Philip A. Harland. "Jewish Associations in Roman Palestine: Evidence from the Mishnah." *JGRCJ* 5 (2008) 200–221.

Jeffers, James. S. "Jewish and Christian Families in First-Century Rome." In *Judaism and Christianity in First Century Rome*, edited by Karl P. Donfried and Peter Richardson, 128–50. Grand Rapids: Eerdmans, 1998.

Jeremias, Joachim. *Jerusalem in the Time of Jesus: An Investigation into Economic and Social Conditions during the New Testament Period.* Translated by F. H. and C. H. Cave. Philadelphia: Fortress, 1969.

Jewett, Robert. *A Chronology of Paul's Life*. Philadelphia: Fortress, 1979.

———. "Paul, Phoebe, and the Spanish Mission." In *The Social World of Formative Christianity and Judaism: Essays in Tribute to Howard Clark Kee*, edited by Jacob Neusner et al., 142–61. Philadelphia: Fortress, 1988.

———. *Romans: A Commentary*. Hermeneia. Philadelphia: Fortress, 2006.

———. "Tenement Churches and Communal Meals in the Early Church: The Implications of a Form-Critical Analysis of 2 Thessalonians 3:10." *BRes* 38 (1993) 23–43.

Johnson, Luke Timothy. *The Acts of the Apostles*. Sacra Pagina. Collegeville, MN: Liturgical, 1992.

———. "Koinonia: Diversity and Unity in Early Christianity." *Theology Today* 46 (1999) 303–13.

———. "Making Connections: The Material Expression of Friendship in the New Testament." *Interpretation* 58 (2004) 158–71.

Josephus, Flavius. *Jewish Antiquities*. Translated by H. St. J. Thackeray et al. LCL. New York: Putnam, 1930.

———. *The Jewish War*. Translated by H. St. J. Thackeray. LCL. New York: Putnam, 1927.

———. *The Life. Against Apion*. Translated by H. St. J. Thackeray. LCL. New York: Putnam, 1926.

Joubert, Stephan. *Paul as Benefactor: Reciprocity, Strategy and Theological Reflection in Paul's Collection*. WUNT 2/124. Tübingen: Mohr Siebeck, 2000.

Judge, E. A. "The Early Christians as a Scholastic Community." In *The First Christians in the Roman World: Augustan and New Testament Essays*, edited by James R. Harrison, 526–52. WUNT 229. Tübingen: Mohr Siebeck, 2008.

———. "The Roman Base of Paul's Mission." *TynBul* 56 (2005) 103–17.

Just, Arthur A., Jr. "The Apostolic Councils of Galatians and Acts: How First-Century Christians Walked Together." *CTQ* 74 (2010) 261–88.

Käsemann, Ernst. *Commentary on Romans*. Translated and edited by Geoffrey W. Bromiley. Grand Rapids: Eerdmans, 1980.

———. *Essays on New Testament Themes*. Translated by W. Montague. Studies in Biblical Theology 1/41. London: SCM, 1964.

———. *Perspectives on Paul*. Translated by M. Kohl. Philadelphia: Trinity Press International, 1991.

Kaye, Bruce N. "Acts' Portrait of Silas." *NovT* 21 (1979) 13–26.

Keener, Craig S. *Acts: An Exegetical* Commentary. 4 vols. Grand Rapids: Baker Academic, 2014.

Keller, Marie Noël. *Priscilla and Aquila: Paul's Coworkers in Christ Jesus*. Paul's Social Network Series. Collegeville, MN: Liturgical, 2010.

Kirkland, A. "The Beginnings of Christianity in the Lycus Valley: An Exercise in Historical Reconstruction." *Neotestamentica* 29 (1995) 109–24.

Kittel, Gerhard, and Gerhard Friedrich, eds. *Theological Dictionary of the New Testament*. Translated by Geoffrey W. Bromiley. *10* vols. Grand Rapids: Eerdmans, *1964–1976*.

Kittredge, Cynthia Briggs. "Rethinking Authorship in the Letters of Paul: Elisabeth Schüssler Fiorenza's Model of Pauline Theology." In *Walk in the Ways of Wisdom: Essays in Honor of Elisabeth Schüssler Fiorenza*, edited by Shelly Matthews et al., 318–33. London: Trinity, 2003.

Klauck, Hans-Josef. *Hausgemeinde und Hauskirche im Frühen Christentum*. Stuttgarter Bibelstudien 103. Stuttgart: Katholisches Bibelwerk, 1981.

Kloha, Jeffrey J. "The Trans-Congregational Church in the New Testament." *CJ* 34 (2008) 172–90.

Kloppenborg, John S. "Collegia and *Thiasoi*: Issues in Function, Taxonomy and Membership." In *Voluntary Associations in the Graeco-Roman World*, edited by John S. Kloppenborg and Stephen G. Wilson, 16–30. New York: Routledge, 1996.

Kloppenborg, John S., and Richard S. Ascough. *Greco-Roman Associations: Texts, Translations, and Commentary*. New York: De Gruyter, 2011.

Knox, John. *Chapters in a Life of Paul*. Rev. ed. Macon, GA: Mercer University Press, 1987.

Koenig, John. "Hospitality." In *Anchor Bible Dictionary*, edited by David Noel Freedman, 3:299–301. New York: Doubleday, 1992.

———. *New Testament Hospitality: Partnership with Strangers as Promise and Mission*. Overtures to Biblical Theology. Philadelphia: Fortress, 1985.

Koester, Helmut. "Ephesos in Early Christian Literature." In *Ephesos, Metropolis of Asia: An Interdisciplinary Approach to Its Archaeology, Religion, and Culture*, edited by Helmut Koester, 119–40. Harvard Theological Studies 41. Valley Forge, PA: Trinity Press International, 1995.

———. *Paul and His World: Interpreting the New Testament in Its Context*. Minneapolis: Fortress, 2007.

———. "Paul and Philippi: The Evidence from Early Christian Literature." In *Philippi at the Time of Paul and after His Death*, edited by Charalambos Bakirtzis and Helmut Koester, 49–66. 1998. Reprint, Eugene, OR: Wipf & Stock, 2009.

Kollmann, Bernd. *Joseph Barnabas: His Life and Legacy*. Translated by Miranda Henry. Collegeville, MN: Liturgical, 2004.

Körtner, Ulrich H. J. "*Markus der Mitarbeiter des Petrus*." *ZNW* (1980) 160–73.

Kraabel, A. Thomas. "Immigrants, Exiles, Expatriates, and Missionaries." In *Religious Propaganda and Missionary Competition in the New Testament World: Essays Honoring Dieter Georgi*, edited by Lukas Bormann et al., 71–88. NovTSup 74. Leiden: Brill, 1994.

Kümmel, Werner G. *The New Testament: The History of the Investigation of Its Problems*. Translated by S. McLean Gilmour and Howard C. Kee. Nashville, TN: Abingdon, 1972.

Lampe, Peter. "Early Christians in the City of Rome: Topographical and Social Historical Aspects of the First Three Centuries." In *Christians as a Religious Minority in a Multicultural City: Modes of Interaction and Identity Formation in Early Imperial Rome*, edited by Jürgen Zangenberg and Michael Labahn, 20–32. JSNTSup 243. London: T. & T. Clark, 2004.

———. *From Paul to Valentinus: Christians at Rome in the First Two Centuries*. Minneapolis: Fortress, 2003.

———. "The Roman Christians in Romans 16." In *The Romans Debate*, edited by Karl P. Donfried, 216–30. Peabody, MA: Hendrickson, 1991.

Last, Richard. "What Purpose Did Paul Understand His Mission to Serve?" *HTR* 104 (2011) 299–324.

Leon, Harry J. *The Jews of Ancient Rome*. 2nd ed. Peabody, MA: Hendrickson, 1995.

Levine, Lee I. *The Ancient Synagogue: The First Thousand Years*. New Haven, CT: Yale University Press, 2000.

———. "The First Century C.E. Synagogue in Historical Perspective." In *The Ancient Synagogue from Its Origins until 200 C.E.: Papers Presented at an International Conference at Lund University, October 14–17, 2001*, edited by Birger Olsson and Magnus Zetterholm, 1–24. ConBNT 39. Stockholm: Almqvist & Wiksell, 2003.

———. "The Patriarchate and the Ancient Synagogue." In *Jews, Christians, and Polytheists in the Ancient Synagogue: Cultural Interaction during the Greco-Roman Period*, edited by Steven Fine, 87–100. Baltimore Studies in the History of Judaism. New York: Routledge, 1999.

Lindemann, Andreas. "The Beginnings of Christian Life in Jerusalem according to the Summaries in the Acts of the Apostles (Acts 2:42–47; 4:32–37; 5:12–16)." In *Common Life in the Early Church: Essays Honoring Graydon F. Snyder*, edited by Julian V. Hills et al., 202–18. Harrisburg, PA: Trinity, 1998.

Linton, Gregory. "House Church Meetings in the New Testament Era." *SCJ* 8 (2005) 229–44.

Llewelyn, Stephen, and R. A. Kearsley. *New Documents Illustrating Early Christianity*. Vol. 7, *A Review of the Greek Inscriptions and Papyri published in 1982–83*. North Ryde, NSW, Australia: The Ancient History Documentary Research Centre, Macquarie University, 1994.

Longenecker, Bruce W. *Remember the Poor: Paul, Poverty, and the Greco-Roman World*. Grand Rapids: Eerdmans, 2010.

Longenecker, Richard N. *Galatians*. WBC 41. Dallas: Word, 1990.

———. "Paul's Vision of the Church and Community Formation in His Major Missionary Letters." In *Community Formation in the Early Church and in the Church Today*, edited by Richard N. Longenecker, 73–88. Peabody, MA: Hendrickson, 2002.

Louw, Johannes P., and Eugene A. Nida, eds. *Greek-English Lexicon of the New Testament: Based on Semantic Domains*. 2 vols. 2nd ed. New York: United Bible Societies, 1989.

Lüdemann, Gerd. *Opposition to Paul in Jewish Christianity*. Translated by M. Eugene Boring. Minneapolis: Fortress, 1989.

———. *Paul, Apostle to the Gentiles: Studies in Chronology*. Translated by F. Stanley Jones. Philadelphia: Fortress, 1984.

———. *Primitive Christianity: A Survey of Recent Studies and Some New Proposals*. Translated by John Bowden. London: T. & T. Clark, 2003.

Luter, A. Boyd "Partnership in the Gospel: The Role of Women in the Church at Philippi." *JETS* 39 (1996) 411–20.

MacLennan, Robert S. "In Search of the Jewish Diaspora: A First-Century Synagogue in Crimea?" *Biblical Archaeology Review* 22/2 (1996) 44–51, 69.

Malherbe, Abraham J. "Did the Thessalonians Write to Paul?" In *The Conversation Continues: Studies in Paul* and *John in Honor of J. Louis Martyn*, edited by Robert T. Fortna and Beverly R. Gaventa, 246–57. Nashville: Abingdon, 1990.

———. *Social Aspects of Early Christianity*. 2nd ed. 1983. Reprint, Eugene, OR: Wipf & Stock, 2003.

Malina, Bruce. *The New Testament World: Insights from Cultural Anthropology*. Atlanta: John Knox, 1981.

———. *Timothy: Paul's Closest Associate*. Paul's Social Network: Brothers and Sisters in Faith. Collegeville, MN: Liturgical, 2008.

Maness, Stephen. "The Pauline Congregations, Paul, and His Co-Workers: Determinative Trajectories for the Ministries of Paul's Partners in the Gospel." PhD diss., Southwestern Baptist Theological Seminary, 1998.

Marshall, I. Howard. *The Acts of the Apostles: An Introduction and Commentary*. TNTC 5. Downers Grove, IL: InterVarsity, 1980.

———. "Congregation and Ministry in the Pastoral Epistles." In *Community Formation in the Early Church and the Church Today*, edited by Richard N. Longenecker, 105–28. Peabody, MA: Hendrickson, 2002.

———. *A Critical and Exegetical Commentary on the Pastoral Epistles*. ICC. Edinburgh: T. & T. Clark, 1999.

———. "Luke's Portrait of the Pauline Mission." In *The Gospel to the Nations: Perspectives on Paul's Mission: In Honour of Peter T. O'Brien*, edited by Peter Bolt and Mark Thompson, 99–113. Downers Grove, IL: InterVarsity, 2000.

———. "Palestinian and Hellenistic Christianity: Some Critical Comments." *NTS* 19 (1973) 271–87.

Marshall, Peter. *Enmity in Corinth: Social Conventions in Paul's Relations with the Corinthians*. WUNT 23. Tübingen: Mohr Siebeck, 1987.

Martin, Ralph P. *2 Corinthians*. WBC 40. Waco, TX: Word, 1986.

———. *Philippians: An Introduction and Commentary*. TNTC 11. Downers Grove, IL: InterVarsity, 1987.

Mason, Steve. "Jews, Judaeans, Judaizing, Judaism: Problems of Categorization in Ancient History." *Journal for the Study of Judaism in the Persian, Hellenistic and Roman Period* 38 (2007) 457–512.

———. *Josephus and the New Testament*. 2nd ed. Peabody, MA: Hendrickson, 2003.

———. "*Philosophiai*: Graeco-Roman, Judean, and Christian." In *Voluntary Associations in the Graeco-Roman World*, edited by John S. Kloppenborg and Stephen G. Wilson, 31–58. New York: Routledge, 1996.

McBeth, H. Leon, "Cooperation and Crisis as Shapers of Southern Baptist Identity." *Baptist History and Heritage* 30 (1995) 35–44.

McCready, Wayne O. "*Ekklēsia* and Voluntary Associations." In *Voluntary Associations in the Graeco-Roman World*, edited by John S. Kloppenborg and Stephen G. Wilson, 59–73. New York: Routledge, 1996.

McKnight, Scot. "Collection for the Saints." In *DPL*, 143–47. 1993.

Meeks, Wayne A. *The First Urban Christians: The Social World of the Apostle Paul*. New Haven: Yale University Press, 1983.

———. "Judaism, Hellenism, and the Birth of Christianity." In *Paul beyond the Judaism/Hellenism Divide*, edited by Troels Engberg-Pedersen, 17–27. Louisville: Westminster John Knox, 2001.

———. "Petrine Ministry in the New Testament and in the Early Patristic Traditions." In *How Can the Petrine Ministry Be a Service to the Unity of the Universal Church?*, edited by James F. Puglisi, 13–33. Grand Rapids: Eerdmans, 2010.

Meggitt, Justin J. *Paul, Poverty and Survival*. Edinburgh: T. & T. Clark, 1998.

Meier, Samuel A. *The Messenger in the Ancient Semitic World*. Atlanta: Scholars, 1988.

Melick, Richard R. Jr. *Philippians, Colossians, Philemon*. NAC 32. Nashville: Broadman & Holman, 1991.

Metzger, Bruce Manning. *A Textual Commentary on the Greek New Testament: A Companion Volume to the United Bible Societies' Greek New Testament*. Stuttgart: Deutsche Bibelgesellschaft, 1994.

Meyer, Marvin W., ed. *The Ancient Mysteries: A Sourcebook: Sacred Texts of the Mystery Religions of the Ancient Mediterranean World*. San Francisco: Harper & Row, 1987.

Michaels, J. Ramsey. *1 Peter*. WBC 49. Waco, TX: Word, 1988.

Mitchell, Alan C. "The Social Function of Friendship in Acts 2:44–47 and 4:32–37." *JBL* 111 (1992) 255–72.

Mitchell, Margaret M. "Concerning Περὶ δέ, in 1 Corinthians." *NovT* 31 (1989) 229–56.

———. "New Testament Envoys in the Context of Greco-Roman Diplomatic and Epistolary Conventions: The Example of Timothy and Titus." *JBL* 111 (1992) 641–62.

———. "Patristic Counter-Evidence to the Claim that 'The Gospels Were Written for All Christians.'" *NTS* 51 (2005) 36–79.

Moo, Douglas J. *The Epistle to the Romans*. 2nd ed. NICNT. Grand Rapids: Eerdmans, 1996.

———. *The Letters to the Colossians and to Philemon*. PNTC. Grand Rapids: Eerdmans, 2008.

Morley, Neville. "The Poor in the City of Rome." In *Poverty in the Roman World*, edited by Margaret Atkins and Robin Osborne, 21–39. New York: Cambridge University Press, 2006.

Mounce, Robert H. *Romans: An Exegetical and Theological Exposition of Holy Scripture*. NAC 27. Nashville: Broadman & Holman, 1995.

Mullins, Terence Y. "Greeting as a New Testament Form." *JBL* 87 (1968) 418–26.

Munck, Johannes. "The Church without Factions: Studies in 1 Corinthians 1–4." In *Christianity at Corinth: The Quest for the Pauline Church*, edited by Edward Adams and David G. Horrell, 61–70. Louisville: Westminster John Knox, 2004.

———. *Paul and the Salvation of Mankind*. Translated by Frank Clarke. London: SCM, 1959.

Murphy, S. Jonathan. "The Role of Barnabas in the Book of Acts." *BSac* 167 (2010) 319–41.

Murphy-O'Connor, Jerome. *Paul the Letter-Writer: His World, His Options, His Skills*. Collegeville, MN: Liturgical, 1995.

———. "Prisca and Aquila: Traveling Tentmakers and Church Builders." *BRev* 8 (1992) 40–51, 62.

———. *St. Paul's Corinth: Texts and Archaeology*. Wilmington, DE: Glazier, 1983.

———. *St. Paul's Ephesus: Texts and Archaeology*. Collegeville, MN: Liturgical, 2008.

Mustakallio, Antti. "The Very First Audiences of Paul's Letters: The Implications of End Greetings." In *The Nordic Paul: Finnish Approaches to Pauline Theology*, edited by Lars Aejmelaeus and Antti Mustakallio, 227–37. LNTS 374. London: T. & T. Clark, 2008.

Myllykoski, Matti. "James the Just in History and Tradition: Perspectives of Past and Present Scholarship (Part I)." *CBR* 5 (2006) 73–122.

Nanos, Mark D. *The Irony of Galatians: Paul's Letter in First-Century Context*. Minneapolis: Fortress, 2002.

Nanos, Mark D., and Magnus Zetterholm, eds. *Paul within Judaism: Restoring the First-Century Context to the Apostle*. Minneapolis: Fortress, 2015.

Nguyen, vanThanh. "Migrants as Missionaries: The Case of Priscilla and Aquila." In *God's People on the Move: Biblical and Global Perspectives on Migration and Mission*, edited by vanThanh Nguyen and John M. Prior, 62–75. Eugene, OR: Pickwick Publications, 2014.

Nickle, Keith F. *The Collection: A Study in Paul's Strategy*. Studies in Biblical Theology 1/48. Naperville, IL: Allenson, 1966.

Nigdelis, Pantelis M. "Voluntary Associations in Roman Thessalonikē: In Search of Identity and Support in a Cosmopolitan Society." In *From Roman to Early Christian Thessalonikē: Studies in Religion and Archaeology*, edited by Laura Nasrallah et al., 13–46. Cambridge: Harvard University Press, 2010.

Nordling, John G. *Philemon*. Concordia Commentary. St. Louis: Concordia, 2004.

———. "Philemon in the Context of Paul's Travels." *CTQ* 74 (2010) 289–305.

Noy, David. *Jewish Inscriptions of Western Europe*. 2 vols. Cambridge: Cambridge University Press, 1993–95.

———. "Letters out of Judaea: Echoes of Israel in Jewish Inscriptions from Europe." In *Jewish Local Patriotism and Self-identification in the Graeco-Roman Period*, edited by Siân Jones and Sarah Pearce, 106–17. Journal for the Study of the Pseudepigrapha Supplement Series 31. Sheffield: Sheffield Academic, 1998.

———. "Rabbi Aqiba Comes to Rome: A Jewish Pilgrimage in Reverse?" In *Pilgrimage in Graeco-Roman and Early Christian Antiquity: Seeing the Gods*, edited by Jaś Elsner and Ian Rutherford, 373–85. Oxford: Oxford University Press, 2005.

O'Brien, Peter T. "Church," In *DPL*, 123–31. 1993.

———. *Colossians-Philemon*. WBC 44. Waco, TX: Word, 1982.

———. *The Epistle to the Philippians: A Commentary on the Greek Text*. NIGTC. Grand Rapids: Eerdmans, 1991.

Ogereau, Julien M. "The Jerusalem Collection as Κοινωνία: Paul's Global Politics of Socio-Economic Equality and Solidarity." *NTS* 58 (2012) 360–78.

———. *Paul's Koinonia with the Philippians: A Socio-Historical Investigation of a Pauline Economic Partnership*. Tübingen: Mohr Siebeck, 2014.

Ollrog, Wolf-Henning. *Paulus und seine Mitarbeiter: Untersuchungen zu Theorie und Praxis der paulinischen Mission*. Wissenschaftliche Monographien zum Alten und Neuen Testament 50. Neukirchen-Vluyn: Neukirchener, 1979.

O'Neill, John C. "Who Buried Peter and Paul?" In *Christians as a Religious Minority in a Multicultural City: Modes of Interaction and Identity Formation in Early Imperial Rome*, edited by Jürgen Zangenberg and Michael Labahn, 103–7. JSNTSup 243. London: T. & T. Clark, 2004.

Oppenheimer, Aharon. *Between Rome and Babylon: Studies in Jewish Leadership and Society*. Texts and Studies in Ancient Judaism 108. Tübingen: Mohr Siebeck, 2005.

ORBIS: The Stanford Geospatial Network Model of the Roman World. "Mapping ORBIS." http://orbis.stanford.edu/orbis2012/#.

Osiek, Carolyn. *Shepherd of Hermas: A Commentary*. Hermeneia. Minneapolis: Fortress, 1999.

Osiek, Carolyn, and David L. Balch. *Families in the New Testament World: Households and House Churches*. Family, Religion, and Culture. Louisville: Westminster John Knox, 1997.

Osiek, Carolyn, and Margaret MacDonald, with Janet H. Tulloch. *A Woman's Place: House Churches in Earliest Christianity*. Minneapolis: Fortress, 2006.

Overman, J. Andrew. "Jews, Slaves, and the Synagogue on the Black Sea: The Bosporan Manumission Inscriptions and Their Significance for Diaspora Judaism." In *Evolution of the Synagogue: Problems and Progress*, edited by Howard Clark Kee and Lynn H. Cohick, 141–57. Harrisburg, PA: Trinity, 1999.

Peerbolte, L. J. Lietaert. *Paul the Missionary.* Contributions to Biblical Exegesis and Theology 34. Dudley, MA: Peeters, 2003.

Peterlin, Davorin. "The Corinthian Church between Paul's and Clement's Time." *Asbury Theological Journal* 53 (1998) 49–57.

Peterman, Gerald W. *Paul's Gift from Philippi: Conventions of Gift-Exchange and Christian Giving.* SNTSMS 92. Cambridge: Cambridge University Press, 1997.

———. "Romans 15:26: Make a Contribution or Establish Fellowship?" *NTS* 40 (1994) 457–63.

Peterson, David G. *The Acts of the Apostles.* PNTC. Grand Rapids: Eerdmans, 2009.

Peterson, Jeffrey. "The Extent of Christian Theological Diversity: Pauline Evidence." *ResQ* 47 (2005) 1–12.

Phillips, Thomas E. *Paul, His Letters, and Acts.* Peabody, MA: Hendrickson, 2009.

———. "Reading Recent Readings of Issues of Wealth and Poverty in Luke and Acts." *CBR* 1 (2003) 231–69.

Philo. *Every Good Man Is Free. On the Contemplative Life. On the Eternity of the World. Against Flaccus. Apology for the Jews. On Providence.* Translated by F. H. Colson. LCL 363. Cambridge: Harvard University Press, 1941.

Pliny, the Younger. *The Letters of the Younger Pliny.* Baltimore: Penguin, 1963.

Plummer, Robert L. "Imitation of Paul and the Church's Missionary Role in 1 Corinthians." *JETS* 44 (2001) 219–35.

———. "A Theological Basis for the Church's Mission in Paul." *WTJ* 64 (2002) 253–71.

Porter, Stanley E. "How Do We Define Pauline Social Relations?" In *Paul and His Social Relations*, edited by Stanley E. Porter and Christopher D. Land, 7–33. Pauline Studies 7. Leiden: Brill, 2013.

———, ed. *Paul and His Opponents.* Pauline Studies 2. Leiden: Brill, 2005.

Porter, Stanley. E., and S. A. Adams, eds. *Paul and the Ancient Letter Form.* Pauline Studies 6. Leiden: Brill, 2010.

Price, Simon. "Religious Mobility in the Roman Empire." *Journal of Roman Studies* 102 (2012) 1–19.

Prill, Thorsten. "Migration, Mission and the Multi-ethnic Church." *Evangelical Review of Theology* 33 (2009) 332–46.

Quinn, Jerome D. *The Letter to Titus.* AB 35. New York: Doubleday, 1990.

Rapske, Brian M. "Acts, Travel and Shipwreck." In *The Book of Acts in Its Graeco-Roman Setting*, edited by David W. J. Gill and Conrad H. Gempf, 1–47. The Book of Acts in Its First Century Setting 2. Grand Rapids: Eerdmans, 1994.

———. *The Book of Acts and Paul in Roman Custody.* The Book of Acts in Its First Century Setting 3. Grand Rapids: Eerdmans, 1994.

Reumann, John. "Contributions of the Philippian Community to Paul and to Earliest Christianity." *NTS* 39 (1993) 438–57.

———. "One Lord, One Faith, One God, but Many House Churches." In *Common Life in the Early Church: Essays Honoring Graydon F. Snyder*, edited by Julian V. Hills et al., 106–17. Harrisburg, PA: Trinity, 1998.

Reynolds, Joyce M., and Robert F. Tannenbaum. *Jews and God-fearers at Aphrodisias: Greek Inscriptions with Commentary: Texts from the Excavations at Aphrodisias Conducted by Kenan T. Erim.* Cambridge: Cambridge Philological Society, 1987.

Richards, E. Randolph. *Paul and First-Century Letter Writing: Secretaries, Composition, and Collection*. Downers Grove, IL: InterVarsity, 2004.

———. "Silvanus Was Not Peter's Secretary: Theological Bias in Interpreting διὰ Σιλουανοῦ . . . ἔγραψα in 1 Pet 5:12." *JETS* 43 (2000) 417–32.

Richardson, Peter. "Architectural Transitions from Synagogues and House Churches." In *Common Life in the Early Church: Essays Honoring Graydon F. Snyder*, edited by Julian V. Hills et al., 373–89. Harrisburg, PA: Trinity Press International, 1998.

———. "Augustan-Era Synagogues in Rome." In *Judaism and Christianity in First Century Rome*, edited by Karl P. Donfried and Peter Richardson, 17–29. Grand Rapids: Eerdmans, 1998.

———. "Building 'an Association (*Synodos*) . . . and a Place of Their Own.'" In *Community Formation in the Early Church and the Church Today*, edited by Richard N. Longenecker, 36–56. Peabody, MA: Hendrickson, 2002.

———. "Early Synagogues as Collegia in the Diaspora and Palestine." In *Voluntary Associations in the Graeco-Roman World*, edited by John S. Kloppenborg and Stephen G. Wilson, 90–109. New York: Routledge, 1996.

Riesner, R. *Paul's Early Period: Chronology, Mission Strategy, and Theology*. Grand Rapids: Eerdmans, 1997.

Rius-Camps, Josep, and Jenny Read-Heimerdinger. *The Message of Acts in Codex Bezae, Volume 3: A Comparison with the Alexandrian Tradition: Acts 13.1—18:23*. London: T. & T. Clark, 2007.

Rives, James B. *Religion in the Roman Empire*. Blackwell Ancient Religions. Malden, MA: Blackwell, 2007.

Robertson, Archibald. T., and Plummer Adolf. *A Critical and Exegetical Commentary on the First Epistle of St. Paul to the Corinthians*. ICC. New York: T. & T. Clark, 1953.

Robinson, Thomas A. *Ignatius of Antioch and the Parting of the Ways: Early Jewish-Christian Relations*. Peabody, MA: Hendrickson, 2009.

Roscher, Wilhelm. "The Status of the Jews in the Middle Ages Considered from the Standpoint of Commercial Policy." *Historia Judaica* 6 (1944) 13–26.

Rosenfeld, Ben-Zion, and Joseph Menirav. "The Ancient Synagogue as an Economic Center." *Journal of Near Eastern Studies* 58 (1999) 259–76.

Rudolph, David J. "Paul's 'Rule in All the Churches' (1 Cor 7:17–24) and Torah-defined Ecclesiological Variegation." Paper presented at the Annual Meeting of American Academy of Religion, Chicago, November 3, 2008.

Runesson, Anders. *The Origins of the Synagogue: A Socio-Historical Study*. ConBNT 37. Stockholm: Almqvist & Wiksell, 2001.

Runesson, Anders, et al., eds. *The Ancient Synagogue from its Origins to 200 C.E.: A Source Book*. Ancient Judaism and Early Christianity 72. Leiden: Brill, 2008.

Russell, Ronald. "The Idle in 2 Thess 3:6–12: An Eschatological or Social Problem?" *NTS* 34 (1988) 105–19.

Sakenfeld, Katharine Doob, ed. *New Interpreter's Dictionary of the Bible*. 5 vols. Nashville: Abingdon, *2006–2009*

Safrai, Shemuel. "Relations between the Diaspora and the Land of Israel." In *The Jewish People in the First Century: Historical Geography, Political History, Social, Cultural and Religious Life and Institutions*, edited by Shemuel Safrai and Menahem Stern, 184–215. CRINT 1.1. Philadelphia: Fortress, 1974.

———. "The Synagogue." In *The Jewish People in the First Century: Historical Geography, Political History, Social, Cultural and Religious Life and Institutions*, edited by Shemuel Safrai and Menahem Stern, 908–44. CRINT 1.1. Philadelphia: Fortress, 1974.

Safrai, Zeev. "The Communal Functions of the Synagogue in the Land of Israel in the Rabbinic Period." In *Ancient Synagogues: Historical Analysis and Archaeological Discovery*, edited by Dan Urman and Paul V. M. Flesher, 1:181–204. Studia Post-Biblica 47. Leiden: Brill, 1995.

Sampley, J. Paul. *Pauline Partnership in Christ: Christian Community and Commitment in Light of Roman Law*. Philadelphia: Fortress, 1980.

Sanders, E. P. *Paul and Palestinian Judaism: A Comparison of Patterns of Religion*. London: SCM, 1977.

Schnabel, Eckhard J. *Acts*. ZECNT. Grand Rapids: Zondervan, 2012.

———. *Early Christian Mission, Volume 2: Paul and the Early Church*. Downers Grove, IL: InterVarsity, 2004.

———. "Mission, Early Non-Pauline." In *Dictionary of the Later New Testament and Its Developments*, edited by Ralph P. Martin and Peter H. Davids, 752–75. Downers Grove, IL: InterVarsity, 1997.

———. *Paul the Missionary: Realities, Strategies and Methods*. Downers Grove, IL: IVP Academic, 2008.

———. "Paul's Urban Strategies: Jerusalem to Crete." *SCJ* 10 (2007) 231–60.

Schnelle, Udo. *Apostle Paul: His Life and Theology*. Translated by M. Eugene Boring. Grand Rapids: Baker Academic, 2005.

Schürer, Emil. *The History of the Jewish People in the Age of Jesus Christ (175 B.C.–A.D. 135), Volume 2*. Revised and edited by Geza Vermes et al. Edinburgh: T. & T. Clark, 1979.

Schütz, John H. *Paul and the Anatomy of Apostolic Authority*. 2nd ed. Louisville: Westminster John Knox, 2007.

Schweizer, Eduard. *The Church as the Body of Christ*. T. V. Moore Lectures, *1962*. Richmond, VA: John Knox, 1964.

Segal, Alan F. "The Jewish Experience: Temple, Synagogue, Home, and Fraternal Groups." In *Community Formation in the Early Church and the Church Today*, edited by Richard N. Longenecker, 20–35. Peabody, MA: Hendrickson, 2002.

Sellew, Philip. "Religious Propaganda in Antiquity: A Case from the Sarapeum at Thessalonike." *Numina Aegaea* 3 (1980) 15–20.

Sim, David C. "Matthew, Paul and the Origin and Nature of the Gentile Mission: The Great Commission in Matthew 28:16–20 as an Anti-Pauline Tradition." *HTS Theological Studies* 64 (2008) 377–92.

Slee, Michelle. *The Church in Antioch in the First Century CE: Communion and Conflict*. JSNTSup 244. London: Sheffield Academic, 2003.

Smallwood, E. Mary. "The Diaspora in the Roman Period before CE 70." In *The Early Roman Period*, edited by William Horbury et al., 168–91. Cambridge: Cambridge University Press, 1999.

———, comp. *Documents Illustrating the Principates of Gaius, Claudius and Nero*. London: Cambridge University Press, 1967.

Smith, Dennis E. *From Symposium to Eucharist: The Banquet in the Early Christian World*. Minneapolis: Fortress, 2003.

Smith, Jonathan Z. *Drudgery Divine: On the Comparison of Early Christianities and the Religions of Late Antiquity*. Chicago: University of Chicago Press, 1990.

Snape, Henry C. "Peter and Paul in Rome." *Modern Churchman* 14 (1971) 127–38.

Son, S. Aaron. *Corporate Elements in Pauline Anthropology*. Analecta Biblica 148. Rome: Editrice Pontificio Istituto Biblico, 2001.

Stark, Rodney. “Epidemics, Networks, and the Rise of Christianity.” *Semeia* 56 (1992) 159–75.

———. *The Rise of Christianity: A Sociologist Reconsiders History*. Princeton: Princeton University Press, 1996.

Stenschke, Christoph W. “‘Not the Only Pebble on the Beach’: The Significance and Function of Paul’s References to Christians Other than the Addressees in 1 and 2 Corinthians.” *Neotestamentica* 45 (2011) 331–57.

———. “Paul’s Mission as the Mission of the Church.” In *Paul’s Missionary Methods: In His Time and Our Time*, edited by Robert L. Plummer and John Mark Terry, 74–94. Downers Grove, IL: InterVarsity, 2012.

———. “The Significance and Function of References to Christians in the Pauline Literature.” In *Paul and His Social Relations*, edited by Stanley E. Porter and Christopher D. Land, 185–228. Pauline Studies 7. Leiden: Brill, 2013.

Stenstrup, Ken. *Titus: Honoring the Gospel of God*. Paul’s Social Network: Brothers and Sisters in Faith. Collegeville, MN: Liturgical, 2010.

Stewart, Eric C. *Peter: First-Generation Member of the Jesus Movement*. Paul’s Social Network: Brothers and Sisters in Faith. Collegeville, MN: Liturgical, 2012.

Stewart, Lawrence Malcom, III. “Communication Networks and Social Cohesion in the Early Church.” PhD diss., Brown University, 1993.

Still, Todd D. “Did Paul Loathe Manual Labor? Revisiting the Work of Ronald F. Hock on the Apostle’s Tentmaking and Social Class.” *JBL* 125 (2006) 781–95.

Still, Todd D., and David G. Horrell, eds. *After the First Urban Christians: The Social-Scientific Study of Pauline Christianity Twenty-Five Years Later*. New York: T. & T. Clark, 2009.

Stowers, Stanley K. “Does Pauline Christianity Resemble a Hellenistic Philosophy?” In *Paul beyond the Judaism/Hellenism Divide*, edited by Troels Engberg-Pedersen, 81–102. Louisville: Westminster John Knox, 2001.

———. *Letter Writing in Greco-Roman Antiquity*. Library of Early Chistianity 5. Philadelphia: Westminster, 1989.

———. “Social Status, Public Speaking and Private Teaching: The Circumstances of Paul’s Preaching Activity.” *NovT* 26 (1984) 59–82.

Stuhlmacher, Peter. “The Purpose of Romans.” In *The Romans Debate*, edited by Karl P. Donfried, 231–42. Edinburgh: T. & T. Clark, 1991.

Sumney, Jerry L. *Identifying Paul’s Opponents*. JSNTSup 40. Sheffield: JSOT, 1990.

———. “Paul and Christ-Believing Jews Whom He Opposes.” In *Jewish Christianity Reconsidered: Rethinking Ancient Groups and Texts*, edited by Matt Jackson-McCabe, 57–80. Minneapolis: Fortress, 2007.

———. *‘Servants of Satan’, ‘False Brothers’ and Other Opponents of Paul*. JSNTSup 188. Sheffield: Sheffield Academic, 1999.

Tacitus, Cornelius. *The Annals*. Translated, with Introduction and Notes by A. J. Woodman. Indianapolis: Hackett, 2004.

Taylor, Justin. “The Community of Goods among the First Christians and among the Essenes.” In *Historical Perspectives: From the Hasmoneans to Bar Kokhba in Light of the Dead Sea Scrolls*, edited by David Goodblatt et al., 147–61. Studies on the Texts of the Desert of Judah 37. Leiden: Brill, 200l.

———. “The Jerusalem Decrees (Acts 15:20, 29 and 21:25) and the Incident at Antioch (Gal 2:11–14).” *NTS* 47 (2001) 372–80.

Taylor, Mark. *1 Corinthians: An Exegetical and Theological Exposition of Holy Scripture*. NAC 28. Nashville: Broadman & Holman, 2014.

Taylor, Nicholas H. "Apostolic Identity and the Conflicts in Corinth and Galatia." In *Paul and His Opponents*, edited by Stanley E. Porter, 99–127. Pauline Studies 2. Leiden: Brill, 2005.

———. *Paul, Antioch and Jerusalem: A Study in Relationships and Authority in Earliest Christianity.* Sheffield: JSOT, 1992.

———. Review of *Paul and the Anatomy of Apostolic Authority*, 2nd ed., by John Howard Schütz. JSNT 31 (2009) 85.

Teeter, Timothy M. "Christian Letters of Recommendation in the Papyrus Record." *Patristic and Byzantine Review* 9 (1990) 59–69.

Tellbe, Mikael. "The Temple Tax as a Pre-70 CE Identity Marker." In *The Formation of the Early Church*, edited by Jostein Ådna, 19–44. WUNT 183. Tübingen: Mohr Siebeck, 2005.

Theissen, Gerd. *The Social Setting of Pauline Christianity: Essays on Corinth.* Translated and edited by John H. Schütz. Philadelphia: Fortress, 1982.

Thiselton, Anthony C. *The First Epistle to the Corinthians: A Commentary on the Greek Text.* NIGTC. Grand Rapids: Eerdmans, 2000.

Thomas, W. D. "New Testament Characters: V. Epaphras." *ExpTim* 95 (1984) 217–18.

———. "New Testament Characters: VIII. Silas." *ExpTim* 95 (1984) 305–6.

———. "New Testament Characters: IX. Phoebe: A Helper of Many." *ExpTim* 95 (1984) 336–37.

Thomassen, Einar. "Orthodoxy and Heresy in Second-Century Rome." *HTR* 97 (2004) 241–56.

Thompson, Alan J. *One Lord, One People: The Unity of the Church in Acts in Its Literary Setting.* LNTS 359. New York: T. & T. Clark, 2008.

———. "Unity in Acts: Idealization or Reality?" *JETS* 51 (2008) 523–42.

Thompson, James. *Pastoral Ministry according to Paul: A Biblical Vision.* Grand Rapids: Baker Academic, 2006.

Thompson, Michael B. "The Holy Internet: Communication between Churches in the First Christian Generation." In *The Gospels for All Christians: Rethinking the Gospel Audiences*, edited by Richard Bauckham, 49–70. Grand Rapids: Eerdmans, 1998.

———. "Paul in the Book of Acts: Differences and Distance." *ExpTim* 122 (2011) 425–36.

Thrall, Margaret E. *A Critical and Exegetical Commentary on the Second Epistle of the Corinthians.* ICC. New York: T. & T. Clark, 2004.

Thurston, Bonnie Bowman. "Paul's Associates in Colossians 4:7–17." *ResQ* 41 (1999) 45–53.

Tidball, Derek J. "Social Setting of Mission Churches." In *DPL*, 882–91. 1993.

Trebilco, Paul R. "Christian Communities in Western Asia Minor into the Early Second Century: Ignatius and Others as Witnesses against Bauer." *JETS* 49 (2006) 17–44.

———. "Early Christian Communities in the Greco-Roman City: Perspectives on Urban Ministry from the New Testament." Paper presented at The International Symposium on the Theological Interpretation of Scripture, North Park Theological Seminary, Chicago, September 27, 2013.

———. *The Early Christians in Ephesus from Paul to Ignatius.* WUNT 166. Tübingen: Mohr Siebeck, 2004.

———. *Jewish Communities in Asia Minor.* SNTSMS 69. Cambridge: Cambridge University Press, 1991.

———. "Why Did the Early Christians Call Themselves ἡ ἐκκλησία?" *NTS* 57 (2011) 440–60.

———. "Women as Co-Workers and Leaders in Paul's Letters." *Journal of the Christian Brethren Research Fellowship* 122 (1990) 27–36.

Tyson, J. B. "The Legacy of Baur and the Recent Study of Acts." *Forum* 4 (2001) 125–44.

Van Nijf, Onno M. *The Civic World of Professional Associations in the Roman East*. Dutch Monographs on Ancient History and Archaeology 17. Amsterdam: Gieben, 1997.

VanderKam, James C. *An Introduction to Early Judaism*. Grand Rapids: Eerdmans, 2001.

Wainwright, Allan. "Where Did Silas Go? (And What Was His Connection with Galatians?)" *JSNT* 8 (1980) 66–70.

Walton, Steve. "Acts: Many Questions, Many Answers." In *The Face of New Testament Studies: A Survey of Recent Research*, edited by Scot McKnight and Grant R. Osborne, 229–50. Grand Rapids: Baker Academic, 2004.

———. "Paul, Patronage and Pay: What Do We Know about the Apostle's Financial Support?" In *Paul as Missionary: Identity, Activity, Theology, and Practice*, edited by Trevor J. Burke and Brian S. Rosner, 220–33. LNTS 420. London: T. & T. Clark, 2011.

———. "Primitive Communism in Acts? Does Acts Present the Community of Goods (2:44–45; 4:32–35) as Mistaken?" *EvQ* 80 (2008) 99–111.

Wallace, Daniel B. *Greek Grammar Beyond the Basics: An Exegetical Syntax of the New Testament*. Grand Rapids: Zondervan, 1996.

Wanamaker, Charles A. *The Epistles to the Thessalonians: A Commentary on the Greek Text*. NIGTC. Grand Rapids: Eerdmans, 1990.

Wedderburn, Alexander J. M. *A History of the First Christians*. London: T. & T. Clark, 2004.

———. "Paul's Collection: Chronology and History." *NTS* 48 (2002) 95–110.

———. "The Purpose and Occasion of Romans Again." In *The Romans Debate*, edited by Karl P. Donfried, 195–202. Edinburgh: T. & T. Clark, 1991.

———. *The Reasons for Romans*. Minneapolis: Fortress, 1991.

Weima, Jeffrey A. D. *1–2 Thessalonians*. BECNT. Grand Rapids: Baker Academic, 2014.

Weiser, A. "διακονία." In *EDNT* 1:302–4.

Welborn, L. L. "'That There May Be Equality': The Contexts and Consequences of a Pauline Ideal." *NTS* 59 (2013) 73–90.

White, L Michael. "Finding the Ties that Bind: Issues from Social Description." *Semeia* 56 (1991) 3–22.

———. "Social Authority in the House Church Setting and Ephesians 4:1–16." *ResQ* 29 (1987) 209–28.

———. *The Social Origins of Christian Architecture: Building God's House in the Roman World: Architectural Adaptation among Pagans, Jews and Christians*. Valley Forge, PA: Trinity, 1990.

Wiarda, Timothy. "The Jerusalem Council and the Theological Task." *JETS* 46 (2003) 233–48.

Wiles, Gordon P. *Paul's Intercessory Prayers: The Significance of the Intercessory Prayer Passages in the Letters of St Paul*. Cambridge: Cambridge University Press, 1974.

Wilken, Robert L. *The Christians as the Romans Saw Them*. New Haven: Yale University Press, 1984.

Williams, Margaret H., ed. *The Jews among the Greeks and Romans: A Diasporan Sourcebook*. Baltimore: The Johns Hopkins University Press, 1998.

———. *Jews in a Graeco-Roman Environment*. WUNT 312. Tübingen: Mohr Siebeck, 2013.

Willis, Wendell. "The Networking of the Pauline Churches: An Exploratory Essay." *ResQ* 50 (2008) 69–78.

Willitts, Joel. "The Friendship of Matthew and Paul: A Response to a Recent Trend in the Interpretation of Matthew's Gospel." *HTS Theological Studies* 65 (2009) 21–40.

Wilson, Mark W. "Cilicia: The First Christian Churches in Anatolia." *TynBul* 54 (2003) 15–30.

Wilson, R. McLachlan. *A Critical and Exegetical Commentary on Colossians and Philemon*. ICC. New York: T. & T. Clark, 2005.

Wilson, Stephen G. "Voluntary Associations: An Overview." In *Voluntary Associations in the Graeco-Roman World*, edited by John S. Kloppenborg and Stephen G. Wilson, 1–15. New York: Routledge, 1996.

Winter, Bruce W. *After Paul Left Corinth: The Influence of Secular Ethics and Social Change*. Grand Rapids: Eerdmans, 2000.

———. *Seek the Welfare of the City: Christians as Benefactors and Citizens*. Grand Rapids: Eerdmans, 1994.

Witherington, Ben, III. *1 and 2 Thessalonians: A Socio-Rhetorical Commentary*. Grand Rapids: Eerdmans, 2006.

———. *The Acts of the Apostles: A Socio-Rhetorical Commentary*. Grand Rapids: Eerdmans, 1998.

———. *Friendship and Finances in Philippi: The Letter of Paul to the Philippians*. The New Testament in Context. Valley Forge, PA: Trinity Press International, 1994.

———. "'Making a Meal of It': The Lord's Supper in Its First-Century Social Setting." In *The Lord's Supper: Believers Church Perspectives*, edited by Dale R. Stoffer, 81–113. Waterloo, ON: Herald, 1984.

———. *The Paul Quest: The Renewed Search for the Jew of Tarsus*. Downers Grove, IL: InterVarsity, 1998.

Wright, N. T. *Colossians and Philemon*. TNTC 12. Downers Grove, IL: InterVarsity, 2005.

———. "Jerusalem in the New Testament." In *Jerusalem Past and Present in the Purposes of God*, edited by Peter W. L. Walker, 53–77. Grand Rapids: Baker, 1994.

Zetterholm, Magnus. *The Formation of Christianity in Antioch: A Social-Scientific Approach to the Separation between Judaism and Christianity*. London: Routledge, 2003.

www.ingramcontent.com/pod-product-compliance
Lightning Source LLC
Chambersburg PA
CBHW060337100426
42812CB00003B/1021
9781532609879